PRAISE FOR
LOVE, HONOR, AND ASPERGER'S

Love, Honor, and Asperger's by April Anderson begins during a timeless era of "gals" on the beach and Armstrong's moon landing. April's summer bliss ends quickly after marrying her summer fling. She tells the dark and debilitating side of being married to a spouse with high-functioning autism. If you are in this kind of relationship, you will find a compassionate friend in this book who sees, hears, and knows your pain. Her truth can set you free.

—**Midge Noble**
Author of Ice Cube Award: Learning to Be Cool under Pressure
and Sheba: Home Is Where Your Heart Is

April's storytelling is both enlightening and informative, carrying the reader swiftly along with her through her experiences with Bruce, her Asperger's husband, as she describes some of the ebbs and flows of the good, the bad, and the ugly of their marriage and the added dimensions of an Aspie-Neurotypical relationship. In her memoir, April illustrates how patience and tolerance are tantamount to a successful marriage and how "understanding your source" is key to your own health and happiness.

—**Lauren Millman**
*Owner of Lauren Wellness in Toronto, Canada;
Certified Relationship and Communications Coach
specializing in Aspie-Neurotypical relationships*

April Anderson captures the struggle with intimacy faced by those who love people with autism. She carefully depicts day-to-day issues that seem senseless and unpredictable. The frustration with trying to address and solve issues with strategies that normally resolve most matters is dealt with directly with true grit. With determination and a sense of humor, the author portrays the quest for a loving relationship that is often one-sided and disappointing. This book can provide support for someone addressing similar challenges while loving someone with autism. Intense and enlightening.

—**Cheryl Nye**
Psychologist and author of Taming Autism

As a woman currently in the process of divorcing a man with (undiagnosed) high-functioning autism, I find so much comfort in knowing I'm not alone in this struggle. April's conversational, and often humorous, writing style immediately drew me in. Hearing her articulate, with grace and humility, so many of the struggles that I've also endured through the course of my own marriage, I can't help but find comfort in the solidarity. The problems I viewed as "unique" to my relationship are far more common than I realized. Everyone needs a friend who truly understands what it is like to navigate love and marriage with someone on the spectrum. If you have no one in your corner, I encourage you to read *Love, Honor, and Asperger's*. You will find that friend in April. I'm so thankful that I did!

—**Nicole Oliver**

Relationships are hard for everyone. Imagine living in a world where everyone is speaking a different language and doing things you don't quite understand. Now imagine being in a relationship with someone who lives in that world. Autism can look different in everyone, and some of the things that make someone different can be special. Many individuals with autism can mask their symptoms of autism for a little while. Sometimes the autism is not identified until much later in life when things are not going so well anymore. Often partners of someone in a relationship will make their significant other see a therapist to "see what is wrong with them" and feel vindicated when there is an autism diagnosis. The truth is, the person with autism is not going to be cured of their autism because of a diagnosis; it's up to the partner to learn how to live with that person. Couples have chosen many paths of cohabitation, including living apart. Ms. Anderson tells one story that is unique to her family. Read about her discoveries that have allowed her to finally find her own happiness.

—**Heidi Mizell**
Family Navigator and Certified Peer Support Specialist,
Autism Delaware

Love, Honor, and ASPERGER'S

Love, Honor, and ASPERGER'S

My Mixed-up Marriage to a Man With High-Functioning Autism

APRIL ANDERSON

Copyright © 2022 April Anderson. All rights reserved.

No part of this publication shall be reproduced, transmitted, or sold in whole or in part in any form without prior written consent of the author, except as provided by the United States of America copyright law. Any unauthorized usage of the text without express written permission of the publisher is a violation of the author's copyright and is illegal and punishable by law. All trademarks and registered trademarks appearing in this guide are the property of their respective owners.

For permission requests, write to the publisher, addressed "Attention: Permissions Coordinator," at the address below.

Publish Your Purpose
141 Weston Street, #155
Hartford, CT, 06141

The opinions expressed by the Author are not necessarily those held by Publish Your Purpose.

Ordering Information: Quantity sales and special discounts are available on quantity purchases by corporations, associations, and others. For details, contact the publisher at orders@publishyourpurposepress.com.

Edited by: Noël King
Proofread by: Nancy Graham-Tillman
Cover design by: Cornelia Murariu
Typeset by: Medlar Publishing Solutions Pvt Ltd., India

Printed in the United States of America.
ISBN: 978-1-955985-49-9 (hardcover)
ISBN: 978-1-955985-50-5 (paperback)
ISBN: 978-1-955985-51-2 (ebook)

Library of Congress Control Number: 2022904462

First edition, May 2022.

The information contained within this book is strictly for informational purposes. The material may include information, products, or services by third parties. As such, the Author and Publisher do not assume responsibility or liability for any third-party material or opinions. The publisher is not responsible for websites (or their content) that are not owned by the publisher. Readers are advised to do their own due diligence when it comes to making decisions.

Publish Your Purpose is a hybrid publisher of non-fiction books. Our authors are thought leaders, experts in their fields, and visionaries paving the way to social change—from food security to anti-racism. We give underrepresented voices power and a stage to share their stories, speak their truth, and impact their communities. Do you have a book idea you would like us to consider publishing? Please visit PublishYourPurpose.com for more information.

DEDICATION

For my Cassandra sisters

CONTENTS

Foreword xvii
Preface xix

1. Whiskey Beach Beginnings 1
2. Something's Missing 11
3. Lucky Fuckers 15
4. Holy Toledo! 23
5. Mom and Dad 35
6. Mother Hubbard Childcare 43
7. Dyspraxia 53
8. Disengage 59
9. RV-ing 67
10. Aspergates: The Mini and the Minor 71
11. Dream Home 79

12. Twentieth Anniversary 87
13. Run to Win............................. 91
14. Sickness and Surgery 103
15. Narcissism 113
16. Verbal Abuse 123
17. Try the Du or Do the Tri 131
18. Cassandra............................. 145
19. Communication 155
20. Fairways and Slopes 163
21. Jekyll and Hyde........................ 173
22. Spirit-Killing 177
23. Demonstrating 185
24. Studmuffin 195
25. Superman............................. 207
26. Thank You Very Much.................. 215
27. Crazy-Making 223
28. Sensitivities 229
29. Fungus among Us 233
30. Obamabago........................... 243
31. Driving Disasters...................... 251
32. Ass What? 263
33. Wasp Stings........................... 277
34. Fights 285
35. Fortieth Anniversary................... 293
36. Name Change 297
37. Major Aspergates...................... 301

38. Moving but Not Grooving 313
39. Burnout 321
40. Travel Troubles 331
41. Things Fall Apart 339
42. Toxic 347
43. Fiftieth Anniversary 355
44. Surrender 359
45. Sort of 367

Epilogue 371
Bibliography 373
Resources for Readers 377
Acknowledgments 381
About the Author 385

FOREWORD

It is a rare privilege to read an autobiography by an ordinary person whose life, when viewed at the correct level of magnification, is extraordinary. In *Love, Honor, and Asperger's*, April Anderson rolls the highlight reel of a half-century of marriage to a man with Asperger's syndrome. Through unabashed humor and unflinching self-reflection, Anderson's story about her husband's neurological condition and her own health challenges becomes a universal fable of loving, trying one's best, and, ultimately, forgiving oneself for plunging headlong into what might have been avoided.

There is scarcely a person who cannot vouch for the "immovables" in any relationship. Arcane habits made sacred by family tradition, precious insecurities to be avoided even at the cost of fun and intimacy, and snoring are a few examples. As Anderson turns on her speakerphone and allows us to vicariously participate in her daily interactions with her husband, the reader finds themselves relinquishing the reigns of the "that'd never be me" high horse in favor of walking alongside Anderson to her gradual recognition that *some things cannot be changed*.

Although most of us do not find ourselves married to an "aspie," Anderson accomplishes the near-impossible with any reader. First, she makes us understand how one can stumble into and remain in such a relationship. (According to the Centers for Disease Control and Prevention, one in forty-four kids is diagnosed with autism spectrum disorder, so stories like Anderson's are about to become very common.) Second, she serves as an example of how the best in ourselves can show up and get us through almost anything (while defunding the delusion that personal strength somehow ennobles walking into oncoming traffic). As an acting teacher, I know that specific behavior on stage translates to an audience better than vague actions that no one actually recognizes as reality.

In telling her story about an aspie relationship, Anderson invites everyone to the table where we can talk, break bread, and weep together about all manner of messy relationships. At the same time, Anderson's commitment to her children, entrepreneurship, and fitness is an inspiring and excuse-removing example of human potential that allows us to get up from the table and move on with renewed energy. Anderson's story makes us belly-laugh without mean-spiritedness, cry with a mixture of sympathy and firsthand knowledge, and, ultimately, thank our lucky stars for the warning.

Jill Richburg
Attorney, life coach, and acting teacher

PREFACE

I had always thought I would get married. That was goal number one for women who came of age in the fifties and sixties. My high school friends and I would inscribe the prefix MRS in pretty cursive strokes in front of boys' names, practicing for our future wifely status. My mother's advice to me as I was dropped off at a college for women in New England was, "The men here"—referring to the inhabitants of nearby Ivy League schools—"are either rich or smart: MARRY ONE!" Well, I didn't, but I guess that was the loose criteria to which I adhered during my single years of boyfriends and dating.

I dated all sorts of the male species, a filing system growing in my head, sorting out pros and cons of potential husband material. Will he cheat? Do we have common interests? Is he fun? On track for a good career? Does he want children? Can I live near my parents? This last issue became important after I fell for an Aussie and nearly relocated to the far side of the planet. Does he have Asperger's—Whoa!...Let's go back. Does he have what? Is he on the autism spectrum? To put it another way, is he neurotypical or not? Are his neuros normal like mine, or are they a-typical?

I certainly never got *this* advice: *watch out for Asperger's*, unless you like the challenge of trying to figure out what is off-kilter with your husband, why your heart is constantly broken, your nerves are shot, your mind is confused, and, ultimately, how it feels to become a "Cassandra," a woman who knows what no one believes.

This book is about my life as an aspie wife. It is not intended to be educational or a manual on how to make a marriage work. It is certainly not meant to condemn anyone for being on the autism spectrum. Indeed, my intention is to entertain and amuse with the eccentricities I encountered in my aspie husband and the adventures we experienced despite the presence of Asperger's in our midst.

At the same time, there is a side to an Asperger's relationship that is somewhat disregarded: the toll it can take on a spouse. This toll includes heartbreak, loneliness, sadness, lack of emotional reciprocity, anger, and stress from trying to overcome or endure Asperger's ever-present challenges.

If you are in a relationship with an aspie spouse or partner like I was, you may see yourself in my stories. If you have never met a person with Asperger's, you may be enlightened regarding the depth and breadth of the syndrome. You may have an "ah-ha" moment and decide that you, too, might be dealing with autism spectrum disorder in your relationship. Knowledge is power, the power to anticipate difficulties and make choices—while you can—that favor a happier life.

Chapter 1

WHISKEY BEACH BEGINNINGS

I should have stayed at home. Why take a day trip to the beach when the weather is bad? I was twenty-four years old, attending the University of Delaware after deciding to improve upon my two-year associate college degree with a bachelor's degree. I filled the so-called gap years with many adventures, from working at a typical *Mad Men*-esque advertising agency in New York City, to ski bumming in Vermont, beach bumming at the New Jersey shore, and working at Harvard University in Boston. But I didn't stay home that rainy day, July 12, 1969.

Off I went with Tom, my casual date, who plowed his car through the flooded roadway, determined to get us to the beach. Looking snazzy in my colorful new beach cover-up and pink floppy hat, little did I guess those clearing clouds would make way for a darker storm, one that would blow and abate but never end.

But then, I was looking forward to seeing friends and hitting the bars and dunes of Delaware's boisterous resort town Rehoboth Beach, a two-hour drive south of my parents' home in Newark's suburbs. Independent and optimistic, I had no reason to worry or fear what the future had in store for me. As Tom and I pulled into the driveway of my friend Maryanne's beach cottage, my only concern was the lack of sunshine. My friend was glad to see me and anxious to get the weekend moving. Despite the lingering dampness, she suggested we check out the scene at Whiskey Beach, the nearby beach where singles were known to meet and party. *Why not?*

Great storm-tossed waves emanated from a dull mist shrouding the shore, along which a few hardy souls wandered. Tom, a former lifeguard and still muscular, could not resist stripping down and plowing into those swells as he had earlier plowed the car through deep water.

I was focused on Tom waging war with the ocean, as I loved riding the waves myself, when a male voice behind me broke my concentration. "Hello," he said. "Nice day." He was being facetious. The mist was spritzing the dark-rimmed glasses peeking out from under his thick brown hair. But he was smiling, he was husky, and he was holding a beer. *Who is this guy? Doesn't he see that I have a date?* His calm demeanor made me feel at ease, though in later life I would see another side.

"I'm Bruce. Are you from around here?" he asked.

"I live a couple hours away."

We seemingly had things in common. Bruce was serving in the navy, attending Russian language school in Washington, D.C., and had come from Minnesota; my dad was from Minnesota. Bruce had graduated from Hamline University, a small Methodist college. My junior college, Green Mountain, was a small Methodist junior college, although Bruce and I were both unaffiliated to any church. He was younger than me by sixteen months—as his mathematical mind quickly deduced—and my mom had advised me to marry a younger man and "train him," as she thought she had done with my dad. Now I marvel how that quick calculation, in addition to Bruce's obtuseness about my date, were inklings of his Asperger's syndrome. There would be no training him, but such thoughts were far from my mind, although it is curious how soon the marriage theme would manifest itself.

Tom was waving at me from his battleground of roiling surf. I waved back, "Good job, Tom!" Bruce and I continued chatting each other up until Tom dragged himself out of the water and up the beach. Bruce disappeared, but we would meet again.

Walking the boardwalk, Tom and I ran into my folks' young neighbors, Debbie and George. The day was still gloomy, so we headed to The Bottle & Cork, a nearby Dewey Beach institution, for drinks and to watch bands play in an afternoon rock 'n' roll jam session. After a break for dinner, we settled in at a table for four back at The Bottle & Cork, now in full musical throttle, and Tom went off to the bar for more drinks.

Above the din, a voice with a recognizable ring surprised me: "April, would you like to dance?"

"Bruuuuuuuce!" I dragged out the *u*'s like the waves rolling in the distance, tipsily responding with the familiarity having been imprinted in me earlier at Whiskey Beach. "Ask me to dance whenever my date gets a drink or goes to the bathroom." I have often wondered since then how I could have blurted this out. I'm not even sure if I meant it, but Bruce took it quite literally—another sign—and he was quite happy to squeeze me—as he would rarely do later—around the dance floor each time his rival left "to pay the rent," as the boys say, until Tom caught on.

Then we almost had a rumble in the jungle as Tom got in Bruce's face with a demand to step outside. "I am going to punch you out, or you are going to punch me out," he declared.

Oops! This isn't going too well.

Fortunately, Bruce had come with a navy friend, who quickly intervened to calm poor Tom down. Simultaneously, Bruce turned to me and said—with deadpan equanimity, by the way—"April, I will see you at the beach tomorrow." I found out later that Bruce had said the same thing to another gal, Susan, after I left the club. She was part of the Whiskey Beach crowd. He had to juggle his attention between the two of us the next day. Nowadays, I'd say this is how Bruce intended to select who would best cover for his personality disorder. I guess she dodged the bullet.

"I wasn't sure your date was going home," he told me later when trying to explain why he had said the same thing to Susan after having told me he would meet me at the beach. And *I* thought we had a *date*! Oh, how this would play itself out in our later life! It turns out this is his typical way of thinking. He does not know if something is *decided*. He won't ask for clarification. He can only concede, "I know we talked about it." During many years of our marriage, I would assume we had settled on a form of action, which could be dinner plans with friends, raking leaves, or buying a new car, and he would not know that it was *decided*. "Bruce," I often complained, "do I have to get a lawyer and sign a contract so you know something is *decided?*"

By the way, it is doubtful, as I would learn later, that Bruce would have butted heads with Tom over someone he had just met. Besides not being a fighter, Bruce had dropped several thousand dollars replacing the row of front teeth he lost in an automobile crash his freshman year in college. He had gotten into the Mercedes of a buddy who, blind in one eye, had missed a turn traveling to a hayride one night and careened into a tree. A busload of nursing students bound for the same hayride were the first at the scene and conveniently had towels to soak up the blood from Bruce's smashed face. He claims the accident is responsible for his low grade on his French oral test. Try saying *Française* without your front uppers.

After Bruce's friend calmed Tom down that evening, Tom left for home to study for an exam, taking his car and bruised ego with him. I thought it would be fun to stay for the rest of the weekend and meet Bruce on the beach, especially since George and Debbie were nice enough to offer me a spot on their motel sofa. Thus, Bruce found himself with two dates at the beach the next day, causing him to scramble back and forth between Susan and me like some seagull scrounging for french fries on the beach.

The following Saturday, July 19, my new traveling companion and cottage roommate, Elizabeth, drove me back to Maryanne's cottage at the beach. I was anxious to find out whether Bruce had called there or even remembered me. As soon as I opened the door, Maryanne announced that I did indeed have a phone call from Bruce. Bruce and I then met up again at The Bottle & Cork and considered that weekend our first real date. It took place at the same time as a very special rendezvous, that between Neil Armstrong and the moon. The whole country was excited, and we had Monday off, to boot. We gathered with a gang in front of their black-and-white TV on Sunday night to see Armstrong's boot sink into the silvery lunar dust.

The country remained under a lunar spell for days. I remember how we gazed up at the moon, slightly dazed from drinking "rusty nails," as we exclaimed, "There's a man up there!" George and Debbie drove down and joined us at the beach the next day and asked me why I said I had the taste of rusty nails in my mouth. They did not know that I was talking about the Drambuie and Scotch cocktail—a drink that Bruce would adopt as his signature drink for all our forthcoming wedding anniversary dinners.

With the long weekend over, Bruce and I were preparing to part and decided to stroll one last time on the beach. I remember turning to look up at him. Around his face was a great frame of blue sky with the gold of sun tracing his silhouette. I heard the words, "I bet we get married" in my head. It was so clear to me that I mentioned this premonition to my mother when I called home to update my arrival time. Crazy as it seems, I have "heard my thoughts" several times in my life, which I believe results from strong intuitive feelings.

When I got home, Mom, Dad, and neighbors Debbie and George were standing on the front lawn excitedly awaiting my arrival. "Are you engaged?" they all asked eagerly.

"Uh, not yet," I stammered, "but I think I will be."

Everybody went inside a bit disappointed. *Geez, it was just my first date!*

First courtship rite: weekend nights dancing at the singles club; days luxuriously lounging around Whiskey Beach. Bruce and I made new friends that summer, and I introduced him to old friends of mine, including my brother, Parker, and future sister-in-law, Sue, who often showed up for the fun and sun. It was as if we had been transported to a 1960s summer beach movie cast with bikini-clad gals, handsome heartthrobs, goofball comic relief, and—maybe this wasn't in the Annette Funicello and Frankie Avalon flicks—plenty of beer.

Center stage was our beautiful brunette, ribbons fastened to her pigtails and matching polka-dot bikini that scarcely concealed her killer body. She was paired with the other half of the archetype, the most handsome guy on the sand, hair-blown hairdo and all. Elizabeth, from whose navel George would lap beer like a slobbering bulldog, was carefree and fun. Finally, there was the clownish guy we called Babe, who entertained us with his masticatory peculiarities. "Hey, everybody," someone would call, "Babe is going to eat driftwood," and Babe would chomp down on a piece of gray wood as if it were a turkey leg.

In addition to beer, we would cart watermelons to the beach and inject them with gin. "I don't drink gin," declared Bruce, "but I will eat it." *What a fun guy*, I thought.

When the dog days of summer came on, so did the jellyfish. Drunken guys would dare each other to jump into the water, but the only one who avoided getting stung was Bruce, who is otherwise extraordinarily accident-prone. The others had to numb their pain with gallons of beer and watermelon gin. Everything was such a youthful dream. I remember when a charismatic dentist in the group, flanked by two attractive girls, inspected my teeth. "You have a beautiful bite," he pronounced, "and a beautiful body." I had a beautiful bite and a beautiful body. Why would I ever worry about an autistic personality disorder? Pass the beer and suntan lotion.

Next rite: meet my parents. The first time Bruce took the train from Washington, D.C., to meet my folks, June and Andy Anderson, he instantly hit it off with them, particularly my dad, who had an easy manner. Bruce loved playing bridge. He loved busing with the folks to University of Delaware football games. He also loved playing golf with Dad. Later, when Bruce and I moved to Delaware as a married couple, Bruce joined a foursome with Dad and two friends, and together they played golf for twenty years.

Penultimate rite: engagement. After the beach season passed, Bruce began coming up to my parents' place on weekends, though he stayed with next-door neighbors Debbie and George. We were saying goodnight one evening in the kitchen, our arms around each other and our bodies balanced against the counter. I told him I wanted a ring like the other girls at the university, who flashed their engagement rings from summer romances. I blurted this out just as I had that first day of our acquaintance when I had told him to ask me to dance when my date was not around. Where do I come up with these ideas? I have only myself to blame.

While he might have expressed surprise or inquired about the logistics of my big idea, ever the practical aspie, Bruce jumped right to the economic nub: "Okay, I will get a job."

The next day he didn't say a word about it: no conspiratorial glances, no special words of affection or commitment. As I drove him to the train station, I wasn't quite sure whether our engagement was actually happening or not. Not all that concerned, I filled the car with the sound of my voice, not knowing that this would be the beginning of a one-way conversation that would go on for five decades.

My only clue was when I dropped him off for his return trip to D.C. "I will call you and tell you if I get a job," he said. That was that.

He boarded the train and left me thinking, *I suppose I am engaged after all.*

After less than a week, Bruce called to inform me that he had a job bartending. He said it as if he were reporting the price of wheat in the commodities market. While I was learning never to assume too much, I did assume—correctly, this time—that our contract was signed.

Bruce wanted to tell my parents, so I kept the banns to myself, anxiously counting the days until Bruce returned to Delaware. There he would break bread at the family table and then play our customary bridge game. There was nothing but pleasantries throughout dinner and into several rubbers. I stared at the ceiling. I sighed. I kicked Bruce in the shins under the table. At long last, as a final trick was collected, Bruce opened up: "I am going to keep you up a little longer." Blank stares. "April and I are engaged." To be proper, he added, "Um, with your permission, that is."

Silence ensued while everyone's mind digested this non-bridge information. A beat. Two. Suddenly Mom and Dad sprang from their chairs, exclaiming joyfully, showering us with tears, and smothering us in a chaos of handshakes, hugs, and kisses. The bridge game was forgotten, and we popped a bottle of champagne. It was October 11, 1969. I had known Bruce for three and a half months, and he had been to our house only five times. Not all that long or that many, but so far the dream had its momentum and was full of pleasure, hope, and fantasy.

Bruce liked to joke that he had been "roped" into marriage since he was on the rebound from boot camp and I was the first girl he met, which he later modified to the first smart girl he met. My unexpressed joke was that I was on the rebound from the dating scene. Evidence that my parents were in on the setup was that my dad knew a jeweler who could get us a good deal on an engagement ring.

It was another two months before I met Bruce's folks, Ralph and Peg, when they threw us an engagement party at their Minnesota home, nestled in a small town among the Mississippi River bluffs.

During our flight out there, Bruce turned to me and said, "I know my mom will like you, because—"

Because you are smart, pretty, and wonderful, said my inner voice, completing his sentence.

"Because . . . I like you."

What kind of joke is this? Or is it a joke?

Peg was gracious and welcoming and gave me a corsage to wear. Ralph didn't seem all that excited, spending the evening in his La-Z-Boy chair with one eye on the TV. My jaw hurt from smiling all day as friends and family arrived to meet the new bride-to-be.

Our wedding day was beautiful with clear, sunny skies—what some call auspicious. The ceremony was held at 2 p.m. at the Newark Methodist church, with the reception at the Newark Country Club. If outdoor or destination weddings had been popular back then, I am sure we would have decided on another venue and held a secular ceremony. My dress was chiffon with puffy long sleeves and a lace bodice, which I had been surprised to see worn by Laurence Welk's daughter on the cover of a movie magazine. I had chosen rainbow colors for the bridesmaids, and the wedding party and family all looked traditional and classy.

We were both under the influence of nascent feminism and dropped the "obey" from our vows. But I could have added a few things: "I, April, take thee, Bruce, to be my husband, to have and to hold from this day forward; to expect no empathy, no emotional reciprocity, no involvement in my or the kids' lives, no understanding of verbal cues or body language, no easy communication, and plenty of crazy-making." Well, if I had read all the vows I could generate with hindsight, I would still have been reading them when everyone else was drinking champagne at the reception.

Chapter 2

SOMETHING'S MISSING

The next two years would transform me from an independent young woman to a woman in the throes of a challenging marriage. I was determined to soldier through all obstacles and forge a loving, successful, and enduring family, beginning with a lovable pooch. Yet, despite some joys and triumphs, there were also the first assaults on my happiness.

Our Bermuda honeymoon was a tropical version of Rehoboth diversions. We met other honeymooners and shared our giddy wedding stories. We spun around Hamilton on scooters, took a rum swizzle cruise, and purchased discounted porcelain dishes to round off our set. Unfortunately, navy duty called for Bruce, so we could not dally the entire week, and we headed home. When my parents picked us up at the airport, we jabbered like little kids while recounting our honeymoon adventures. Within a few days, Bruce and I were off on the long slog to Texas.

San Angelo-bound, we hauled a dowry comprising two standard flatware settings Bruce had snagged from his bartending job, two suitcases stuffed with clothes and toiletries, and my black miniature poodle, Jasper, repository of my heart and family memories. We had christened Jasper the "Tinsel Fairy" due to his habit of chewing the tinsel off my parents' Christmas tree. Having run the tinsel undigested from one end through to the other, the Tinsel Fairy would balance on his front legs like some canine circus clown, back up to the neighbor's chain-link fence, and deposit his business. It was glittering and kind of pretty if you ignored the brown stuff. It lasted till spring. Dad observed that "Jasper likes to strain his poop."

Jasper was not only the acrobat of poop but a hairy Houdini when it came to escapes. Once, when I was slowly driving down the road near my house in Delaware, I glanced in my rearview mirror and spied a dog standing in the street. *Wait a minute; that looks just like Jasper,* who was supposed to be in the back seat, where I had provided just a crack in the window for air. *What the heck?* My curly-haired pet had squeezed himself through as a mouse slips under a door and was off on a puppy promenade.

As narrow as we made his air vent on the road to San Angelo, Jasper still escaped more than once—at a rolling plains gas station, for example. There the locals watched two Easterners chase their little doggy around the pumps, hollering at each other and trading blame for their lack of diligence.

We were in for a shock when we arrived at the address of our rental apartment in San Angelo. It was in a sketchy area of town, above a garage with a steep stairway to the door. The place was so hot that I wrote thank-you notes for wedding gifts in my underwear, all the while trying to keep sweat droplets from ruining the stationery.

One evening we hooked Jasper on his leash and went out for a stroll. We were a block away from our lovely apartment when I heard an odd rustling, snorting sound. Bruce and I turned around to see a pack of dogs aiming to make a meal out of Jasper and maybe one of our arms or legs. I am not sure I have ever been so afraid. We knew that we couldn't outrun them, so we picked up our walking pace and, in the nick of time, grabbed Jasper, bolted up the stairs, and slammed the door to the apartment. The poor creatures moved on, and so did we, deciding to spend all our wedding money on a nice apartment on the other side of town.

Once settled into our Texas routine, we got braver with Jasper, who seemed to have become less impulsive. We would even take him rafting on Lake Nasworthy, which we renamed "Lake Nasty Water" due to its muddy hue. Jasper sat contentedly between us, tied to a leash. Beguiled by his good behavior, we took him with us to the tennis court. Still cautious, we checked all four sides of the fence for holes and then proceeded to swat tennis balls. We had barely worked up a sweat before I exclaimed, "Oh, I don't see Jasper!" *Gone again!*

We flew out the gate and took off down the street. When we spotted the dog, Bruce went into a full sprint, yelling, "Jasper, stop!" This command we expected Jasper to ignore, as usual. But this time he stopped short and sat on his haunches, catching Bruce by complete surprise. Bruce careened past Jasper, arms pinwheeling and sneakers screeching as he spilled nastily onto the pavement. He looked up, and Jasper bolted again.

Jasper was to be my consolation in Texas and beyond since Bruce began to manifest an inexplicable distance in San Angelo. I knew romance was likely to simmer down as responsibilities kicked in, but something else was going on. During the road trip to San Angelo, Bruce would often take my hand and look at me with love and affection. The next time he displayed such tenderness was five years later, on a wedding anniversary, when we were driving to dinner and he reached for my hand with the same look. I remember how surprised I was. Now, when I take myself back to that earlier trip, I feel like a canary set to be the cat's lunch rather than a bride, more like a prize Bruce could deposit on his parents' doorstep. Maybe it was all a charade that he could drop once we arrived in Texas. Then, he could withdraw into himself, the only companion he felt comfortable with.

Except for that one instance after a five-year hiatus, I never got that look again.

I tried to rekindle intimacy with what I thought were wifely gestures. For dinner, I would stick a vase of flowers or a candle on our little kitchen table, but he did not get the hint. Wasn't there more to share about how we felt as newlyweds, happy in the springtime of our marriage? He just glanced at my lovingly prepared dishes as though they were a portion of mush, gulped them down without any conversation, and then headed for the couch to recline in front of the TV. My uneasiness vacillated since we socialized with other navy families and seemed to live a normal life. Yet he was always off to golf or off to class, with no loving looks or hugs or taking my hand. As Bruce continued to disappear into himself, a deep loneliness began to spread its roots in me. He probably could not help it, but his disappearing act starved those roots in a way that drained my life energy, leaving me ever more vulnerable to the toxins that life had in store for me.

After only two months of marriage, I felt compelled to write to my mother. That letter was my first cry for help with my marriage. She must have intuitively felt my pain, as only a mother can feel about her child, because she addressed a return letter with "Dear Baby April," her sentimental nickname for me. In the years since then, I have searched for that letter and her response through dusty basement boxes of old love letters and Mom's journals. Where could that letter be? And where is the response from Mom? Like eating sour grapes, reading that letter might prove too painful, I rationalized. Still, I remember that Mom attributed my loneliness to being far away from home while adjusting to married life.

There was no way she could have known that I was in the beginning stages of what some call Cassandra Affective Deprivation Disorder, an Asperger spouse's counterpart malady, named for the lonely Cassandra, whose suffering is discounted and dismissed. Apollo granted her the gift of prophecy, but when she shunned his love, he put a curse on her: no one would ever believe her.

Chapter 3

LUCKY FUCKERS

"You lucky fucker!" shouted Bruce's sergeant as his finger reached Bruce's name on the list of reassignment orders. Communications school had ended, and rumors flew that most of the men were being assigned to remote bases in Rota, near Gibraltar in Spain; Ankara, Turkey; or Alaska's Adak Island, halfway out the Atlantic Aleutians to Kamchatka. None of these places would have accommodations for wives or family as husbands completed long tours of duty far from home. Everyone was extremely anxious as we approached the day new orders would be handed out.

There were no cell phones or texting in those days, so I had to wait nervously at home for Bruce to arrive. I couldn't bear to hear the news. When Bruce opened the door, I held my breath. "We're going to Chesapeake, Virginia," he announced.

Say what? My brain could not compute this information. *Like here in the United States of America? Like Virginia as in four hours south of Delaware?* I asked again for clarification of this unbelievably fantastic news.

Well, it was true. Bruce and one other lucky guy had been assigned stateside. My parents would be spared the inconvenience of having Jasper and their daughter boomerang back home. I couldn't wait to call them. "Guess where we are going!" I said to Dad when he answered the phone. Not waiting for his response, I yelled, "Chesapeake freaking Virginia!" Dad let out a big whoop and a holler. We were all thrilled.

Bruce and I drove to Delaware, via Minnesota, figuring we had time for an extended visit with Bruce's parents on the way to my hometown. Then, after gathering some meager belongings and celebrating our perfect assignment with my parents, we drove to our new place in Chesapeake, Virginia. This whole area contained the Norfolk, Portsmouth, and Little Creek navy bases. Jets laid contrails across the sky as ships sailed in and out of port throughout the region. Bruce's base was a radio station located just over the state line in North Carolina in an area called "The Great Dismal Swamp," where, as a Russian linguist, Bruce listened to Soviet Union ship communications off the US shore.

We lived in a rented ranch duplex in what was, at that time, a rural parcel in Chesapeake. Both our front and back yards were sizable, which Jasper loved. We made pals with the young naval couple who rented the other half of the house and socialized with other military couples, playing board games and cards and going to Virginia Beach. With my parents residing reasonably close, we would often scoot over the Chesapeake Bay Bridge-Tunnel and head up the Delmarva Peninsula.

Old and obstinate Mrs. Carlson lived next door. At our backyard intersection, I encountered hard-core racism in person for the first time. I had certainly witnessed such attitudes on the radio or television, but I'd never come face to face with such blatant hatred. She hated Black people, Jewish people, and most of all, Catholics. She even dubbed the dogs owned by the African American families down the street as "nigger dogs" and cursed them when they dared approach her property.

Initially, Mrs. Carlson took a big liking to us. We had casually told her about our recent wedding at a Methodist church. Being a Methodist herself, she was excited to have people in the neighborhood who she assumed would be like-minded. It took her a while to catch on that she had pegged us wrong. We were not religious, and we had no stomach for racism. She habitually tucked her Sunday church programs in the crack of our front door, goading us to mend our ways.

I was twenty-six years old, and in the 1970s, twenty-six was deemed time to start a family. We thought that was a good idea ourselves, and we figured, *Why not have a baby on the navy's dime?* We planned to go to Delaware for Thanksgiving weekend, stopping to pick up my brother, who was undergoing National Guard training at Fort A.P. Hill in Bowling Green, Virginia. Since we had a few hours to kill, we decided to try to get pregnant.

Well, I didn't get my period the next month, so we went to the infirmary. I got a quick examination and peed in a jar. No one said a thing, but as I checked out, the receptionist gave me some iron pills. That was that. Bruce and I looked quizzically at each other as we walked the long sidewalk back to the car. Finally, it hit us—we were having a baby!—and we jumped up and down with a cheer. We both agreed it was magic, though the magic was not to stay with us the second time around.

Bruce worked shift hours at the communications center, and I got a job teaching third grade. It was my chosen field, which I would pursue when I established a string of childcare centers in Delaware decades later, but this was a difficult beginning, especially for a young, untried, and pregnant rookie. The school was understaffed, and I had fifty-two students crammed shoulder to shoulder in a classroom built for thirty, max. They had cut the gym and art programs that could have enriched the lives of my students, all of whom were from an underprivileged neighborhood. At this school, bored and restless children got smacked on their hands with a paddle. Most of them had skipped breakfast, and many came with no lunch. I brought crackers with me to stave off morning sickness, but I ended up giving them to the kids. I had no support managing these rowdy youngsters, and, eventually, I was let go because I was pregnant.

Nine months later, I found myself riding up the elevator at the Portsmouth Naval Hospital with a towel stuck between my legs.

"Honey," said a woman with a rack of cleaning supplies, "your water's broke." As I left the elevator, she shared a knowing look with her companion as if to say, "She ain't gonna like this." I sure as hell didn't.

My labor was not advancing, so the doctors decided to induce. However, a big aircraft carrier had been in port precisely nine months before, and the wailing, laboring wives of sailors were overwhelming the staff and facilities. They were on the birthing assembly line, while I, sleepless and slow to labor, was shunted to the warehouse, so to speak.

Meanwhile, my parents rushed four and a half hours down the Delmarva Peninsula from Delaware to be present when their new grandchild arrived. They needn't have hurried. I was not put in the queue until the following afternoon. Still, having them join Bruce for the long wait gave me some comfort amid the pain and lack of sleep.

It turns out that my baby boy was in the posterior position, hence the problem with contractions. When I was finally in labor, Bruce was surprisingly helpful, rubbing my back expertly. He had been attentive in our Lamaze class and followed the doctors' instructions perfectly. If he had not performed so, I believe the doctors would have booted him from the labor room, as they did once I was in delivery. As soon as Reid was dragged into the world with forceps, he was whisked off to an Isolette incubator.

Numbed and weary, I still had the presence of mind to notice the view out the window of navy ships in dock and, through the stirrups, my doctor's blue, Paul Newman-esque eyes. "You have beautiful eyes," I remarked as he sutured my wounded vagina.

"Thanks," he muttered, with a tug.

Reid was born on Labor Day, and I had not slept for fifty-six hours. If this had been the only hit on my adrenal glands, my life might have been different, I suppose, but Bruce began to manifest the remoteness and agitation that would wear on me even more than childbirth.

All seemed A-OK during Bruce's first year spying on Russian ships, while I took a training course in Lamaze and proceeded to teach the technique to more than fifty couples. We were a typical small navy family, making do on a meager income. We entertained a growing circle of friends and managed to visit our parents from time to time. Still, when we prepared to head to the beach on Bruce's days off, I was unsettled by the way he would slam the beach gear and playpen into the car. The road to the beach would be a battleground, as Bruce sped the narrow two-way roads, cutting close to oncoming traffic and skirting the curves. *We have a baby on board. What's the hurry?*

"Bruce, will you please slow down?" I'd plead, pressing an imaginary brake on my side of the floorboards.

"Do you want to drive?" he would snarl.

I was shocked at his behavior. Bruce seemed incapable of imagining how I perceived his recklessness or how I felt. In fact, once we had arrived at the beach and he had cracked his first beer, he would settle down and go about the day as if nothing had happened. Even though I suggested he cut down on some of his evening cocktails, I was happy to see him relax and build mini-swimming pools in the sand for our little boy, so I swallowed my distress and let it slide. This I learned to do again and again, not understanding the cost to my own well-being as I focused on our mutual aspirations instead.

Bruce had always wanted to go to law school, but, as with so many other young men of that tragic era, Vietnam had put his plans on hold. Warned that his draft number was coming up, Bruce enlisted in the navy. As the end of his enlistment neared, he eagerly began applying to law school, along with hordes of other Vietnam-era GIs with the same ambition. Before the war, he had almost been guaranteed a spot at the University of Minnesota for his top LSAT scores, but his less-than-admirable college grades and the fierce competition erased that opportunity.

Rejection letters piled up. We began to lose hope. Then one night Bruce's mother called as we finished dinner. I bounced Reid on my knees while Bruce listened to his mom. And then he appeared to be crying into a dishtowel. *Did someone die?*

He hung up the phone and left me hanging for several moments until he looked up at me. "I got in."

"You got into what?" I asked, flummoxed by what this meant in the context of the bad news I anticipated.

"The University of Toledo Law School," he said.

Of course! He had used his parents' address on his University of Toledo application, so his mother had to call him with the good news. Holy Toledo! I began singing into Reid's ear, "We're going to Toledo! We're going to Toledo!" I was so excited for Bruce. "Where the heck is Toledo?"

It turns out that he had not been crying. Burying his face in a dishtowel was his way of expressing his emotions, where others might have let out a "Woo-hoo!" After dreaming for so long, after delaying his dreams in the navy, after missing his chance at the University of Minnesota, and after nearly giving up, Bruce was facing the chance of a lifetime.

Those nonstellar grades came back to bite him on the ass, however. He would have to attend night school, but he was in. All he had to do was finish getting out of the navy.

Once his enlistment was up in 1973, Bruce wrote, "I'M OUT!" in bold, black lettering across his US Navy sailor's cap. He wore it brazenly all over the base as he finished his official discharge procedures and accepted the jealous handshakes of his shipmates.

More signs—I'M OUT! and GOODBYE NAVY—decorated our car in celebration of our newly gained freedom as we headed off to our new life in Toledo. Along our way up the Delmarva Peninsula, we were regaled with honks and waves from those in other cars, many of whom were military.

We made a quick stop at my parents' house in Delaware. We had planned to march around Mom and Dad's living room with our signs, but as we pulled up to the house, we discovered Grandpa Parker's car parked in the driveway. My maternal grandfather had been a proud lieutenant commander stationed in Hawaii during the Second World War, and he had worked for the State Department afterward. He had a different perspective on war and service than our generation did.

"Hide the signs!" I said.

We suppressed our true feelings from Grandpa Parker and his wife, Lorraine, and bemoaned Bruce's separation from the navy. "Look," I said to Grandpa Parker, changing to a more agreeable topic, "your great-grandson is here!" Luckily, Grandpa Parker and Lorraine were on a tight schedule. After they left, we grabbed our signs—the first of many we would create over the decades—and marched around my parents' house chanting, "NO MORE S.O.S.," the military nickname for "Shit on a Shingle" that refers to the monotonous breakfasts of creamed chipped beef on toast. Hurray! We're off to a new life!

Bruce flew to Toledo to find housing and leased us a small, two-bedroom apartment on the first floor of a townhouse. The new place would turn out to be an adventure in itself, our third home in two years of marriage, and this time in an older urban neighborhood.

Unlike so many others during that tragic era, Bruce never had to experience combat, escaped the military system alive and with his limbs intact, and had a promising career before him. We were lucky fuckers, indeed.

Chapter 4

HOLY TOLEDO!

The US Navy paid for the van carrying our five pieces of crappy furniture from our Virginia abode to our bottom-floor townhouse flat on a quiet, tree-lined street in Toledo filled with older homes in a variety of American styles. We had some variety upstairs, too, we were about to discover.

The movers—we called them Mutt and Jeff—were hauling our sofa into our flat. Just then, the upstairs tenant clambered down the stairs, threw open the door, and jogged to the street, dressed in a full football uniform—including pads, helmet, and a pack of Marlboros folded in the sleeve of her white T-shirt—and straddled her motorcycle. As their jaws dropped to their collarbones, Mutt and Jeff almost dropped the sofa as well. She primed the carburetor a couple of strokes, then kicked the engine into a roar before careening down the street. We all exclaimed, "Did you see that?"

Something told me that I was not going to be having tea with this woman. Turns out she was a quarterback for a professional football team, which I think is cool, but she was mean. Her roommate sister was precisely the opposite, a timid waif of a girl whom we imagined cringing in the corner as Quarterback noisily pounded on the walls when she was angry; she even punched a hole through the drywall by the front door during one outburst.

I used to tie escape-prone Jasper to the front door so he could get some air without running away, but Quarterback hated the dog, who cowered instinctively as she stomped by. When I heard her coming, I would grab Jasper and dash back into my place before she could kick him.

Bruce could sleep through almost anything, but I don't think I slept for the entire year that Quarterback stomped the floors at all hours like Frankenstein's monster. Boom! Stomp! Stomp! *It's midnight! Cut us a break!* When she finally decided to settle in, we would hear only one motorcycle boot drop, and then——nothing. For the longest time, Bruce and I would lie in bed waiting, eyes rolled up to the ceiling and holding our breath. Even Bruce could not sleep until the other boot, with an uncanny lag, finally thumped to the floor.

Her bedtime signaled other disturbances, however, when her attractive girlfriend spent the night. Then it was squeaking bedsprings. Bruce threatened to leave a can of WD-40 by her door so she would get the hint. I had to explain that this would not be socially acceptable, and besides, "Are you crazy? We can't piss this gal off!"

I envied the lovers upstairs as they chatted and laughed for a long time after sex. They were having fun, sharing and bonding, kinda like going to lunch with your girlfriend, just with an added dimension. All I got from Bruce was *Zzzzzzz*.

We needed to augment our income, so, thinking I might get Reid a playmate in the bargain, I put an ad in the paper offering at-home childcare services. The first mom to interview me expected me to have references. Before I could persuade her that her little darling would be safe with me, Reid promptly bopped the boy on the head with a toy. She grabbed her tyke's hand and left in a huff.

My second interview with Sharon, a nurse and mother of two kids, went much better. She and her husband, Bill, would become our good friends, and her kids were great with Reid. I had my first childcare business.

As we were settling into the neighborhood, I noticed the crappy condition of our lawn. "Bruce, our front yard is mostly weeds and clover, unlike our neighbors'."

"It's green, isn't it?"

"And the grass is spreading over the sidewalk."

Was this a red flag that Bruce might never care much for lawn care?

I was recruited as an Avon Lady by Nancy, a new acquaintance on our street. She was a mom, as well as an eager salesperson. Soon I was dragging two-year-old Reid around my district to ring doorbells and sing, "Avon calling!"

During this era, I was exposed to the world of consciousness-raising, stimulated by conversations we women were having with each other over books like *The Feminine Mystique* by Betty Freidan, *The Women's Room* by Marilyn French, and articles by Gloria Steinem, founder of *Ms.* magazine. Almost overnight, we experienced what it was to "get it," to be aware of the pervasive sexism in our society. Being a feminist and fighting for women's rights became a significant part of my life. Working for Avon in this spirit, I touted women's rights and raised consciousness as much as I peddled lipstick and eye shadow.

Eventually Quarterback moved in with her lover, leaving her sister to her own devices. Soon the sister had a parade of Toledo dreamboats trooping through, so the bed was still squeaking.

Relief came on the heels of someone else's misfortune. A few blocks away lived Dickie Pickett, a man with Down syndrome. Dickie's live-in caregiver went through a psychological crisis, strewing cornflakes all over the house and wandering the streets searching for the pope. Dickie's siblings, who had hired the caretaker, were in a lurch, so they asked their next-door neighbor and my Avon associate, Nancy, for help, and she recommended Bruce and me.

The next thing we knew, we were living with a handicapped person in a nice, rent-free house that also was free of squeaking bedsprings. Bruce and I became quite fond of Dickie, who was short, round, and gray-haired, as well as mute ever since a fall from a window. He was also fond of stroking Bruce's newly grown beard and trying to give him a hugely puckered-up bedtime kiss, which Bruce singularly deflected. It was the time of Richard Nixon, and we came to call our charge "Tricky Dickie Pickett."

I never received such affection from Dickie, but we spent a lot of time together, especially in the evenings when Bruce was in school or studying. Rocking in our chairs in front of the TV after Reid had gone to bed, I would say wistfully, "It's just you and me, Dickie." Dickie, though, seemed to see someone else in the room, as he fanned his face with his fingers and smiled at his imaginary friend on the stairs. *My* friend, Bruce, wasn't imaginary, but he could be even less present than Dickie's.

Caring for Dickie meant that I had to learn to deal with surprises, abandon norms of modesty, and compensate for Dickie's distinctive behavior. For example, while Dickie was at school on weekdays, I would go about my business, most of the time forgetting when he would arrive home. When the bus dropped him off, he would do a quiet penguin walk right up behind where I stood, usually in the kitchen. Suddenly I would hear his wheezing right in my ears and gasp in fright. *Don't sneak up on me like that!*

At dinner, Dickie would eat and eat and never get full. He would stop only when he got sick. Hence, we had to monitor his food carefully. We learned the hard way that he was allergic to pork. He would lose control of his bowels and throw his loaded underpants down the laundry chute for me to find ripening later.

When Bruce was gone, bath duty fell on me. Our ritual began with me filling the tub while Dickie disrobed in his bedroom and then emerged au naturel at the bathroom door. Still looking the other way, I would hand him the bar of soap, hide down the hall for ten minutes, and return to retrieve what was left of the soap. Dickie would lather himself up until either I took the soap away or the bar had dissolved. Then I would figure out how to rinse the foam off and get him out of the tub all sleek and clean.

During the summer, we would take Dickie on day trips to a public beach on Lake Erie. He was fascinated with Black people and would blatantly point at any African American he would see. Then they would point back. It would be an uncomfortable pointing match. "Who you looking at?" one of the folks would say.

"Please excuse us," I would stammer in apology." He doesn't mean anything."

I had tried to apply at public schools before we arrived in Toledo, but there was a hiring freeze. Fortunately, a law school spouse who worked at the University of Toledo preschool got me a job there, and I could bring Reid to work. The proprietress ran a string of preschool centers, a serendipitous circumstance.

We made friends with neighbors on our little city street and other law students, but Bruce was constantly preoccupied. He worked all day for DeVilbiss, a medical equipment company, went to class at night, and studied every other waking minute at his little basement alcove, which I decorated with pictures of luxury cars, big homes, and yachts to inspire him. He decorated the entrance with strings of his beer can tabs and collected more from the neighbors. When you pushed through, it would tinkle like a beaded curtain in the Casbah. Alone in his sanctuary, Bruce would feed peanut butter to a little mouse friend when it popped through a hole in the wall.

I might have been a law school widow, but I had the company of Jasper, my impetuous dog. Bruce and I often had friends over, which once almost cost me Jasper. Bruce was cooking popcorn for some guests, but he let the fire get dangerously high. I soon caught the unmistakable odor of smoke and heard the kitchen door fly open as Bruce ran out with a pan of blazing oil. Jasper heard it, too, and he flew out the door behind Bruce, disappearing into the neighborhood for the night and the next day.

Bruce and I rode our bikes around the street for hours, checking backyards and praying we would not find him crushed in the gutter. Finally, we spotted him, alive but disheveled, and hauled him home. Poor Jasper was famished.

Bruce enjoyed some unexpected advantages after the economy took a downturn in 1972. He was laid off, but with unemployment benefits. This was a boost to his studies, and he made it into the day program at law school with an award for most improved grades.

I could understand why the studious Bruce was insular but not why he was incommunicado. Most afternoons I put Reid in the kid's seat on my bike to meet Bruce halfway back from his classes. Then the three of us would ride home together and talk. I wished that Bruce made more time to spend with Reid, and I often felt frustrated trying to persuade him. Prioritize our child, not the newspaper. Such frustration was not the only crack in our relationship.

For our fourth anniversary, Bruce and I talked about going to a new restaurant in town called Red Lobster. A friend of his had recommended it, and it seemed like a good idea. Then one evening, I was standing in the driveway chatting with Nancy as Bruce was preparing to ride to school. She told me that Red Lobster was a big chain, not a local restaurant. Bruce and I had always tried to avoid chain restaurants and seek out local establishments. Before he got his bike out the driveway, I said, "Bruce, guess what? Red Lobster is part of a chain." He became furiously angry and took off on his bike.

I was shocked, and I chased him down the street, yelling, "Bruce, I don't care if you really want to go to Red Lobster! It doesn't matter. Can you stop a second?" But he didn't stop. Instead of resolving the situation, Bruce simply cut off communication.

Deeply hurt, I bundled up Reid, our PJs, and the dog and took off to stay with the family of a young woman who had been my babysitter.

I can't recall how I explained why I was there, but she welcomed me with no questions. I had a very restful sleep and then returned home the next morning.

Bruce came home to an empty house. He thought I had driven back to Delaware, and he called both of our parents. I was horrified that he had involved them, and now I needed to call and try to explain our fight. He told me that he had slept on the kitchen floor with the phone on his chest in case I called. *Geez, do you think he really cares or loves me?* This was the most attention I had gotten in a long while.

We spent the afternoon with our neighbors while the kids played at the playground. Bruce was cheerful and affectionate. I was very happy; everything was back to normal after the Red Lobster fiasco. We all decided to have a spaghetti dinner and separated into our own houses to prepare our part of the meal. Sometime during these preparations, however, I seemed to lose Bruce again. Although he was with me, he was no longer *there*. I could feel him slipping away into his own isolated, noncommunicative world, and I was alone again, pondering this inexplicable breakdown. *What happened? Am I imagining things?*

When neighbors decided to have a street party, Bruce and I were tagged as organizers. As the mavens of merriment, we planned all the details. We passed out flyers inviting neighbors nearby to what we called "The Rathbun Ruckus," named for Rathbun Drive, where we lived. Our house was the base, and about a dozen attended. Kids under the age of five were shepherded down the street and placed in the care of our neighborhood's teenage babysitter. The rest of us toured an older home to get a feel for community history and got to know more of our neighbors. Festivities had begun with a cookout in the late afternoon, and in spite of the fun and as the evening wore on, I became concerned about Reid and told Bruce I needed to go pick him up. I found the kids tired and crying at the overwhelmed babysitter's house, their fingers wrapped in the chain-link fence, waiting for moms and dads while getting bitten by mosquitoes. I grabbed Reid and hurried home. "Bruce," I said, "it's a good thing I left when I did, as Reid is very tired and crying and—"

Bruce glared at me with a horridly altered face, as if he were a different person, dark and sinister, and turned his back. He was angry again. No hug for his child. I tried to talk to him, but he ignored me. I can still remember the fear and confusion I felt. I put Reid to bed and walked around in a daze for the rest of the night. Bruce was fine in the morning and denied my concerns. Maybe he just did not like parties to end. For my part, I was unnerved and frightened.

He reacted similarly after playing cards with Nancy and her husband, Doug. I saw that they were tired and knew they preferred going to bed at a specific time. But Bruce missed all the social cues. I went to the kitchen to get the cake and coffee that signaled the end of the evening. He followed me into the kitchen and sneered, "Go ahead and serve your precious pound cake!" By then I had begun to feel that something was really wrong. These incidents were mounting up, although Bruce denied that they even happened.

To this day, Bruce remembers our happy experiences but not our difficulties. But he knows I have my stories that I can't forget.

There was a more benign aspect to my hubby's idiosyncrasies: his willingness to be unconventional or outré, at least when I prompted him. For example, one year he dressed for a Halloween party as the Jolly Green Giant. He painted his face and arms green and wore green-dyed long underwear, a leaf mantle over one shoulder, and a shaggy leaf wig. We decided he needed a prop. So, while costumed, Bruce strolled into a supermarket to explore the aisles and retrieve a can of Green Giant peas. He lined up casually with more conventionally dressed shoppers and paid a chortling cashier.

Such outlandishness got a positive reaction from my folks when we returned to Delaware for Christmas. Bruce had grown a beard, and he showed up at my parents' house wrapped in a sheet and carrying a staff like Jesus and said, "Can you direct me to the manger?"

My parents, *joie de vivre* types, loved it. Their openness to Bruce's quirks would provide us considerable relief in our roller-coaster marriage.

The magic and ease of Reid's conception made Bruce and I optimistic about further building our family.

It was wintertime during the first trimester of my second pregnancy, and the streets were icy in Toledo. With three-year-old Reid in my arms, I slipped and fell at a crosswalk. Trying to keep Reid away from the pavement, I let my body take the full force of the fall. Soon afterward, I began to cramp and bleed. The doctors placed some painful device in my cervix to secure the fetus but to no avail. They then performed a standard dilation and curettage, which we had been used to calling a "dusting and cleaning," or a "d & c," but it was even more serious. When they took a biopsy of the fetus, they discovered that I had had a molar pregnancy; in other words, there had been an unviable growth that could have metastasized to cancer. X-rays showed I was okay, but we were warned not to get pregnant again for six months. I will never know if the fall affected my pregnancy, but I felt it dislodged the fetus.

After the doctors gave the go-ahead, we tried again and hoped for a daughter this time. Every few hours I would check my temperature for ovulation and then grab Bruce and direct him to perform: "Right now!"

After a few months, we were expecting our second child.

If it weren't for the miscarriage, we would have followed the advice of a popular book of the time, *Your Baby's Sex: Now You Can Choose*. In short, X-chromosome female and XY-chromosome male sperm thrive in different environments. We joked that guys need to freeze their balls for a boy and fry them for a girl. Instead of science, however, I relied on tradition and good omens. For example, I received a mail flyer advertising baby blankets. Their sample was monogrammed "Sarah," the name we had chosen for a girl. Other signs were the baby's slow heart rate and the fact that I was carrying my baby weight around my middle. Were we primitive or what?

Reid was excited about becoming a big brother, crying, "We have to remember how happy we are!" I needed naps, so Reid would occupy himself by assembling 100-piece puzzles while mommy rested.

Men in our circle were becoming more involved in the nine-month adventure. When our friends threw us a surprise baby shower, the guys fed each other mock baby food (pudding) and competed to see who could change a diaper on a baby doll the quickest.

I went into labor at three o'clock in the afternoon and gave birth to a girl three hours later. I was thrilled, exclaiming, "The first woman president of the United States!"

With the birth of Sarah (quickly nicknamed *Sally*), hope was in the air. Bruce finished his last law classes, and friends and neighbors gathered to celebrate, marching around our house singing, "For He's a Jolly Good Fellow!" Our family was complete, and Bruce began to think about getting a vasectomy.

Our friend Larry had had a vasectomy and knew a crackerjack urologist named Dr. Richard Tapper, who, in our many mirthful retellings of this story, we call "Dick Tapper." Larry recounted his experience at dinner one night at our house. While I faint at the sight of a needle, Bruce is generally unfazed by medical procedures. Larry informed the dinner party that he had not recovered well. When he went in for his checkup after surgery, he was asked to drop his trousers so the doctor could check his scrotum and testicles. They were so purple and swollen, Larry explained, that Dr. Tapper shouted, "Oh my God!" Bruce, who had been listening dispassionately, turned deathly pale and ran out for air.

Nonetheless, Bruce did not want to chicken out and lose the right to brag about getting his vas deferens detached by Dick Tapper, so he got up early and took himself to the hospital, a block from our houses.

He came home taciturn and without complaint of complications. My neighbor Nancy remarked that he would not be riding his bike to class that afternoon.

With law school behind us, my parents secured a clerkship for Bruce with a well-respected attorney in Delaware. I still felt a residue of apprehension about Bruce's tendency to drift away when we moved to Newark, but I figured my droll and fun-loving parents would draw Bruce into their social fold.

Chapter 5

MOM AND DAD

Bruce won the brass ring when he got my parents for in-laws. June and Andy Anderson were not average or typical: a perfect fit for Bruce, and another cover for his Asperger's lack of social skills and craving for attention. Everyone loved my folks, and Bruce joined the crowd. Their constant talking, joking, and game-playing camouflaged his lack of communication skills, as he could hardly get a word in edgewise. All he had to do was sit back and watch us entertain him as if he were watching a movie.

Bruce enjoyed bus trips from the local country club to the University of Delaware football games, Bloody Marys in hand, and hours of tailgating with my folks ahead. To this day, he is a fervent Blue Hens fan. He so loved golfing with my dad that he joined in a jocular foursome with Dad's friends, a squad that lasted for twenty years. And his quirky genius for numbers gave him an advantage in bridge games. Years later, as Bruce's distance and rigidity began to cool our relationship, I accused him of weaseling his way into my family's life.

I found out later that Bruce had literally listed seven goals for a mate and then checked them off when he met me. Applying such a rational method to matters of the heart is a red flag for Asperger's. Apparently I checked out. Meeting my parents cemented his belief that he must marry me.

Dad was born on the Fourth of July, and he loved to claim that all the fireworks were meant for him. He insisted we throw him a big party every year at one of our houses. Our homes always included large backyards, good for Roman candles, skyrockets, and our "dance of the faeries," a synchronized display of sparklers cutting fire trails in the night.

My dad was an only child, although he had a cousin, Glenn, who was like a brother to him. Glenn became an acrobat who performed live with Spike Jones and on the TV show *You Asked For It*, during which he walked on his hands down the steps of the Washington Monument.

Dad's father, Henry, was only in his late forties when he died of a stroke, right in Dad's arms. His mother was a beautiful Swedish woman, Grandmother Myrtle, from whom Dad got his good looks. Her family had emigrated from Sweden to Minneapolis and then moved on to Los Angeles. She worked in the lingerie department of Bullock's Westwood and collected autographs of movie stars; Jane Fonda's was my favorite.

My mother and her sister were born in Burlington, Vermont, where my grandfather built a comfortable life for his family, with a nice house and two cars. Grandfather Parker took a big hit in the crash of 1929, however, and became risk-averse when it came to financial advice. He warned my parents against buying AT&T stock, which left them wishing "if only" forever after when that blue chip continued to soar. Sadly, my grandmother Ivy died of colon cancer when my mom was only sixteen. The pain in my mom's voice and eyes when she spoke of her mother has marked my life with a sense of sadness. I would love to have known Ivy.

My parents met on a blind date in Albany, New York, and married soon after. Mom was dazzled by Dad's Swedish good looks and wavy blond hair, and he was smitten by her dark eyes, brunette tresses, and striking beauty. So exceptional was she in personality and looks that her college crowned her queen of both their Winter Carnival and Spring Fling. Dad began working for Cargill, while Mom was a photographer's assistant. Her expertise with cameras proved valuable to Dad when he took an interest in photography himself.

During WWII, Dad joined the Army Air Corps. Stationed in Orlando, Florida, his job was to plant himself in the bombardier section of airplanes and take photos to teach map reading. A Minnesota man, Dad said he had never been so cold as he was when standing on the tarmac in Florida.

Hip, hip, hooray! It's a wonder that Dad was another "lucky fucker" who kept missing deployments to Europe. When the Air Corps finally cut his orders to the war zone, the war ended. During all the missed deployments, my parents decided they might as well try to have a baby. I was born in Orlando, Florida, on October 22, 1944, a vaginal breech birth that would have been a C-section today. Because it was such a rare and challenging birth, Mom's bruised vagina was put on view to a clutch of interns and residents for teaching purposes, a story my mom loved to tell.

After the war, they bought a small photography business in Poultney, Vermont, home of Green Mountain College, which both Mom and I attended. Students at the college and local weddings provided the bulk of their business. Dad took the photos, and Mom hand-colored them out of her little tubs, each bearing dabs of pink, sienna, or green paint grooved by her swab or brush. I was fascinated by the darkroom while watching Dad develop film, pictures emerging magically from the stinky chemicals. His fingernails were always a slight brown hue.

Friends convinced Mom and Dad to move to Delaware, where there were better schools for my brother and me. Unfortunately, small photography studios encountered stiff competition as stores like JCPenney and Sears began offering inexpensive pictures. So Dad gave up his photography business and became a traveling salesman for Swift's Instruments. The job was a bad fit. Mom suspected him of golfing more than selling. Finally, he settled into real estate, where he did quite well, thanks to his extroversion and smarts.

He still took portraits—one client was Mrs. Delaware of the time—but his focus was on woodworking. He made beautiful tables and frames for my mom's oil paintings, which she began to produce after taking courses at the University of Delaware. They were hung all over the house, making it a congenial site for their frequent, boisterous, and fun-loving parties.

Come-as-you-are parties were popular in the fifties and sixties, and Mom and Dad loved to throw them and catch everyone unprepared. Something about everyone sitting around in their grubbies and dirty hair made it more hilarious. At one party, the guests took turns donning one of Mom's tams and smocks and painted part of an abstract picture on a canvas set up on an easel in their living room. This wonderful creation was passed around from house to house so that everyone could enjoy it.

The party games my folks played were a hoot, and Bruce and I adopted them for our own revels. One game was called "Choo-Choo." First, a guy and a gal would conga around the room, and then the gal would pick a second guy to join them. Off they'd choo-choo like a train to a bedroom out of sight. The first guy would kiss the gal, and when the second guy puckered up for his kiss, he got smacked in the face with a powder puff. Surprise! They went back into the living room, and the second guy would pick up an unsuspecting female victim. Then the first guy would kiss the second gal, who kissed the second guy, who of course smacked the poor new gal in the kisser with the powder puff. Everybody thought it was hilarious.

Another game was a more risqué version of *Pass the Orange* or *Apple* (under the chin) called *Pass the Plate*. Two teams would line up.

Gals would put their hands in the guys' pockets and, holding onto a plate, pass it over the guys' privates, and the next gal would grab the plate. Sometimes it got a little dicey if we got too close to the family jewels, especially if pants were tight, but in those days guys usually had big pockets and loose-fitting pants.

We heard stories of a game where a gal was blindfolded and told to spread her legs and walk over a so-called bridge made of couch cushions. "Don't fall in the water!" she was warned. When the gal finished the walk, a guy would lie down on the cushions. It was a shock when they removed her blindfold and she saw the fellow lying on the cushions with a big grin on his face, as if he had been looking up her dress the whole time. One time, things went awry when a woman got so angry that she slapped the poor guy across the face. Hey, this was the fifties!

My parents' stunts and pranks were the stuff of legend. One Halloween, instead of trick-or-treating with an empty shot glass, they decided to entertain their friends with a shocking performance. Wearing a blond wig à la Bridgett Bardot, Mom covered her bathing suit with a big towel wrapped around her torso, giving the illusion that she was nude. Dad, meanwhile, dressed as a dirty lusting devil in long red underwear. So scandalously accoutered, they would knock on a friend's door, and then Dad would chase Mom screaming through the friend's house to the back door. As she flew out the exit (and just out of sight), Dad would snatch off the towel, leaving the results up to the gawking audience's imagination.

My uncle Wayne was a professional piano player and encouraged us all to learn to play. I took lessons and did pretty well, but Dad learned only the first couple bars of "Begin the Beguine." One Christmas, Dad set Uncle Wayne down to entertain us with his skill. With great flourishes, Dad began to play the keys, but then Mom called out from the kitchen, "Andy, I need you here quick." Sighing, Dad stopped playing, answered her call (while Uncle Wayne twiddled his thumbs impatiently), and finally returned to play the same introduction.

"Andy! I can't lift this turkey!"

And then, "Andy, quick help me get this hot casserole out of the oven!"

A few seconds later, "Andy, where is the baster?"

Finally, Wayne yelled into the kitchen, "June, will you let him fin—Oh, Andy, you son of a gun, you don't know any more, do you?"

While Dad did not tickle the ivories himself, beyond those two bars, he was a fabulous dancer. He taught me ballroom dancing, especially the two-step, which he also taught to Bruce for our wedding dance. I believe that Dad's instructions are why Bruce and I have enjoyed doing the two-step on dance floors for five decades. And Dad could intuitively pick up the newest dance craze. From The Frug to The Twist to The Mashed Potato, could he jitterbug! When I was attending Green Mountain College and Dad accompanied me to a local club, all the girls would vie to be his partner.

One of Mom and Dad's most memorable capers was at a dance club in New Jersey. Frustrated by the thick crowd on the dance floor, Dad enlisted a friend to whisper to the bandleader that they were a professional dance team called "The Parker Anderson Duo." They would be delighted to perform, he suggested, if the bandleader were to introduce them. He did, and the "Duo" glided around the dance floor, making dips and turns to loud applause. I have a video of their last two-step in the lobby of the Grand Floridian at Disney World to a piano version of "Begin the Beguine," their favorite song, but I never have the courage to watch it. Reid and I would go on to choose the same song for the mother-son dance at his wedding.

Bruce was amazed at how my mom contrived bookkeeping. She decided what bills to pay by drawing them from a hat, as in a lottery. She would joke that any creditor who persisted in dunning her wouldn't even get into that hat.

She also was famous for writing what she called "no checks" to prevent overdrafts. Inept at reconciling a checkbook, she would write herself checks in odd amounts. She never cashed them, although she still deducted the amount from the checkbook, thereby leaving a cushion for the bills she did pay. She had another tactic for her dentist, who was astonishingly quick to send out a bill for service. Once as she was checking out, she cocked an eyebrow and interrogated the clerk, "So, is your bill going to get to my house before I get back?" The joke was oft-repeated at the dental office.

Mom was no more into housework than she was into accounting, and she expressed her aversion dramatically. She once dumped all of Dad's dress shirts on the floor and danced The Twist on them, spinning the arms of the shirts like pinwheels and chanting, "I hate to iron! I hate to iron!" Nonetheless, she taught me how: first the yoke, then the collar, now the sleeves, blah blah.

The house was not dirty; it was just that most of the countertops were buried in clutter. Mom's one concession to housewifery was to leave a vacuum cleaner standing in the middle of the room. If company should knock on the door unexpectedly, she planned to claim, "I was just about to clean." As one might guess, I lacked training in the distaff arts. I learned to clean by reading the list on a bottle of 409 of things it was good for: "fixtures, blinds, floors," etc., etc.

Bruce and Dad were as close as any card-table, golf-green, or football-stadium buddies could be, and Bruce spoke at Dad's funeral. Following the burial, everyone set out for a restaurant by the riverside, where we danced our "dance of the faeries" with sparklers and set off memorial firecrackers.

My parents' passing has left a big hole in my heart. I would have dearly loved their ongoing support as I continued to struggle with Bruce's idiosyncrasies and my chronic illnesses. Mom would have understood and believed the Asperger's diagnosis in a heartbeat; she harbored a deep feeling that Bruce was different. He was not abusive or mean when we were with my parents, but maybe that was because he knew instinctively that they would not respond well to any mistreatment. Or maybe he was just happy and relaxed with them. It was a different story, however, when we were in the company of *his* parents.

Chapter 6

MOTHER HUBBARD CHILDCARE

The year of our nation's bicentennial, 1976, I was back home in Delaware, the Diamond State, the First State, the not-quite-as-small-as-Rhode Island state. Some say you can't gain much in the game of life stuck in such a postage-stamp playing field, but Bruce and I were to build our careers there, raise our children there, and damn near go to pieces there.

Bruce began law clerking for Ed Sobolewski, the attorney my parents knew, while studying for the Delaware Bar Examination, known nationwide as a dream-wrecker for aspiring barristers. Fifty percent of hapless law school graduates fail the Delaware bar and have perpetual clerkships to look forward to. Bruce chose to rehearse for this exam by taking the District of Columbia bar exam. For several weeks that winter, he commuted by rail to D.C. for evening bar review classes, often arriving home early the next morning due to frozen track switches or some such impediment, until he finally took the test. He was at work when I got the letter that he had passed, and I posted a big sign at the door: "Congratulations, Counselor!"

One year after his graduation, Bruce passed the Delaware bar, a terrific relief dollar-wise as well as mental health-wise. My parents threw an impromptu celebratory party.

Most of the guests were my parents' friends since we were new in town, but they were thrilled to support Bruce and me. One of them wrote a poem called "On Passing the Bar." The first few lines went thus:

> On this Thursday, October the twenty
> Our minds were sure occupied with plenty
> Did he pass? Did he fail?
> To counsel others from going to jail?
> Bruce anxiously awaiting his score in law
> When published was delighted with what he saw
> His number was there: yes, there's forty-nine
> Hopes not diminished, now everything's fine.

We were all tickled pink and quite joyous. I even puffed on a big cigar!

While we were driving home from the party with our two young children aboard, the car sputtered and stopped on the dark roadway. No gas! And then some guy came up out of nowhere.

"Stay in the car," Bruce said as he got out, which only unnerved me more. The guy told Bruce that he was on neighborhood patrol. *We have a neighborhood patrol?* My mind was racing about how I would take down this dude if he tried to rob Bruce. Turns out, the stranger *did* have a gas can full of gas. Bruce paid him five bucks and off we went, glad to be away from this scary encounter. However, Bruce continued to be gas challenged throughout the years.

Then we had a pitiful loss, although I certainly can't blame it on Bruce.

One evening, we were outside with my parents, who'd come over for a cookout. Jasper was frisky as a gremlin on steroids, jumping and dashing back and forth on his rope. He seemed particularly annoyed at being constrained and was driving me crazy, so I gave in and unsnapped his hook. I am forever guilt-ridden for aiding Jasper in his final escape.

He bolted across two small yards, ran straight into the street, and was instantly run over by a car driven by a woman blinded by the afternoon sun. Horrified, I watched his little black body roll under the car, and I collapsed to my knees, crying and screaming. Bruce ran off to the veterinarian with our wounded pet, but Jasper had to be euthanized because his back had been broken.

A kind neighbor took the kids to the playground so that they did not have to witness my tears and could be removed from the fray. Bruce comforted me at the time, but a few days later he coolly pointed out how I had looked hysterical crying in the street. What was my resolve after that remark? *Next time I see my beloved pet get killed, I'll stiffen my upper lip and take it like a good soldier. Better that than to look foolish and embarrass Bruce.*

Within a few days, we answered an ad for another miniature poodle and drove to a dilapidated house in a town nearby to purchase her for twenty-five dollars. We named her Governor, after a golden retriever that used to dash back and forth in our backyard when we lived in Virginia. We got quizzical looks when people heard her name, as if she were a Chihuahua named King. We had Governor for twenty-three years, and my grieving for Jasper was eased by the sweetness of this little dog.

We bought our first house in 1978, a townhome in a development called Four Seasons, where other young families had their starter homes. Although this was the same development where we had rented a townhome upon our arrival in Delaware, I never walked by the scene of Jasper's demise.

This was also where I first encountered one of my life's most joyful passions. Some neighbors we got acquainted with were runners; one even did the Ironman in Hawaii. At some point we went to a Marine Corps Marathon to support a friend. It was then that I decided to start running and took Governor along with me. That was the beginning, and since then I have continued the practice for over forty years.

Although other parts of my life were going well, my marriage was heading in a negative direction. Bruce routinely joined his boss, Ed, after work, hitting the local bars. He didn't bother to call home first, which I guess was smart on his part because it wouldn't have sat well with me. At a loss for what to do about this behavior, I focused on keeping the kids happy, fed, and tucked into bed while I hid my distress. One night Bruce wandered in at 11 p.m., late even for him. I was worried and angry, but his only comment was that he had thought it was 8 p.m., as if that were a reasonable explanation. It was a deplorable situation for me to try to handle by myself, but I soldiered on, trying to keep peace and a good family environment for the kids.

While living in that townhome, I went with my mom one night to a NOW meeting (I had joined the local chapter as soon as I had arrived in Delaware), and it proved to be a singular event, with the speaker talking about women going back to work. Mom leaned over to me and whispered conspiratorially, "Childcare."

Childcare! The word reverberated in my brain.

I had once sent for information on daycare when we lived in Virginia. In Toledo, I had operated a childcare business in my home and taught at the University of Toledo preschool. I also had a BS in elementary education. I'd recently applied for a job at a daycare in Four Seasons, but I was turned down. Now I hurried myself to the Small Business Administration, where I got great advice and encouragement from a woman who told me, "If you want a daycare, you can have a daycare." But it would be difficult, so she recommended that I begin with an in-home "family daycare."

And that's what I did. I turned my basement into a playroom and soon had a neat little business going and made good friends in the bargain. My two-year-old daughter had friends, too, and Bruce was supportive, greeting the early arrivals at the door before I was out of bed.

Still, I wanted a real, stand-alone daycare. We found an ad for a daycare center for sale and called, but after waiting days and weeks, we never got an answer. After a few months, I closed my family daycare and began working afternoons in another center, but I kept looking for a place of my own. It was like the labors of Hercules.

Even with my lawyer husband and Realtor father, it was daunting to find a site for daycare that met all the state, county, and city regulations in Delaware. Maryland had a category called "group daycare" with requirements we could satisfy, so we began looking just over the Delaware line. We found a raised ranch-style house that, while not the Ritz, was ideally situated across from an elementary school. Bruce found the place so ugly that he called it "The Box in the Gulch," a name that stuck with us. Still, he accepted that it was time to focus on *my* career, even though I had hoped for something better.

Soon Bruce and my father were hard at work in Bruce's office, completing the paperwork to seal the deal for The Box in the Gulch. Outside the building, low winter clouds had turned the sky a dull gray. The same clouds began to shed snowflakes over Four Seasons and all over northern Delaware. In minutes, it turned into a full-blown storm. I knew what that meant. School would close early. Reid was only in first grade, and after school he stayed at a friend's house a few miles away. When his bus dropped him off, she would still be at work, so I would have to hurry to find him.

I had just bathed Sally, so I had to stuff her wet hair into a stocking cap. I threw on some big boots and a long coat, which flared out behind me like some Russian Cossack jacket as I rushed for the door, grabbed the knob, and yanked it open.

The phone rang.

I was about to rush out when I thought, *Maybe it's my friend who watches Reid.*

I dashed back and snatched the receiver: "Hello! . . . What? . . . Hello?"

A man's voice responded, "Are you interested in buying a daycare center?" *Are you kidding me?*

"Oh my God!" I must have sounded like a maniac. Composing myself, I answered as professionally as I could manage, "Oh yes. I am very interested," and "Oh yes, I do have a staff lined up," and "I am qualified, and I have a degree in education," finishing with "I will be in touch with you right away."

Holy shit! I want that damned daycare. I have to tell Bruce to ditch The Box in the Gulch! And I have to find Reid!

The tire treads were barely gripping the snow as I gingerly urged that big blue Buick onward to intercept Reid, with Sally, in her winter wraps, sitting behind me in her car seat watching the snowfall. When I finally made it to my friend's street, I spied him through the tumbling flakes: my little kid walking toward the empty house.

Relieved, I hopped out of the car, gave Reid a quick hug and a kiss, and told him, "Mommy's going to Daddy's office. Let's go!"

How do you hurry in a blizzard? So-o-o slowly, but I finally slid into a parking space behind Bruce's building, unsnapped Sally, and rushed up the stairs to his office with kids in tow. As I burst in, Bruce and Dad were scratching away at a pile of paperwork, preparing to put in the offer for The Box in the Gulch. "A guy . . . he called . . . daycare." They looked at me in astonishment as I finally spat the words out. "A guy called about buying a daycare. It's the one in our neighborhood!"

Bruce scraped up all the papers in both hands and jubilantly tossed them into the air. "Saved by the bell!" he shouted, as the documents rained down in disarray. He immediately went into lawyerly high gear, first phoning the man back and then drawing up an Agreement of Sale contract. We understood that we might be facing stiff competition to buy this daycare, so Bruce raced into the raging snowstorm to get to the seller before other potential buyers. It's amazing when I think about it. If that snowstorm had blown up more quickly, if I had gotten out the door one minute earlier, if I had ignored that phone call to get to Reid sooner, this would not have happened. The universe had rained lucky charms.

Bruce reached the seller's office one step ahead of another buyer and clinched the deal. We did it! I'll just call it *Mother Hubbard Childcare* after moi.

We opened on April 2, 1979, and Sally celebrated her third birthday at my center later that month. It turned out that this was the place that had rejected me for a job six months before.

We were all moving forward. Bruce had done settlements for the owner of Caravel Farms south of Newark, and we bought a new home there. Bruce built us a pool from a kit after all the pieces were delivered to our backyard by a huge truck. His uncle, who was an electrical engineer, visited and volunteered his services with the electrical work. Our kids became active in all sorts of activities and made loads of neighborhood friends, who flocked to our pool. We had pool parties, played Marco Polo and pool volleyball, and raced each other. Whenever I had to leave for the daycare center, I kicked the kids out.

At this point, Bruce was a full-blown lawyer, and childcare was in demand, so we concentrated on growing the childcare business. We scouted a property a mile from the first small center, bargained with banks to fund a new lot, and built our own modern, one-hundred-kid childcare center.

There was almost a disaster before we opened, however, thanks to Bruce's inability to stay alert to vital details. We had to cart some metal sleeping cots in the bed of a small pickup we were using, but Bruce failed to tie them down securely. I was following him as he pulled out of Four Seasons and began breezing down the highway. Suddenly, several cots lifted from the truck bed and flew up in the air behind him as if they'd been sucked up by a tornado. I don't know how I dodged those somersaulting cots. It was a miracle that no other cars plowed into them, either.

Still, it was an exciting morning when all my little guys and gals were transported to the new facility. One little boy, who had been with us for several years, walked in with me, looked around at the colorful walls, toys, and brand-new child-size furniture, and said, "This is bootiful." Thinking of the excitement and joy we all felt warms my heart to this day.

During that time, our lives were so busy that I couldn't deal with Bruce's screwups. The emotional consequences for me, however, would be for keeps.

Before long, a band of parents who were losing their own daycare approached us to open a daycare in nearby New Castle, a charming town known for its colonial buildings, cobblestone streets, and the landing of William Penn. We found a suitable building for sale, but it needed renovation, and we needed both a new zoning law and a variance. With Bruce's lawyerly skills and the cooperation of the city council, we soon had our second daycare. After renovating, we built an addition that we could rent to other businesses.

The universe kept working for us. The owner of our first center in Strawberry Run asked us if we wanted to buy out his place in another complex. We did. Now we had three centers, and eventually, after developers approached us to create centers in new office complexes, we got up to five.

Every weekend, however, was dedicated for repairs of one sort or another. Bruce drove a 1950 faded green Chevy pickup truck, which we nicknamed the "Mother Hubbard Maintenancemobile." Sunday-morning polka music blared from the radio as Bruce rattled around town, making pit stops at different facilities.

The Maintenancemobile also served Bruce with the rentals that we had acquired. University of Delaware students rented the apartments, and "move out" time was hectic. Bruce did an excellent job of dealing with routine tenant problems. Some were not so routine, as when inventive college kids put their beer keg on the roof or when roommates were squabbling. It struck me as odd that he could handle his clients' and tenants' problems but was distant with our family issues.

My first director was a talented and experienced teacher and administrator, Clementine Hayburn. One of her four sons attended the little family daycare in my home, and Reid and one of her other sons played soccer together, so we often had time to dream and plan. The day we signed the Agreement of Sale for our first center, I called her and said, "Name your price, Hayburn!"

"You *got* it!" she exclaimed.

Clementine helped me immensely during the learning phase of being a childcare owner. As my centers grew, she went on to run an early childhood program at a large private school, but we would remain close friends and colleagues.

I loved being a business owner, but when the business is kids, it allows us grownups to stay in a childlike state. In his book *Your Erroneous Zones*, Wayne Dyer (2001) provides all kinds of advice, using psychological terms such as the id, the ego, and the child. We were heavy on the child, a fun-loving and carefree state. The motto for Mother Hubbard was, "Kids are people too."

We were laid back and laughed a lot. Holidays were especially happy for us adult people because we shared them with kid people. My employees were lighthearted, and we were like family. My last director, Karen, made my sixtieth birthday special by presenting me with a lime green T-shirt printed with "Sixty and Still Running." The only snag with the gifts was that she gave me a fake lottery ticket. I thought it was my lucky day, but when I called to cash in my $10,000, the clerk asked me if my ticket said "State of Delaware" on it. It didn't.

It seemed to me that my daycare parents could use some tips on how to deal with childcare. Their kids would fuss when they were dropped off and be uncooperative when their parents were in a hurry to retrieve them. While Clementine was still working with me, she and I decided to collaborate on a self-help book for parents. Before long, we self-published *Daycare Parenting: How to Have a Successful Child Care Experience* through Four Seasons in 1985. We sold it to some local bookstores, where it got the attention of a small private publishing company that printed it as *Daycare Parenting* (Hubbard and Hayburn, 1988). We got an advance and publicity in our local newspaper and gave talks to interested groups, including a lecture at a local community college.

Over the next dozen years, we were to see our lives expanding bountifully: growing our businesses, touring in recreational vehicles (RVs), moving to finer homes, and running competitively. Add bridge, golf, and University of Delaware football with my folks, and what could go wrong? These experiences would weave our lives together, even if Bruce's inexplicable behavior tended to unravel the tapestry.

Chapter 7

DYSPRAXIA

When they were still small, Reid and Sally loved to hear Bruce tell them stories of his scars, the yuckier the better. "Start at your head this time, Dad!" Reid would urge, as opposed to his feet; Bruce's head has taken insults from his crown to his occiput, including his neck bones.

When Bruce was only six, his father, who was hammering down plywood on a new roof, asked Bruce to climb up the ladder and bring him some nails. Negotiating the slanted roof, Bruce fell through a gap in the plywood and crashed onto the concrete ten feet below. He was in a coma for twenty-four hours!

And the teeth that got knocked out in the car driven by his one-eyed friend were implants. The originals had been knocked out years before by a heavy tin can, which a playmate had been enthusiastically swinging from a stick. Is it any wonder Bruce hadn't wanted to fight for a girl he had just met at the beach and go through a third round of front teeth replacement?

Bruce liked to fiddle with knives and hatchets. The knuckles on his hand are scalloped with various circular and half-moon scars, acquired from having whittled or shaped soapbox derby cars. At the tender age of eight, Bruce wanted to crack open some agate rocks he had collected to see which one was the prettiest. He explained to Reid and Sally how the rocks looked rather plain outside but dazzling inside. However, one time while aiming the blunt end of a hatchet at a rock, Bruce drew back so eagerly that he momentarily lodged the sharp end in his skull. His folks were not home, so he ran to a neighbor's house, blood streaking down his face, and they hurried him off for medical assistance.

It seemed to me that Bruce and his two brothers had little parental guidance at the home of his grandparents Daisy and Jesse in Portsmouth, Ohio, where, incidentally, his brother Ralph had gone to first grade with Roy Rogers. Daisy and Jesse had raised ten children of their own in a small wood-framed house with no running water, but the kids took care of themselves. During one visit, Bruce and his brother were chasing chickens back to their coop, and Bruce ran into the low galvanized tin roof, slicing his forehead, across his eye, and down his cheek. He was lucky not to lose his eye, but he carried a rather sinister scar, which, if it had not faded over time, might have been off-putting to his clients.

To the consternation of his elementary school teacher, Bruce once dangled by his ankles from the gymnastic rings in the school gym and slipped loose, managing to miss the mat and crash on the hardwood floor. Much later, he told me he would never take up bungee jumping.

On another summer trip to Ohio, Bruce's uncle had him ride on a pickup running board on the way back from a swimming hole while the rest of the gang crammed into the truck bed. Unable to hang on over the bumps, Bruce fell onto a gravel road, which scraped the skin off his right side. I know how much a skinned knee stings, and I can't imagine the pain of a partially skinned body, but luckily he suffered no broken bones. The lengthy healing time of his raw flesh ended his swimming for the rest of the summer, however, which was especially hard since he lived across the street from beautiful Lake Winona, where everyone went to swim.

The kids and I were particularly grossed out by the hayride tale. This mishap occurred when Bruce was on an autumn night hayride through the Wisconsin countryside, across the Mississippi River from his hometown. As the hay wagon wheeled into the parking area for the teenagers to disembark, Bruce jumped off before it stopped, and he propelled himself onto a barbed-wire fence, severely slashing and puncturing his legs. *Ouch!* Being familiar with barbed-wire fences from traipsing around Vermont farms during my childhood, I had gingerly avoided getting stuck with the dagger-like metal.

One plus of Bruce's pervasive absence from our lives was that our kids were spared injury most of the time, but there were a few memorable incidents, like the time we were strolling the boardwalk in Ocean City, Maryland. Bruce was carrying two-year-old Reid on his shoulders, oblivious to the fact that he had to duck down when he entered a souvenir store to allow room for Reid's head, thus smacking him into the overhang. This was one of those incidences when the child's mouth opens in a silent scream before a piercing sound is emitted into the ears of anyone in the vicinity, and I did my best to assuage the whole kerfuffle.

Fast forward to Reid's graduation from law school in Miami, where we hired a small U-Haul trailer to move his belongings back to Delaware. The trailer was hooked up to the RV, and I watched in horror as Bruce backed up to a loading position, unaware that the trailer would collapse like an accordion. Reid was guiding him and about to be crushed between the two vehicles. Sally and I were waving our arms and screaming, "Stop! Stop!" Fortunately, Bruce finally realized something was wrong and hit the brakes, while Reid jumped away at the last second. My heart almost jumped out of my chest as my nerves took another hit.

Bruce and I visited Sally at The College of William and Mary when she performed with the marching band. We were particularly excited about her upcoming fire twirling show, and Sally asked her dad to dip the cloth-covered batons in oil and shake them down. She performed a spectacular half-time show for an appreciative and enthusiastic crowd. When it was over, however, Sally was trembling and in tears because Bruce had not shaken off the excess fuel, so hot oil had splattered her as she twirled. She told us she had been terrified of being badly burned. Bruce said nothing. After she persevered for a response, some sympathy, a hug, or an earnest apology, he finally conceded, "I'm sorry."

One of the first things Bruce said to me when we discovered the diagnosis for Asperger's syndrome was that he wanted to find out why he could not follow instructions. He should not have been put in that position, and I feel bad now that he was, but I did not understand at the time that this task was beyond his ability.

As I learned later, it is not uncommon for people with Asperger's syndrome to exhibit symptoms of dyspraxia, or developmental coordination disorder, which affects fine and gross motor coordination. Disrupted messages from the brain to the body affect a person's ability to perform movements in a smooth, coordinated way. While Bruce has several of the traits associated with this disorder, most pronounced is his lack of awareness of body position in space and spatial relationships, which results in his bumping into things, tripping over things, and dropping and spilling things. Unfortunately, I have been the victim of a lot of bumping and dropping of things, with many of my poor cook pans, picture frames, and endless other articles smashed to pieces.

Bruce did support my interests as well as my business. He never complained about any new creature four-footing across our threshold, and at one point we had two dogs and nine cats. Bruce once saved a family of kittens from an abandoned car, getting bitten and having to take a tetanus shot in the process. He is a good guy, right?

When I was going off to women's marches in Washington, D.C., Bruce took Sally and me to several of them, and he supported my feminist agenda. Thomas Jerfferson said "Men of quality are not threatened by women of equality." That was a plus for me.

Bruce never forgot my birthday, Valentine's Day, Mother's Day, or anniversaries, giving me pretty flowers and cards with beautiful sentiments. Since they were such a disconnect from our real life, I have no idea whether he truly felt the words in the cards or thought they would make me happy. I had a business to attend to and kids to raise, so the days and years sped by with the vagaries of our less-than-ideal relationship taking a back seat. When we contracted to build a new house, which was exciting and occupied most of our time, I hoped that things would change for the better and keep us coasting on the upper tracks of our marital roller-coaster ride, at least for a while.

Chapter 8

DISENGAGE

On the surface, where all could see, we were hunky-dory. Business was blossoming, our kids were doing well in school, and Bruce went off to work each morning and came home like a responsible hubby, most of the time, although sometimes he did come home in an inebriated state. But not every pain is evident to others, like a rash or rasping cough. Under the surface or out of sight, something in the totality of Bruce's behavior left me deeply distressed. You see, much of the time he just *had* to be somewhere else: at a road race, a golf outing, or anywhere but home. When I brought this up with Bruce, his reaction appeared reasonable on the surface, but it was the old passive-aggressive subterfuge: "Do you want me to stay home? I don't have to go; I'll stay home if you want me to." Meaning, the kids and I can have his company, but it comes with his resentment. This so confounded me that I caved in like a statue with feet of clay.

So it was I, pregnant with Sally, who pitched baseballs to Reid when he was a little tyke back in Toledo. He could hit the ball back at me so hard I had to turn around and duck to protect my big belly.

But when I took him to Little League tryouts, he kept missing pitches. How could that happen? When all seemed lost, he tossed his bat down and said, "I don't like this bat." He picked another and whack! He hit a home run!

I asked a woman next to me—the coach's wife, it turns out—whether she thought Reid would make the team. "Are you kidding me?" she exclaimed. "With a home run hit?"

When Sally was no longer a tot, I took her to the Little League field to sign up for tee-ball. It turns out she was too old by two months. She'd have to play in a more advanced division, where kids swung at pitches whizzing by their heads instead of at balls resting on a post. I had no idea where Bruce was, but I dashed home to toss Sally a hundred pitches until she caught on, and we headed for tryouts. She made the team—number 1 on her Angels jersey! I took her to dance classes, where she learned to be a baton twirler. I remember how excited I was filming Sally marching in a parade, the smallest kid on the street, twirling her flashing baton. She continued twirling in marching bands through high school and college.

On the surface, Bruce seemed engaged in these adventures, attending plenty of soccer matches, baseball games, and twirling events. What I saw and felt, however, was his preoccupation with fraternizing with other parents. Under the radar, Bruce rejected all my cajoling and insistence that he help the kids with homework, school projects, or sports.

One instance was especially unsettling. Each season that Reid played soccer, he experienced terrible leg cramps due to the high intensity of practice. He would wake up at night screaming in pain, so we had to leap out of bed and fly to his bedroom with a pain pill and a heating pad. Each year I tried to enlist Bruce to help Reid build up his leg endurance so that he would not suffer so, but Bruce could not be bothered. When I did manage to drag Bruce along to the practice field, he halfheartedly kicked the soccer ball to Reid with me coaching, but as far as helping with the painful cramps, it was a waste of time.

During these years in Caravel Farms, I began telling people that something was not right with Bruce. For example, whenever I dared to voice a concern, he would get all in a huff, as if he were being attacked. Hence, most problems involving him remained unresolved. If I had no alternative but to address an issue with him, I had to brace myself for the storm that I knew was coming. Even though I was trying to maintain calm both inside and outside, I was walking on eggshells in both spheres, and my nervous system began to run steadily on overdrive. If I mentioned that he was using a loud tone of voice or seemed to be in a bad mood, he would deny it and say that I had been in a bad mood first. His favorite line was, "I just don't want to cause a problem." What problem was he trying to prevent? Was I unreasonable or impossible to live with?

I had no idea at the time that he had been born with a condition that would make him super sensitive to anything he perceived as criticism. He would react like a coiled rattlesnake.

One time, we took a quiz from a magazine, and one question was, "Do you make mistakes?"

"No," Bruce answered confidently.

That was odd, I thought.

We all learned to keep Dad Bruce on an even keel. When Dad fried hamburgers for the kids' dinner, he was prone to burning them because he set the burner too high. The kids would peer up at me from their plates of blackened burgers, afraid to say anything, such as "Dad, the burgers are burned."

"They are not burned!" he would spit back if they did venture to say anything.

If it were me, I would just say, "I can't believe I burned them again. I better get a new pan or stop cooking the burgers." Not Bruce.

My girlfriend, who needed cheering up after her divorce, came for dinner one evening. Much to my distress, the pot roast that Bruce had purchased was tougher than a rubber doorjamb. Bruce freaked out in front of her, even though I insisted that it wasn't his fault but the fault of the grocery store. That made a bad situation worse, and I wore myself to a frazzle trying to mollify Bruce. This little dinner party certainly did not lift my friend's spirits!

We became close with our next-door neighbors in Caravel Farms, Dan and Brenda. They had a son and daughter our kids' ages, and we shared our lives and extended families. I envied the way they collaborated on projects, chatting about this and that as Dan worked on a repair while Brenda stood by at the ready, handing him nails or screws. If Bruce washed the dishes and I offered to help dry, he would respond, "No need for both of us to do it."

These guys were into computers and tech before anyone else and had a VCR player. Once, Dan was kind enough to tape a TV show for me, and I watched it in his family room with him, while he actually made comments Their daughter was on Sally's Little League team, and Dan would cheer and gab next to us on the bench during a game, while Bruce sat mute. I was getting the sense that not all husbands were like Bruce. Some did chat and share.

Folks might have seen Bruce and me as crewmates on a love boat, but belowdecks Bruce was on another cruise, and I began to detach emotionally and physically. To Bruce, I was invisible. He was steeped in his own agenda and lost in his own world. He had no interest in what the kids and I were doing, whether he was at work or off with his diversions. When I would reach out and ask him what he thought about a subject, he would reply, "You know what I think." Bruce seemed to have no idea that we each had thoughts of our own. I told him I had no idea what he was thinking. When we watched TV, he never said a peep, and he sat silently with his hands folded in a tent before his face.

Apparently he didn't get the memo that a partner and companion is supposed to communicate, laugh, touch, joke, reminisce, plan, or hash out concerns and problems. There was an uneasy tension sitting with him in the same room.

I figured, *Why stay around him watching TV this way and be ignored?* So I began going upstairs to my bedroom each evening to read a book. After a couple weeks of this, even he could sense that things were not quite right, and he trekked up the stairs to talk to me. Sitting on the bed and watching me read for several minutes, he did not say a word.

Finally, he asked, "What are you doing?"

"I'm reading."

I could not frankly explain my unhappiness. If I had, Bruce would probably have denied my concerns, turned the blame on me, and there would have been a big fight. He was visibly relieved that I did not seem angry and that there was no threat to his fool's paradise. Our relationship was off the rails, but neither of us knew the reason.

Every September, when the first day of school arrived and school sports also typically began, Bruce insisted on taking an annual bike trip to the beach for days of manly carousing with his boss and friends, who called themselves the "Mums." Bruce seemed unaware of any reason to be there to help his children develop their athletic skills or to salute milestones. Once, when I insisted that he come back from his barhopping, he told me the other guys said he was "pussy-whipped."

This behavior drove me to enlist my mother in a campaign to give my husband a taste of his own medicine. She understood how Bruce's behavior was unacceptable and went along with the plan. I called Bruce to tell him that Mom and I would not be home until late, but even after a long night and my returning home after midnight, Bruce did not change. All I got for my trouble was a hangover.

Since I had more success handling my business than my husband, I thought I might try some tactics I had learned in a management class. I wrote up an improvement plan, told him that he was taking the kids and me for granted, and informed him that I expected change. He tried to ratchet himself up to a higher level for a while, but he was soon in the same old trough. Our roller-coaster relations got more extreme, especially the troughs. I began to say to him or the walls or anyone who might listen, "You shouldn't have gotten married, had a wife, kids, a house!"

I got to be an actor! Okay, just a background artist or an extra, but I got a paycheck of ninety-five dollars for fifteen hours of work from the Screen Actors Guild! Our neighbor was a casting agent, and she recruited me; Sally; my mom and dad; my sister-in-law, Sue; and our friend Buzz to be the audience in the theater scene for the 1989 movie *Dead Poets Society,* starring Robin Williams. Reid and a few of his high school friends were also background artists. By chance, Sally, Dad, and I sat in the theater just a few rows from an action scene, so we spent more time on the set than the rest of the audience. When Dad arrived, friendly and funny as usual, he remarked to director Richard Weir, "We have lights, camera, and now we have the action!" to which Weir gave a hearty laugh.

We had to sit still, be quiet, and look interested in a nonexistent performance. My friends would suggest that that was not typical behavior for me. Still, afraid of wrecking the scene, I held fast to the director's instructions. Reid's acting entailed kicking a soccer ball back and forth to another student on the school's front lawn, with the pond as a backdrop. After repeating this movement all day while the actors in the foreground did their thing, Reid got blisters from the street shoes required by his costume. Sally got itchy from her period wool clothes. Mom got blisters from her ill-fitting shoes, which were only held on by tissue paper.

Mom, representing a 1960s theater goer, was placed in the front row because of her gray hair and mink stole, the mink inherited from Grandpa Parker's wife, Lorraine. I volunteer for anti-fur activism with PETA, but the producer wanted fur, so we dug it out of the attic, and it is hopefully now keeping a homeless person warm. The front row of the audience was not let go until dark because they could exit only after the main characters.

Our job finally over, we huddled outside the theater, shuffling around in the fake snow, and prepared to whisk Mom off for some relief. When she came out to join us, she admitted that the last time she had walked up the aisle she had banged on the vintage cigarette machine prop, hoping an old pack of Camels would fall out.

We moaned when the director said, "Cut!" and rejoiced when he said, "It's a wrap." To our delight, Robin Williams did a little skit for us to keep us from getting antsy while the crew set up a scene. I learned that filmmakers deserve every penny they make, as we were exhausted after only a couple of days.

The troughs in our roller-coaster marriage were aggravating, to put it mildly. There were compensating heights, however—children, business, sports, a brief career in moviemaking, and knocking around the country in RVs—that made life tolerable at least.

Chapter 9

RV-ING

Our lifetime love of RV-ing began at a Little League end-of-the-season barbecue at Reid's coach's house. Overspreading his driveway like a giant seagoing galleon was a thirty-foot motor home. We were intrigued by this movable hotel suite on wheels.

Bruce always spoke fondly of his childhood road trips, and I cherished the memory of my parents driving my brother and me cross-country to California. We could repeat history with our kids! Who cared that we had no idea how to drive or operate a motor home? We made a rental deal with the coach. I devised a tight travel budget, and in April 1983, we rattled and rocked Santa Monica-bound down the road in our ship of the highways, where Parker, Sue, and my new niece, Brooke, lived.

We had a steep learning curve, and avoiding catastrophes was first on the agenda, mainly by battening down the hatches of our asphalt [ship]. If we did not secure our cabinets, a can of beans or a pot [would land] us on the head. Anything left on the counters might end [up on the deck], banging back and forth against the bulkheads. If the refrigerator was not locked, food would spill out. This old RV had a shag rug, and more than once I had to sop up orange or tomato juice absorbed by the orange and auburn fibers, which at least were the same color. We learned to announce when we were going into the commode, so the driver could warn us to hang on around the curves or sudden stops and not get pitched out the door with our pants around our ankles and a goose egg on the noggin.

A great way to amuse our kids on the rolling waves of a long-distance RV voyage was playing board and card games. If we could keep the games on the table, that is. We'd also stumble around the RV and roll toy cars or rubber balls back and forth. Once we got our sea legs, we entertained ourselves with a daredevil game we called "motor home surfing." As the RV careened around bends or bounced on highway rough spots, we would spread our feet, refrain from holding on, and wobble like surfers trying to stay in the wave barrel without bailing on the sofa. It was rad! We didn't get the parent award for safety back then. Now all the seats have belts.

I learned to drive the thing in a big parking lot out West, and soon I was sailing long stretches of the interstates.

When we got back from our virgin cruise, we bought the first of nine RVs we were to possess, this time a used twenty-eight-foot Pace Arrow. It was old, cold, and rickety, but it got us to Disney World, me riding with my stocking hat pulled over my head. A few days after we saw Michael Jackson's thrilling Victory Tour show at JFK Stadium, we took our parents with us in that ice bucket to see a dramatic launch of the Challenger on October 5, 1984. On that journey, Kathryn D. Sullivan became the first American woman to make a spacewalk.

RVing met our needs perfectly. I had never liked hotels, with the noise of people in the next room, the rumbling in the hallways, the chemical scent, and the elevator doors wheezing open and shut. Campgrounds are quiet, and I loved the scent of pine needles in the morning or walking the dog around when we first arrived. We rare put out the awnings, set up chairs, cooked out, or stayed long. We just traveled in style, saving money on galley-cooked breakfasts and lunches so we could indulge ourselves with fine dining in the evenings. The process entailed my running into the restaurant in my sweats or shorts to see if they had a table available. If they did, we would get decked out in our swellest clothes inside the RV and head back in. Sometimes the staff didn't even recognize us because we cleaned up so well. We would set sail early the next morning for golfing, skiing, running races, and more dining. The RV was our base-in-port. Reid's birthday fell on Labor Day weekend, and for years we drove him and his friends to the beach in our RV for a summer's last blast.

Later we were to take our RV to visit Reid when he went to college in Florida and Sally when she went to college in Virginia. Our favorite RV was an Airstream Land Yacht, a gleaming, stainless steel, twin-axled, streamlined wonder with leather seats, solar stone-guard windows, and a dump station light, among other luxuries. Compared to the ones in the past, RVs today are fancy, sleek, and high-tech, but in those days, when we pulled into a parking lot with our Airstream, people acted like the circus had come to town. *Haven't you ever seen an RV before?* Often folks would ask to peek inside to see what it was all about or with ambitions of becoming RV-ers themselves. Many craved a tour, so Bruce would hold them off while I threw underwear in a drawer, covered the sheets with the bedspread, and grabbed dirty dishes off the counter.

"How many does it sleep?" was the most common question.

"How many people do I want to cram in here?" I would respond. We traveled sometimes with both pairs of our parents, but they usually spent the nights in motels.

When my daughter graduated from college, we parked the RV near the campground pool, which was in a remote area obscured by trees. We topped off the festivities with a farewell skinny-dip, such was the derring-do inspired by our RVs.

We experienced temporary relief from our obscure and indefinable marital problems when we traveled, because that was when Bruce was the most relaxed and, therefore, less prone to anger and defensiveness.

Chapter 10

ASPERGATES: THE MINI AND THE MINOR

What is one more mess-up in the realm of things? I am not maimed, dead, or hauled away by the men in white coats. At least not yet, but all the screwups over the years have put me closer to the edge of insanity. When Bruce makes mistakes that affect only him, he wrangles out of them most times, with no seeming damage to himself. When Bruce's actions affect me, I have come to call these aberrations "aspergates." Lack of interest, a dearth of listening and communication skills, carelessness, and an inability to "make connections" (Bruce's phrase) are the usual mainsprings for these calamitous actions. None are intentional on his part, but the nerve-racking effect and damage are the same.

I often thought that Bruce processed information into many minuscule segments, like in the sixties when we would flip through pages in a Crackerjack miniature book prize that we dug out from the bottom of the box of caramel popcorn. Looking at one page does not give the whole story. It is only a slice of information, which does not allow the viewer to grasp the sequence from the beginning to the end. It's like watching Road Runner's legs spinning in the dust as he is chased by Wile E. Coyote with no understanding of how the bird got himself into the predicament or how he will eventually save himself from Wile E.'s clutches. How is one to visualize and understand past or future events with snapshots of information? One can't, and that is a formula for mishaps, mistakes, and aspergates.

During fifty-plus years of marriage, I estimate I have been aspergated 20,000 times, give or take a few thousand. Some instances are insignificant and pass through my brain in a nanosecond, causing a slight tensing of my neck and shoulder muscles. I have taken to categorizing aspergates: the mini, a mere trifle were it not one among thousands; the minor, an acute annoyance; and the major, a calamity that inflicts the greatest harm on my body, brain, nerves, and health. I describe a few of these deleterious proceedings below.

MINI ASPERGATES

Bruce inadvertently mowed down a tomato plant. What makes this an aspergate is the preceding conversation:

"Bruce, look, a tomato came up from last year. A *volunteer*, your mom would call it."

I look out the window ten minutes later, and he has mowed it down with the riding mower. "Why did you do that?" I yell.

"How am I supposed to know what a tomato plant looks like?" Bruce yells back.

Were those rows of fragrant tomato plants you tended for your parents invisible? Where did the bags of tomato sauce I made each year come from if not our tomato plants, like the one you just lopped off at the ground, claiming you never saw one before?

The older kids were having great fun on the waterslide of our new pool. Afraid our two-year-old grandson would slide too fast with the hose running, I turned it off. From inside the house, I heard Bruce turn it back on, so I ran out in a panic, yelling, "Turn it off!" Too late. The child had sunk like a stone under water and coughed and cried pitifully in my daughter's arms. Sally was distraught and decided the slide was not appropriate for a two-year-old. And I had been so excited about introducing our new "spool playground."

We hired a guy to help us plant bushes, azaleas, roses, holly, and crepe myrtle around the huge perimeter of our new house on Mason Drive. The pickup truck was crammed full of plants from the landscape nursery. Bruce had no idea where any of them went, but that didn't stop him from dumping them helter-skelter around the place before I could get there and show him. "What the hell are you doing?" I cried.

"I just wanted to get started," Bruce mumbled.

The poor hired guy had to pile all the plants back in the truck while we were fussing and arguing. *Thanks for making another project double the trouble and making the guy think we are two looney tunes.*

From around the mailbox, Bruce kept digging up the purple clematis, one of which I had spent two years nursing. I devised a plan to hide a new clematis plant from Bruce by planting it by our garden fence. Bruce yanked it out while weeding. Was fate telling me that I dare not plant clematis?

The white annual vinca flowers needed to be pulled out at summer's end. They surrounded a white rosebush, which complemented another one on the other side of the landscaped area in front of our house. Bruce tackled the job and didn't say anything about thorn wounds, so for a few days I didn't notice it was missing, but when I did, I cried, "What happened to my rosebush?" Bruce jumped in fear, tore off to the woods, retrieved the rosebush, and crammed it back into the ground. Lucky for him, it survived.

When we bought the property for the new house we were going to build, I thought we could plant flowering trees before the building began to ease my sadness at making the move from our old house. We spent a lot of money on dogwood, weeping willow, magnolia, and others. Bruce routinely drove over to the property to water them. Wandering around the property one day, I gasped when I noticed the $500 Robinson cherry tree was dead as a doornail. Somehow, Bruce had passed by it every time he had come over to water. I still see the stump and feel so sorry for the thirsty tree, which slowly succumbed to a man-made drought.

MINOR ASPERGATES

I run tapes over the things Bruce has dropped, broken, and maimed: A baby bird in a bush that he weed-whacked to bits, its sibling skittering away pathetically, making me frantic. A favorite photo of two-year-old Reid knocked off the shelf and torn, with no negative to replace it. My good serving dish dropped and broken on the front walk, spilling out our intended contribution to a football tailgate lunch. For a wedding memento, Sally gave us a professionally rendered painting from a photo of herself, Reid, Bruce, and me. As Bruce carried it into the house during the move, he scraped the portrait against the door frame, leaving an indelible scar across the bottom.

For my seventieth birthday, Bruce picked up the cake from our local bakery. I wanted my birthday color theme to be lavender, pink, and white even though it was fall, not spring. My beautiful flower arrangements, balloons, and decorations were lovely with these soft colors. Before we got into the car, I peeked at the cake, which Bruce had put in the trunk. It was frosted with garish Halloween colors of bright orange, black, and brown. I went into a tizzy fit, having assumed the cake would be white. Why hadn't he called me from the bakery? He calls about every other little thing until I am crazy, but this time he didn't ask—and I didn't think to check and stay one step ahead of him.

I use a device called a PAX for vaporizing cannabis buds. It looks like a long cigarette lighter, with a little stove area at the top where I put in the grated cannabis. It needs to be periodically cleaned with isopropyl alcohol. After the old material is picked out with a toothpick or small tool, I use my little finger's nail to poke out the remains. Bruce offered to help but accidentally turned it on before I stuck my finger into the stove area, which by now had heated to 350 degrees. I danced around the RV, squeezing my poor scorched pinky; relaxing early in bed with a book was not to be.

One December Bruce and I were invited to a dinner party in a fashionable Staten Island apartment overlooking Manhattan. The hosts were smart, world-traveling friends, and I wanted to present them with an impressive gift. Bruce makes these delicate Scandinavian cookies called "rosettes." They require a special iron or mold that you first dip in the batter and then hot oil, where it breaks loose and fries to a golden crispness. For such a specialty, I purchased a decorative box, but the pièce de résistance was an indigenous-crafted peace dove that had been affixed to Christmas wreaths produced by *Pacem in Terris*, the Delaware peace chapter. I attached the dove to a ribbon that I wrapped around the box. As we entered our swanky friends' apartment building, I glanced at the tin. The dove was missing, and I was devastated. We searched the sidewalk. We looked inside the car, but we didn't find it. Luckily, it was on our garage floor, where Bruce had knocked it off when he had put the box in the car. I ended up mailing it to our friends, but the perfect gift now lacked its masterstroke.

Bruce reads the local obituaries every day. I think it is gruesome, but when he was still working as an attorney, he said he had to keep up with deaths and estates, and the habit has continued in retirement.

I don't particularly want to know about death when it is 8 a.m. Bruce doesn't know how to gauge the severity of his death announcements, so they sometimes cause me to go into a temporary panic over the mother of a person I hardly knew. Whereas Bruce's inability to feel empathy makes this kind of information simply factual for him, I end up feeling bad in the midst of making breakfast.

One death announcement truly saddened me because it was a fellow who had worked for us as a handyman at the daycare center and our other properties for years. He was a Woodstock hippie who hovered between survival and destitution. But he was extremely likable, very funny, and full of platitudes and truisms like Yogi Berra.

"Tommie Sadlowski died," Bruce said.

"That is terrible! I wonder what happened. I really liked Tommie."

"The visitation is tomorrow at Bones and Jones Funeral Home, and I think we should go."

The next day, dressed in my customary black funeral outfit that is usually stuck in a basement closet, I arrived at the funeral home before Bruce. My son called while I was sitting in the parking lot, and as we chatted, I was astounded at the quality of the cars and expensive attire of the people I saw descending on the place. *You should see these fancy cars, Reid.*

Guess we hadn't known Tommie as well as we had thought. I went in and stood in line to sign the register, then wandered around and looked at Tommie's childhood pictures. *I guess it looks like him.* It was hard to tell as I peered at each photo. Tommie had been rough-looking with long hair and a beard when I had known him.

People were hugging and shaking hands, greeting each other with sorrow and tears. Something was off around here.

For crying out loud, this is not the same Tommie Sadlowski! How many Tommie Sadlowskis could there be in this small town!

I felt like such an idiot! I lowered my head and made a beeline for the door before a mourner could ask me, "How did you know Tommie?"

Well, I had no idea who the deceased was and didn't like being a funeral crasher. I had crashed a wedding once and had done the electric slide with a bunch of drunken strangers, but I could do without funerals for strangers.

I called Bruce, who was on his way. "It is not Tommie Sadlowski! Well, it is *a* Tommie Sadlowski but not ours." We lost track of our handyman, who most likely is in hippie heaven without having received the big, fancy send-off bestowed upon his doppelgänger.

I was driving the RV back from a trip and pooped out for the night while Bruce called a campground for a reservation. After he got off the phone, he told me that the office attendant had mentioned that a group of people was staying there for a church choir conference. He gave me the impression that the event was occurring in the nearby town. *Why should we be concerned when we're just staying for the night?* As we pulled in, my eyes focused on a huge white tent, music booming from loudspeakers. *Something is fishy about this place.* A born-again Evangelical revival was in full swing. It was not, as I had imagined, just a group of the kind of ordinary folks who usually compete in traditional sing-off competitions. No wonder she had tried to warn Bruce. Her comments had not registered with him, and he had not accurately conveyed the conversation to me. As a nonreligious type, I would have been more comfortable on another planet than up close and personal with this crowd.

We had been assigned a Tom Thumb site with no room for our slide-out because a group of redneck guys were heavily into beer drinking and playing horseshoes within an arm's reach, and I didn't think they would appreciate us sliding into their space and wrecking their game. Where did these people come from? *We are in Pennsylvania, not the Deep South.*

"I can't take this," I said to Bruce. "Get us outta here." We made parting excuses to the horseshoe crowd and headed back to the campground office. The attendant, remembering us from the Obama campaign days—when we had boisterously stumped for the eventual forty-fourth president—was downright hostile as we pleaded for another site, but she finally relented, slamming the pen down on the desk for me to sign.

She sent us to a far-flung field, and we settled in and relaxed with a drink. At least it was quiet. A couple of glasses of wine later, I proposed that we sneak over to the big tent and check out the activities. We strolled past a line of huge travel trailers flying American flags of a size that suggested big guns inside.

We approached the entrance to the tent and tried to blend in, although we were a bit slimmer around the midsection than most of the occupants and not wearing a T-shirt, baseball cap, or jewelry decorated with a religious logo. One woman caught my eye, and we smiled at each other. *I guess I'm okay.* I was leaning toward buying a cross necklace with flashing lights from a vendor just outside the tent but decided to inch up to the entrance and take a peek. Various performers were singing and playing guitars inside, as it was an intermission of some sort. I guessed that we had missed the preachers saving souls, talking in tongues, and wrestling with snakes, so we wandered back to our RV. At dawn, we were eager to make a quick getaway—except the RV failed to start. It rolled over once, twice, three times, and then roared into life. Hallelujah!

Chapter 11

DREAM HOME

Bruce told my dad he felt like he was on vacation when we moved to Amaranth Drive on St. Patrick's Day, 1989. It was a far cry from our meager beginnings, when we had lived with crazy neighbors, roaches, and wooden cable spools for furniture. Our dream house was situated in a private cul-de-sac on seven semi-wooded acres with a winding river in the background and wildlife to photograph. The design had been featured in a magazine that I happened to pick up at a hair salon. We liked it so much we sent for the architectural plans. It was, indeed, awesome and unusual.

From our upper deck, we could view the flagstone path leading to a pond filled with lily pads, purple and yellow irises, frogs, and snakes. We gave up stocking the pond with fish after a great blue heron gulped them all down one summer. The pool seemed exceptionally beautiful, lined with ceramic tiles, a jacuzzi on one side, and a peach-colored deck. We thought it was fun for guests to pick black raspberries to top off their ice cream and eat dessert in the jacuzzi. Next to the upper deck was a screened-in porch, which provided shelter if a pool party got rained out. Our white, wrought iron bar inside was a great place to set up drinks.

That splendid view was available from the inside, too, with an open layout and multiple windows opening up the wall and providing light for every room. The living room was crowned with a cathedral ceiling, which, along with the 1930s-style glass block walls that divided several rooms, added spaciousness throughout the house. I loved to sit reading on the floral wicker loveseat in the pretty yellow sunroom filled with succulent plants. In our basement wine room, Dad built a floor-to-ceiling wine rack. We furnished it with comfy chairs and wine-themed accents. Every so often, we'd mount an expedition to restock our supply with fifty or more bottles of wine for every occasion. And with three decorative fireplaces adding ambiance and warmth, our home was a cozy place to relax with a cocktail during the winter months.

Mirrors graced the dining room on several sides. One was set into bookshelves built by Dad, another over a small bar area, and a third over the fireplace surrounded by more bookshelves. At dinner parties, we joked that the vainest guests could admire themselves luxuriating in mirrors on three sides.

Since our decorating expertise was limited, we copied the furniture pictured in the magazine where I had found the design for our home. We were able to acquire almost everything from High Point Furniture Sales of North Carolina. With Dad contributing the carpentry and Mom designing silk flower arrangements and providing oil paintings, we were starting to look so upscale. Was this really us? We had to pinch ourselves! The family who moved in next to us became dear friends, and we shared our lives in our peaceful cul-de-sac in all manners and forms.

Some of those manners were more uproarious than tranquil, however, especially when they took the form of our famous parties.

Particularly uproarious was a mystery-themed party we called "The Grapes of Frath." The character of Mr. Frath was the victim of a murder aboard a yacht. Accordingly, we decorated our Amaranth home as a luxury yacht, converting the windows to portholes, and the guests came dressed up as characters. There was Captain Mal de Mer (French for seasick) as well as a famous opera singer, bellowing off-key in coloratura. Bruce dressed as a race car driver, wearing goggles, a tan suit, and a little mustache. I was a Jazz-Age princess, attired in a pink flapper dress and crowned with Sally's twirling tiara. All of us had to read our lines, examine the evidence, and deduce who was the guilty party. The victim was portrayed on a section of paper roll, complete with a fat mustache, and hung over the fireplace.

Then there was our famous Lethal Luau fest. Everyone took on comical names and wore Polynesian attire: scuba gear, hula skirts, and leis. The house was decorated with hibiscus and other tropical flowers. Bruce ruled as Chief Wiki Wacky, while I ruled as Queen LaeLani, wearing a pair of coconuts for a brassiere and a grass skirt over my hips. When I wanted to get anybody's attention over the din of ukuleles and Hawaiian singing, I would knock on my coconut shells with a pen.

Since we had such a lovely backyard, pool, deck, and patio at Amaranth, many of our parties were barbeques or cookouts. At that time, outdoor grills were not the large, high-tech, sleek machines that resemble small submarines or private jets, but they were functional grillers of delicious steaks, kabobs, burgers, dogs, and chops. Bruce, however, created his own unique grill from empty beer kegs. One keg stood upright, and he bolted the second one horizontally to the top of the first. He sawed a large opening out of the midsection of the second keg, ruining quite a few hacksaw blades in the process, but he could open and close that section, which held the charcoal. He confiscated abandoned shopping carts to use as the grill.

Our poor guests, after a few drinks, ignored the grit that accumulated on the grill, which was cleaned only by a few feckless swipes of a wire brush. Bruce was dangerously free with the lighter fluid as he soaked the charcoal, so a huge flame often soared above our heads when he lit the match. To protect the guests from getting scorched, I would yell, "All clear, fire in the hole!"

With our having very little ability to regulate the heat, a lot of the food was crisp on the outside and raw on the inside. It took a lot of management to produce edible dinners, but we used this method of grilling for years. Often we had to drink a whole keg of beer at a party to acquire a replacement part, and Bruce sometimes slunk around the grocery store parking lot to snag a new shopping cart.

Our glorious existence came to a crashing end a year and a half after moving into our new home, when I started to get sick. My body ached, and it was difficult to function at a normal level. I couldn't imagine what was wrong with me. As my quality of life deteriorated, I became frightened, disheartened, and anxious.

My doctor thought it was the flu, and I would tell people that I had some sort of viral infection. I took antibiotics often, just in case it would make a difference, although I typically felt worse from August until December. I became very disheartened, but I would get a small break from the symptoms in the winter. My doctor, having no clue what was wrong, decided I had chronic fatigue syndrome (CFS). I had no idea what that vague diagnosis could mean, except that I was stuck with this illness, though I seemed to experience some relief when I stayed at our beach condo.

A strange thing would happen when we would travel to Virginia or Florida to visit the kids in college. I would get better. Upon arrival, I would roll myself off the RV couch and stagger around in an attempt to participate in the activities. And, after a couple of days, I would feel well. One year, my husband and son entered a parents' weekend golf tournament, with me going along for the ride. Waiting for our turn to tee off, I rested my head on my arms on top of my golf bag.

Reid was concerned. "Mom, are you sure you can do this?" he asked.

The day and the golf course were beautiful, and suddenly I noticed I felt good. The horrible sickness had vanished, *poof*, just like that. I was so happy to feel healthy, and a bonus was that Reid and Bruce won the tournament. On the way back from Florida, Bruce and I golfed, dined, and saw the sights in historic Beaufort, South Carolina, including the house where they filmed *The Big Chill*. It was great to feel normal, but as soon as I got home, I was sick again.

At the same time as I was experiencing this puzzling condition, a lawyer with whom Bruce had a professional relationship was also sick with an illness that eluded diagnoses. He described symptoms to Bruce that seemed a lot like mine. He was a highly accomplished author, worked at one point as assistant attorney general for the state of Delaware, and was a crackerjack trial lawyer, but his career had become sidelined due to this malaise. Bruce suggested I go to this lawyer's doctor, who also didn't have any answers. He insisted that Bruce's friend had an immune disorder but inferred that I had CFS. He told me to come back in two years, as they didn't know much about the disorder.

Boy, did he miss the mark!

Early on, an allergist gave me a clue. He told me, "Something around your house doesn't agree with you." I was eager to delve into this possibility with Bruce. I hurried home with the doctor's theory, but I received no response from Bruce. Deflated by his disinterest, I slunk into the house to rest.

In 1994, after we had lived in the new house for five years, four of which I had been sick, Bruce said something to me about his lawyer friend having reported mushrooms growing in the basement of his office building. Bruce has only a vague memory of this conversation. I still remember picturing odd toadstool forms sticking out of the dirt of his friend's dank basement, and I could not think of the relevance to my situation. I did not have mushrooms sprouting from my basement floor concrete!

The answer to my illness was still elusive, so I tried to ignore my fatigue, brain fog, and body aches as much as possible and continue with working, golfing, skiing, running, and socializing.

Sadly, my days were getting shorter, and I became unable to either plan or participate in our celebrated revels. Depleted by 7:30 p.m., I found myself going to bed early and waking up exhausted twelve hours later. My workdays had to end at noon or early afternoon when I began to wear out. The mantra that I repeated almost hourly was, "I don't feel good."

My relationship with Bruce drove me toward a new mantra. Even with a beautiful new house, Bruce was rarely home. Sally was in high school, Reid had gone off to college, and I was increasingly sick, but Bruce's interests were not with us. Even worse, he was becoming more and more reactive. It seemed like the easiest conversations would end in discord, and communication was breaking down. If he acted grouchy after work, he blamed his behavior on me, saying that I was in a bad mood when he came home. I became hesitant to discuss any concerns for fear of getting into a fight. Often, when he became angry and confused, I would think, *If I had known such and such would upset him, I wouldn't have said it!* I had no clue what would set off his rage. What would make him go so rapidly "from green to red," as Louise Weston put it (Weston 2010)? Only later would I encounter this term in Weston's helpful book *Connecting with Your Asperger Partner: Negotiating the Maze of Intimacy*. Bruce said that things were building up, but I couldn't imagine what was building up. In terms of our home and our socializing, we seemed to live a normal life. I began repeating my new mantra: "You should never have gotten married, had a wife, had kids, had a house."

I grew to hate it when Bruce would sometimes declare something stupid with unquestionable certainty. *There will be no traffic on the highway on Thanksgiving Day because everyone will be eating dinner.* And then we'd be stuck in bumper-to-bumper traffic on the way north of New York City to my daughter's in-laws' house. *No one goes out West in the summer, so there is no need to make campground reservations.* It turned out the whole country travels to the Canadian Rockies every summer, and we had to change campgrounds each night and hope for a spot to open up. *It will not rain.* But our golf cart got stuck on a flooded path with lightning strikes all around. It is okay to make a mistake, but he never took responsibility. It seemed that he would say anything to stay in control, especially if he felt backed into a corner. I had to suck up any illogical comment to avoid an argument that never went anywhere. And if I did try to explain my reasoning, he would say, "You are not going to make any points with me." Now I know that I wasted my time, because no matter how many analogies or examples I gave him, he would never agree.

The realization set in that Bruce ignored me because he was obsessively sticking to his agenda while lost in his many thoughts.

"April, I am always thinking," he once said to me.

And I wondered, "What is he thinking *about?*"

He didn't muse or discuss abstract philosophy or disclose much about his day-to-day life. Bruce would rest in his chair, eyes glued on the TV, and fold his fingers into a tent over his nose, as if to signal that he was not to be disturbed. Observing that kind of body language, I often thought an elephant could walk across the living room and he would not notice. Once, I conducted a three-day experiment during which I spoke to him only about picking up a kid from sports, taking out the trash, what time dinner was, or whether someone had an appointment. He didn't pick up on the fact that we had no significant conversations. Mentally I called him a "Boy Scout robot" because of his strict code of behavior. He performed every action robotically, speaking pedantically or in monotone like Stephan Hawkings' electronic voice. He rarely displayed any emotion or passion for anything. Bad news, good news—even touchdowns by his favorite team—did not faze him.

He seemed preoccupied with his routine. Mornings, when he was getting ready for work, he stuck to an agenda. I had to insert myself into his movements to get his attention if I had an issue to discuss. He would drink coffee, read the paper, go to the bathroom, get shaved and showered, and off he'd go. It took me some time to realize that he could not get his keys, money clip, wallet, and change off the mantel in our bedroom and then remember or hear anything I said to him while he did so. He did not even hear my voice. Apparently I needed a megaphone and a marching band.

Life was a challenge. I was trying to both cope with an unknown problem with my husband and deal with my still unknown illness. If I tried to explain these difficulties to anyone, I was not understood, but I had to carry on. On top of this, my parents were having health problems.

Still, we had plenty of things to keep us busy. Bruce and I shared the same mindset when it came to helping people. He was very generous with his time, pro bono law work, and money. I would come to him with stories of folks in need, and he would attend to their problems. We helped employees, our son's friends, and other folks who crossed our path with whatever we could: an extra bedroom, an apartment, an automobile, cash, and bill payments. Most notable for Bruce was his regular donation of bags of aluminum cans that he hauled to a fellow's house so that the man could turn them in for cash. Bruce picked up discarded cans along roadways and added his own beer cans to the contribution. As for me, I financed school clothes, soccer registration, and a uniform for a grade school girl I met doing volunteer work and needed a leg up. Bruce arranged a suitable guardianship with her aunt and now she is a college graduate We also took in a high school girl who was estranged from her family. I taught her how to drive and helped her get her license, and Bruce worked out a reconciliation with her father.

There were the kids' colleges to visit. We cared for a herd of rescued pets, managed our businesses, and continued to throw parties. I had ten gardens, replete with beautiful flowers and butterflies.

On the surface our life looked so beautiful, like the sun reflecting on our pond. But with respect to the state of our marriage, it was murky and dark below.

Chapter 12

TWENTIETH ANNIVERSARY

When our twentieth anniversary, June 20, 1990, came around, I racked my brain to think of a fun celebration. The marriage was continuing its roller-coaster ride of ups and downs, loneliness, and fights. Still, with Reid finishing his freshman year at college, Sally wrapping up a busy year at Newark High School, Bruce busy with his law practice, and my Mother Hubbard Childcare centers humming along, I decided to look on the bright side.

An idea popped into my mind that it would be fun to remember our first goofy meeting at Rehoboth Beach. I pulled out our old typewriter and onionskin typing paper and proceeded to write a script or, as we called it, a "reenactment" of the fateful meeting. Like I know how to write a script, but I did the best I could, writing the dialogue of our first conversation, adding descriptive phrases to the scenes, and typing many typos.

Our friend Peggy was a new Rehoboth resident, so I recruited her to play Susan, the other gal on the beach. Sally took the part of Maryanne, the friend who owned the cottage. Reid and his friend Brian were spending this summer at the beach, so we grabbed them to play my date, David, and George, Bruce's navy friend, who broke up the fight. We used the RV for a base, and, because it was early in the season, the beach was relatively deserted. Nevertheless, it was a lovely day, mild and sunny, reminiscent of our wedding day.

```
REANACTMENT **** JUNE 20, 1990 **** 20TH ANNIVERSARY

SCENE I  WHISKEY BEACH

MARYANNE - April, this is Bruce.
Bruce - Are you from Wilmington?
April - No, I'm from Newark. Where are you from?
Bruce - I'm in the Navy, stationed in Washington, but I'm from Minnesota.
April - Oh, my father's from Minnesota. He lived in Minneapolis.
Bruce- I'm from Winona, south of Minneapolis. Where did you go to college?
April - A small Methodist college in Vermont that you have probably
        never heard of, called Green Mountain and now I go to U. of D.
Bruce - I went to a small methodist college in Minnesota that you
        probably have never heard of called Hamline.
April - You're right.
Bruce opens his wallet and April looks at his drivers license and s
sees his birth date 1946.
April- I don't believe that you are 2 yrs younger than me.
Bruce - When were you born.
April - Oct 22 1944
Bruce - You are only 16 months older.
April - My date is leaving at 9 to study for finals, maybe I'll see you
        at the Bottle and Cork.


       SCENE II  BOTTLE AND CORK  later that evening

Bruce - April would you like to dance?
April - Bruuuuuuce! Anytime David goes to the bathroom or gets a drink
eat   b  ask me to dance.
After several dances
David - I'm going to lay you out or you're going to lay me out!
Bruce - Whoo dude! I'm not going to fight you, what would that prove?
George - Come here Dave, let's not have any trouble here with cops.
Bruce - I guess I'll see you on the beach tomorrow.
April and David leave and Bruce uncovers his false teeth.

     Scene III  Beach the next day

Susan who was anther part of the group and at the bar last nite meets
Bruce at beach

Bruce - April do you want to go swimming?
April - ok
Bruce - Susan, do you want to go in the water?
Susan - sure
  repeat 4 times
April - I'm getting sick of him.
Bruce - April, do you want to go for a walk?
April and Bruce kissing at waters edge  very romantic
```

```
April - See you next weekend.

At April's home in Newark
April - Guess what? I've been making out with a sailor on the beach.

END
SCENE III   Next weekend on beach Astronauts walk on moon Sun nite
            April has premonition and hears voice
            I BET WE'RE GOING TO GET MARRIED!

Arriving home JUne and Debbie say   When are you getting married
after April called on phone earlier
April - I don't know when, I just think we will get married.

AND THEY LIVED HAPPILY EVER AFTER!
```

At the bottom of the script are these innocent, uninformed words:

AND THEY LIVED HAPPILY EVER AFTER!

When we acted this out, was I still cruising on that Egyptian river of de-Nile? There was some kind of cognitive dissonance going on here.

The little play worked out well, and afterward we piled into the RV and drove to Ocean City, Maryland, for dinner at a favorite restaurant, one with a piano bar overlooking the boardwalk.

Chapter 13

RUN TO WIN

One source of light that kept the darkness in our relationship at bay was running. Since Four Seasons, when we had driven to the Marine Corps Marathon to support our neighbor, I had been running, my first jog with our poodle Governor at my side. Through all my physical and emotional difficulties, I have striven to remain fit. Bruce was another story. By the time we had moved to Caravel Farms, I was disturbed and mortified to see Bruce waddling across the yard with his white shorts riding up his rear in full view of my next-door neighbor, Brenda. Hints about his sagging physique and carb-rich appetite did not work. I resorted to tough love.

"You're the fattest guy in our crowd!" I told him.

Bruce's idea of dieting was a special regimen of beer and popcorn, which only served to keep him drunk and gaseous.

Still, my prodding got him to try to slim down. He decided to run a 5K road race, "Run For Bruce," in memory of a University of Delaware student who had passed away. Unfortunately, my Bruce was so pooped out when he got to the finish line that he decided to chuck racing for good. Three more years of beer, popcorn, and gas lumbered by before he gave it another try, and this time he was hooked. He enjoyed getting chummy with the local runners in a low-stress ambiance, where all he had to yak about was today's race, yesterday's race, and tomorrow's race. Bruce began to exhibit a newly fit and trim physique. When people asked him how he had lost weight, his standard quip was, "All my weight goes to my ass, and I run my ass off."

Bruce turned the tables on me and mentioned how fit and fun runners were. He thought I might enjoy racing, too, instead of just jogging around the neighborhood with only the dog for company. So after we settled into Amaranth Drive, I ran my first race at Brian's Run in West Chester, Pennsylvania. Bruce was right. We did meet fit and fun people, and we established lasting new friendships. Often we would motor together to races in our RV. We gave our little crowd a name, YARRA—Young and Restless Road Running Association. We even had our own cute blue-and-orange shirt printed with our name and an image of fun-loving runners.

Dick Beardsley, the great runner, said, "Once you cross the finish line, your life will change forever." In my case, it sure was true. Crossing the finish line exhausted and exultant is a near-religious experience, especially with all the endorphins floating around. Running makes a person strong in mind and body. It teaches you not to quit and to endure, not only with running but with all of life's ordeals. My thighs got firm and slim, and my legs shaped up into "runner's legs." Soon I could spot runner's legs from a mile away. And I began to understand why runners say they run because they like to eat.

I loved running outfits and shoes, nerves at the starting line, the sound of the gun or horn, passing mile markers, grabbing a cup of water for a quick drink, and smashing the cup to the ground on the run. We would roll our fists and encourage each other with shouts of "Way to run!" and "Go, April!" I loved the trophies, medals, plaques, gift certificates, beer mugs, glasses, race shirts, hats, and swag that we were collecting.

Bill Rodgers, the great marathoner from Boston, awarded me my first trophy at an event in Delaware. He ran like a gazelle, and I was in awe of his long strides and fluid form. His wife, Gail, created a writing contest in *Running Times* magazine called, "The Slower We Run, the More We Like Trophies." I could not pass up the challenge. I wrote about why I liked trophies: there were few sports for women when I was in high school and college, I explained, and I never had a chance to compete for awards like all those jocks. I typed it up and sent it in. And my essay was published! Also, I got another trophy, a neat paperweight as an award, which I displayed in my growing collection.

There were not as many gifts and mementos for running as for other sports like golf. So I opened a novelty business for runners called The Finish Line. First I went about collecting an inventory. A jeweler in the Jewelers' Row District in Philadelphia created gold and silver earrings and bracelets from my design of runners and running shoes. I fashioned earrings out of running charms, and we sold sweaters, pillows, flags, calendars, belts, ties, bags, and shirts with running designs. I was especially enamored of the future marathoner T-shirts I designed for little kids. I designed runner widow and runner widower T-shirts and runner support shirts for the families and friends of competitors. These were printed with a flag on which I inscribed the competitor's name with a marker, so a friend or family member could wear it at the race.

Handsome Reid modeled an embroidered sweater for the cover of my small catalog. Dad did the photoshoot after flying to Florida, where Reid was in college. Sally helped package my orders when she was home on Christmas break. My novelties were gobbled up.

Five years into my Finish Line business, we exhibited our wares at the 1994 Marine Corps Expo in Washington, D.C. Oprah was there, creating a special sizzle. Also, it was my fiftieth birthday. Bruce snuck away from our table and told the announcer, who broadcasted this information over the public address system. Simultaneously, Bruce presented me with a large diamond ring to replace the small engagement ring I still had from a quarter century before. Everyone knew it was me because my T-shirt said, "I am not fifty, I am thirty-five with fifteen years of experience." I flashed my ring and told bystanders that I had just gotten engaged! We shared a bottle of champagne with our fellow vendors.

Another announcement came blaring over the floor that a marine was unable to run the marathon because she had been shipped off to Okinawa and her number was for sale. Bruce, who had not trained one minute for this race, ran over and snatched it up. That meant I would have to watch the whole marathon.

Walking to the start, Oprah looked small under the umbrella held by her boyfriend Stedman Graham. Poor Oprah was just trying to meet her goal while everyone wanted to brag about beating her. Unfortunately, it was a rainy day, and I mostly hid inside the Lincoln Memorial, where I memorized the Gettysburg Address to kill time. I was starving and drooled as I watched a mom and daughter eat a picnic lunch. If I had been a little bolder, I would have asked, "Are you going to finish all of that?" I ventured out into the rain to see Bruce and Oprah splashing across the finish line, although not together. Oprah received cheers and adulation from the crowd, thrilled to see this much-loved star.

The sun came out and lit up the monuments with a blaze of marble white, too late for the soaked marathoners. We drove off in our RV with the remainder of our wares while Bruce hollered out the window, "Last chance to buy a pillow!" The business took in a lot of cash, but Bruce figured out that with the cost of the product, the expo table fees, and travel that I had only broken even. Ever the businesswoman, when I saw that bottom line in zero territory, I thought it was time to wrap it up. It was fun, though, and I still wear many of my creations. Runners have often asked me, "Where did you get those cool earrings?"

We still had other diversions related to running to look forward to. An acquaintance once exposed her naïveté about our passion, claiming, "Do runners drink beer?"

Do bears poop in the woods? Some might think eight or nine in the morning would be too early for beer, but not for runners. After burning all those calories and expelling all that sweat, it was perfectly normal for us to replenish our bodily fluids with more than water. Beer, wine, margaritas, and screwdrivers became as common as sweatbands, and races evolved into major social roundups. For example, one of our summer races held an after-party bash in a big picnic area with a rock 'n' roll band, beer, burgers, hot dogs, and dancing. We jitterbugged and slow danced in bare feet and flip-flops, kidding and laughing with friends.

While I was digging out garden weeds the next morning, I called my friend and said, "Boy, ain't this a drag; it's 10 a.m., and we're not drinking and dancing!" Another plus to races is that you can party and socialize without dealing with invitations, cleaning the house, preparing the food, and washing the dishes.

Sally began to run with us, but she accused me of child abuse once I hooked her into training with me. One time we passed another mom, trailed by her teenage daughter, and I said, "Look, another mother abusing her daughter!"

I was thrilled when Sally joined us at races. We ran together, but when she showed some extra steam at the finish, I cried, "Go, Girl!" and loved seeing her ponytail bouncing back and forth as she took off. One snowy morning she was cuddled under her comforter in her brass bed when I woke her and said, "We have to go running! It is a magical snowy day with big soft flakes flying around." How I convinced her to get out of her cozy bed and head out, I don't know. Still, it was a glorious winter run, our noses freezing while our bodies steamed under our clothes.

We were excited to run with Sally when she was in college in Williamsburg and in law school in New York City. Reid joined in occasionally, and we even ran as a family marathon team. I decided the team's name should be "Family Fun," which the kids thought was dorky. Our motto was, "A family that runs together stays together."

Sally went on to run the Marine Corps Marathon and Staten Island Half Marathon. Reid would eventually join a local running group. Meanwhile, Bruce had become our family's major marathoner.

The Boston Marathon is an elite race, and to finish Boston is a lofty goal for only the highest-caliber runners. You cannot just register for the Boston Marathon; you have to qualify, and the qualifying times—though they are adjusted for age—are daunting. Bruce began to contemplate a qualification run after running marathons and getting faster times with each race. There was a lot of pressure from our running crowd, especially from Bruce's good friend, Chip, who had been running Boston for years. Bruce speculated that he might qualify each time he ran a marathon, but it wasn't happening. I thought it would be fun to have a surprise party prearranged for him when he finally qualified, and I organized friends to be ready with Boston baked beans, Boston cream pie, and Cape Cod oysters, in anticipation of the great event.

Chip's advice was to get strong in body, not just train for running, so Bruce got a trainer and began hoisting weights. In one marathon, he cramped up from his leg-lifting exercises, so it was a bust. In another marathon, it was so windy we could hardly heave our car doors open. Dad had come to watch, but we knew it was futile that day, with strong headwinds slowing everyone to a slog. Then Bruce ran the Philadelphia Marathon, with everyone at the ready to party once more. I waited at the finish line with Bruce's friend, Buzz. The clock seemed to be ticking double-time as Bruce pushed on to the finish: too late again. Bruce collapsed from the effort, and I was cussing in the stands, people wondering, "What is wrong with this woman?" *I have a party to cancel!*

Finally, I sat Bruce down at the kitchen table and told him that I had planned a party each time he had tried to qualify. I was sick of giving thumbs-down to the neighbors and making secret phone calls of cancellation.

Bruce answered, "I *might* qualify."

Well, I "might" bowl a 300 or do a triple axel. I guess anything "might" happen. I still knew nothing at this point about Asperger reasoning.

I took matters into my own hands, circled an ad for coaching in *Runner's World* magazine, and hired an Olympic marathoner from California names Mark Conover. He faxed a training program to Bruce, which Bruce followed scrupulously. In February of 1995, Bruce entered a race at the Aberdeen Proving Grounds in Maryland named "Last Train to Boston," so called because it was the last Boston-qualifying marathon of the year. There were four loops to the race, so if people knew they were behind the qualifying time, they could drop out. Bruce had tried it before and failed. One year, I ran the half-marathon there—two loops—for the heck of it.

Chip decided to pace alongside Bruce for the first three loops even though Chip was sick with a bad cold. Sally and I sat in the car, protected against the chill, and jumped out to cheer when the two ran by. They were on track, and we were sweating it out. Maybe this was the day! The Boston baked beans waited in the refrigerator for the results.

Chip bailed out of the last loop with 6.55 miles to go, declaring, "It's up to you, Bruce!"

Bruce seemed strong and resolute, but anything could happen. It was a long, nerve-racking wait. We watched the clock and peered down the road for a sign of Bruce. It was getting down to the wire. Where was he? Minutes and seconds were ticking away on the digital clock. Finally, we saw him, racing to beat the clock, pushing himself on, until he cut across the finish line with two minutes to spare; he needed 3:25, and he got a 3:23! Bruce gave Chip a huge bear hug. Sally and I were cheering, but somehow, I did not get a hug.

We pulled the beer, baked beans, and pie from the fridge and put on a grand party, Bruce basking in congratulations from friends. As a gift, Chip's wife, Doris, had cross-stitched a runner with "Boston" emblazoned across the top. Chip gifted Sally and me with his cold. It had taken Bruce ten marathons to qualify, and he went on to run

Boston five times, one of which was the hundredth running, an electrifying race we are so proud to have been a part of.

Each year, traveling to Boston for the marathon was a fabulous experience, with all the fanfare, huge expo, and great dinner with the Delaware gang, who always came up on a bus. After one such dinner, we crammed twenty-three runners into our RV and headed for the "*Cheers* bar."

One year, we parked the RV in Hopkinton, near the starting line. After Bruce executed another successful marathon, he crashed on the RV couch while I watched the news coverage about the race. It was so warm that spring that the medical support had nearly run out of IVs. We decided to hit a local bar, which was in full party mode, as the marathon is run on Patriot's Day, a holiday. I let slip to one partier that Bruce had run the race. Word passed around that there was an actual competitor in their midst. I ran to the RV to get Bruce's finisher medal, and the band leader introduced him to the crowd, which responded with boisterous claps and cheers. Bruce was in his glory. At one point, he leaned against the bar flanked by women on both sides, who were plying him with questions about his training, fitness, and other marathons. Bruce seemed to feel more happiness qualifying for Boston than he had felt for his kids' births or for our wedding. I think that was the happiest I ever saw him.

Bruce ran almost every day, even Christmas Day, when there was a break in the action. He began donning a Santa beard for the special day, which evoked a jubilant response from people cruising by in their cars. Eventually he bought a full Santa outfit, and Sally and I would run a few paces behind him dressed as elves. After a few Yules, Sally bailed out, so I got myself a cute Mrs. Santa Claus outfit, and the tradition has continued for twenty-five years. We don't run as far or as fast now, but our "fans," as I call them, still love to see us on the road as they take pictures, beep horns, and wave. Ho, ho, ho! Merry Christmas!

Throughout the year we now run a road in our nearby state park, White Clay Creek. The road and trails are adjacent to the beautiful creek, which is wide and winding, with white water rushing over rapids, old stone railroad trestles protruding from the banks, and birds and wildlife keeping us company.

We belong to a group of runners who run the Creek Road—the Creek Road Runners—and have a logo, website, and branded running clothes. Bruce ran this route from his downtown office at lunchtime. Running by the creek is a calming experience, but one time I had a bad fall there and skinned both my knees. I knew it meant that more scars would be added to my already scarred knees and legs. At the time, the road was drivable, so I got in my car that I had parked in the parking lot and headed to town instead of home. I have no idea why. After a mile, I spotted Bruce walking just ahead. He had blood streaming down his legs from cuts on his knees, and he was holding his hand, which he had wrapped with his headband because it was also bleeding from a deep cut. He was relieved to see me, as he needed medical attention and stitches. We shared stories and realized we had tripped on the same outcropped rocks only a few minutes apart! After his ER visit, Bruce sledgehammered the tops off the rocks, and now I think of that coincidence every time I run over the worn remains.

Bruce and I had to acquire some new running skills when our friends Sue and Jerry Bergman, who live in Buffalo, New York, convinced us to come up to run the "Police Chase," a benefit for their police department. The first race was a two-mile couples race followed by a 5K. The trouble was that we would have to run handcuffed in the first race. Bruce and I practiced on Creek Road by tying his headband around our wrists. We tied his left hand and my right hand and then my left hand and his right hand and settled on the former. We felt foolish when we passed other runners who were out for an evening jog and gave us weird looks, as if we were into some creepy running bondage. To run fast and not stumble over each other, though, we had to pull together and finetune our locomotion. If only we could have applied such a technique to our marriage.

We made it to the evening race in Buffalo in the nick of time, driving the RV up from Delaware that day. A police officer handed handcuffs to Bruce and said, "Don't snap them too—" SNAP "—tight!" Unaware of Asperger's syndrome at that time, I didn't have the forethought to protect myself. *Ouch*, they were tight, and right then and there I vowed never to get arrested. We were near the back of the pack with the young couples running together, but we ended up with a huge red-white-and-blue trophy, adorned with white plastic handcuffs because our combined ages gave us first place.

After getting the darn handcuffs unlocked by a cop, we scurried to the start of the 5K. It was an odd feeling to be sweaty and flushed at the start of the race. We ran in downtown Buffalo, where people party by the lake in the summer. I landed first in my age group and got another trophy.

Jerry, who hadn't realized that I was going to do both races, said, "April, you animal!"

What a compliment! But I unintentionally messed up the points in the local women's series, as some irritating woman in my age group pointed out.

We again traveled to Buffalo to participate in the Niagara Falls half and full marathons, Bruce and Jerry running the full and me the half. I was eager, as the results from the previous year for women in my 55–59 age group showed I would have placed first with my running time. Before sunrise, we had to board buses that would take us down river to the start lines. Bruce and I separated because he was going 26.2 miles and I was going 13.1. It was dark, cold, and drizzly. I found a semi-dry spot in a corner of the holding tent, tucked my knees under my chin, and waited for the announcement to head to the start. At that point, I began wondering what the heck I was doing there at this early hour, tired and chilled with only a garbage bag to keep me warm.

As usual I was on the lookout for my competition, but with my training times and past results I felt confident enough that my odds for placing were good. Runners were talking quietly among themselves, but I heard snatches of conversation that I suspected might be German. A group of fair-haired, strong, tall, older people wearing high-tech running clothes and shoes stood out like an advertisement for the TV shows "The Great Race" or "Survivor." *I don't like the looks of this*, I thought. Laughter came from their camp. They couldn't have been happier standing in the mud and killing time. I imagined the god-like creatures saying, "We're going to whip the asses of these Americans! Ha Ha!"

The Amazonians thundered off at the start, and I could only keep them in sight for a few seconds. High school kids wearing fun, colorful outfits entertained the runners with songs and cheers at every mile. I yelled to the cute guys who were bare-chested, "You guys look fab!" I ran my second-best half-marathon and would have easily placed in past years, but the Germans were no match for me. They gobbled up the first three places, and I took fourth and no award. We later found out they were from an elite running club, touring around making mincemeat of American runners. When I was sixty-one, I went back to Niagara Falls and placed third.

It seemed a great idea for our whole Family Fun team to run the Rock 'n' Roll Half Marathon in Virginia Beach because it fell on my son's thirtieth birthday, September 2, 2002. We wrote 30TH BIRTHDAY TODAY with a marker on the back of his calves, and being a good-looking guy to boot, Reid got a lot of attention, congratulations, and singing of "Happy Birthday" all along the course. Sally and Bruce took the lead. Reid was not as well-trained, and I was sick with my mysterious illness, so we lagged behind. I can't imagine how I made it the whole 13.1 miles, but I often have raced while sick. Rock 'n' roll bands were blaring at every mile. It is an awesomely fun race. Reid and I got our picture taken with Elvis at the finish line.

Although there was entertainment on the beach afterward and a concert later, I had to crash early in the RV.

We competed in road races almost every weekend, trucking up and down the East Coast and pulling off races from Maine to Florida. It was fun to get to know runners from other states and running clubs, three of which we belonged to. We combined our running with golfing, sightseeing, shopping, and gastronomy.

Running was the glue that bound us together and the light that contained the dark. I doubt we could have endured those many years without running.

Chapter 14

SICKNESS AND SURGERY

A new millennium! A thousand years to run, to ramble in RVs, corral kiddies in childcare, rabble-rouse for peace, and maybe endure a plague or two.

We rang in 2000 at a Rehoboth Beach dinner dance with our old friend John; his new bride, Merle; Chip (the fellow who made Bruce bulk up his running muscles); Chip's wife, Doris; and other friends. It was kind of warm and soupy for late December, all the better for our midnight cardio. Halfway through the festivities, Bruce and I deserted our pals to join a band of local running club runners for a midnight jaunt on the boardwalk. With Bruce in his suit, me in my black dress and lace sleeves, and both of us in running shoes, we jogged past bonfires on the sand and fireworks over the glistening waves.

As usual, we'd brought our RV, so with Chip and Doris aboard and the party over, we retreated to the campground, plowing through the pea-soup fog. There we festooned a pole next to the RV with holiday balloons, decorated the RV with hats, silver leis, streamers, and champagne glasses—loot we snagged from the dance—and crashed.

The next morning we walked to the beach and held our shoes in our hands as we waded in the sea. I dragged my bare toes through the cool sand and traced a gigantic "2000" just beyond the water's edge. It felt like a magical time, a perfect welcome to the new century.

The generous young year had more happiness to dole our way as we headed for the Walt Disney World/EPCOT Marathon Weekend and met up with our friend Buzz, who lived in Florida at the time. The guys would do the whole marathon, and I would do the half. Already amped for the race, we decided to hit the golf links the day before. The course was unexplored territory to us, however, and as the sun was sneaking away, we got lost trying to find our way back to the clubhouse. With Bruce and me in one cart and Buzz in the other, the more we zoomed around the course, the farther we seemed to be from the nineteenth hole. The course was hill and dale, and Buzz would suddenly appear on top of one rise like Lawrence of Arabia on the dunes. Then we would lose him for a minute, only to have him appear again around some knoll. We sped through sprinklers and skirted the trees, our carts snagging Spanish moss on their roofs. We were as comical as Keystone Cops. What amazed me was that Bruce was laughing, really laughing. I had never heard him belt out such a hearty, unrestrained, resounding laugh before. Then—holy fuck!—I almost got slammed into a tree by my aspie-assed husband! Another aspergate dodged by a hair.

For the spectacular 2000 Walt Disney World Marathon, we had to be at the starting line by some ungodly hour like 4 a.m. At one point, the PA speakers blared, "May you live a thousand years!" That was the plan.

Unfortunately, some poor Swede got no farther than a few hundred yards from the start when he collapsed and died. His wife was told that tragic fact when she crossed the finish line.

I loved my Donald Duck finisher medal. Bruce and Buzz both got a Mickey Mouse. After the race, we ate a celebratory lunch at an Italian theme park called Portofino. Still high on the race, I drove most of the way to Punta Gorda to visit friends. How I had the energy I do not know. Maybe, because my illness is better in the winter, I had just what it took to make it. Maybe I WILL live a thousand years.

Come Memorial Day weekend, Mother Hubbard Childcare was sponsoring the "Glasgow Dragon Draggin'" to benefit the honor society at my son's high school. However, one day after the 5K, I was bedridden with a high fever and terrible body aches. I thought I'd come down with the plague.

"Just a virus," the doctor said.

Then my fever hit 103, and we rushed to the ER. Curiously, they inquired whether I had gotten an insect bite. *Not that I know of.* For another two weeks, my joints burned, my muscles ached, and I continued to grow weaker and weaker.

One day I looked at my inner arm. I had been tested for tuberculosis so that I could help coach the Glasgow girls cross-country team, and I wanted to see if I was positive. Right where I had gotten the test, there was a faint circular trace. *I have TB?* Then I noticed more rashes on my right arm and leg.

Bruce drove me to the doctor, who looked again at my rashes. I was so debilitated at the doctor's office, I had to lie flat on the table. "Oh," she said calmly, "I suspected Lyme disease."

How long was she going to keep me in the dark? How long was she going to wait to get me tested? I did end up testing positive for *Borrelia burgdorferi*, the dreaded Lyme bacteria, and ehrlichiosis—a double whammy of tick-borne infections. With the antibiotic doxycycline, I got better right away, but I was still weak as a rag.

A few days after the diagnosis, I was resting in bed when Bruce peeked in and announced that I was to receive the Runner of the Quarter Award from the Pike Creek Valley Running Club. I struggled to focus my eyes on Bruce and absorb what he was telling me. Wow! I hoped I would make it to the presentation.

I got better, but not as well as I'd been a decade ago, having been hit by CFS and other health issues. The conventional wisdom this time was that I had *chronic* Lyme disease. I attended a support group and heard terrible stories from people whose live shad been destroyed by Lyme, but I didn't seem to fit the mold. Still, my inflammation and illness might have begun with a tick bite I never noticed after moving to a wooded lot ten years before. I was determined to get rid of this, so we went to "Lyme-literate" doctors, attended lectures, and read Lyme-literate research. With few Lyme-literate doctors in Delaware, we went to an osteopath recommended to us in New Hope, Pennsylvania. He gave me more doxycycline and advised probiotics. I got stronger, but I was still sick. The osteopath ordered an MRI on my brain in case spirochetes were invading my gray matter.

The MRI results were sent to a neurologist and my primary care physician, but nobody told me anything. Back in the osteopath's office, I picked up vibes as if I had antennae sticking out of my head, and I saw the shock in the doctor's face as he read the MRI results. I tried to remain calm as he gave me the news: "You have three aneurysms in your brain, and you need to go to a neurologist immediately."

"Shit a brick!" as my cousin Lynda is fond of saying. Shit three bricks! I don't want those things in my brain. I don't know much about aneurysms, except that Joe Biden almost died from one.

Next stop: a brain surgeon at our local hospital. I was scared shitless by the diagnosis that the aneurysm was in my brain-feeding carotid artery, but the proposed treatment terrified me. First, to locate the aneurysm precisely, they'd give me an angiogram. That meant they would anesthetize my groin, slice open my femoral artery, and slide a long tube all the way up my torso to my brain, which they would stain with a contrast dye visible to an X-ray machine. While they were doing the deed, I projected myself out of my body, out on some ski slope, but I was still uncomfortable. Afterward I was stuck lying on my back for eight hours so that all of my blood would not bleed out through the incision. I couldn't pee lying with the darn pan under my butt, so I had to be catheterized.

Two nights after the angiogram, I could not sleep because of the pain in my bladder. Bent over with cramps, I staggered into the family room to tell Bruce. Without taking his eyes off the TV, Bruce said, "You should call a doctor." *Why can't he? I'm the sick one.*

I got a prescription from the on-call doctor, and Bruce picked it up at the drugstore. I needed him to do something more, to say something sweet and comforting. Whenever I was in need, Bruce would check out emotionally. "Take a pill," he would say whenever I had a headache. This time I was too far gone for pills to help. Bruce had to drive me to the emergency room. As the streetlamps streaked by the windows, each tire-thumping pebble told my burning bladder how soon I would have to pee again. It was the worst night of my life.

Just a few months before, life had been good. The millennium had been off to a roaring start, but now I was bottoming out, and Bruce was not there to hold my hand. Old thoughts of leaving him floated up, like an old log that uproots from the mud, but with my brain surgery coming up, I'd have to leave that idea just beneath the surface.

Bruce was chewing gum, and I swear he was in a trance because he never looked at me or said anything. He was so odd and so cold. Earlier, when it had been I who was driving him to the ER with kidney stones, I had kept asking him how he was doing, telling him we would be there soon—just staying in touch.

Bruce had acted the same way with our ailing pets. When my poor old dog was dying as we drove him to the vet, I got hysterical when the dog froze into a coma on my lap. He never made it home. A few days later, I overheard Bruce asking someone, "Can you believe April wanted me to go through a red light?"

What is he talking about? It was night. There were no cars at the intersection.

Another time, we came home from an RV trip to find one of my cats staggering in the throes of a heart attack. We raced to the vet, me in the back with the cat, who was writhing in pain, paws clinging to the front of the carrier. I was telling Bruce what was happening in the rear, and he never said a thing. She expired just as we arrived.

Bruce evaporates into himself when I need him, just as he did as we were heading to the ER. Once there, I learned that they had three triages ahead of us, and people were helicoptering in with hopes of saving their lives after several car crashes. I would have to wait and wait. My heart rate was so high that I thought I might die of a heart attack, and I had to pee every few minutes. Bruce would help me to the bathroom, but he would not talk to me.

Each hour seemed to drag by more slowly than the last. It was horrible. After I was finally seen by medical personnel, we were admonished for having chosen to come to the hospital; we should have gone to our urgent care facility five minutes away, where we would have been in and out in a jiffy. As for me, I could not clear the fog from my pain-raddled brain or drag myself from the depths of fear and despair about my upcoming surgery. My only thought had been to go where I had received the catheter. I needed Bruce to be involved in my strife emotionally and intellectually and to take the initiative.

We got out of there at 4 a.m. or so, and then crawled back to see a neurosurgeon at 9 a.m. the next day. We were so tired, and I was miserable as the neurosurgeon pulled the paper down on the examining table and sketched the carotid artery in my head and the aneurysms lurking there. He recommended that I see a surgeon at Jefferson Medical Center in Philadelphia.

Coincidentally, my surgery was set for April 2, the anniversary of the opening of Mother Hubbard Childcare Center. I should have been anticipating this milestone, but for three months, my mind kept going over the gruesome details of the operation, as if I had PTSD in advance. I was told that they might have to saw into my skull if the procedure done through a catheter, called "endovascular coiling," was unsuccessful.

I was given a balloon occlusion to see if my brain could even stand all this messing around. Once they had the balloon in my brain, they woke me up and told me, "Talk." I began trying to set up the nurse with Reid, and they knocked me right back out. It turns out that I was good for the main event.

When I awoke from that surgery, I was thrilled to find my head still intact, but my leg would be strapped down for the next two days. My incision was left open, just in case they had to dash back in for emergency repairs, so I couldn't move. Bruce was puzzled why the surgery should be such a setback for me. *Hey, who just got impaled from her crotch to her brain, not to mention having both hands punctured black and blue from IVs?*

Bruce's lack of empathy and compassion are amplified when I am ill. When I had a hysterectomy in 1994, Bruce acted the same as he had the night in the ER when I suffered the bladder infection—disconnected and cold. He couldn't figure out why I was nervous. *Umm, I'm only getting a major organ removed.*

On another occasion, one of the at-home injection treatments caused intense burning on my skin. I didn't know the cause and feared anaphylaxis, but I was still breathing. We headed to the local urgent care, but then I thought perhaps the allergist would be better. I was scared, but instead of trying to calm me down and help me decide the best course of action, Bruce reacted with annoyance and kept irritably turning the wheel back and forth from one route to the other. "Make up your mind!" his actions clearly stated to me. Turns out it was a niacin flush.

Years later, when I had a blood pressure problem and didn't know where to go for help, I finally decided on the urgent care center, but in the parking lot I worried that it might not be a true emergency. Bruce gave a big sigh, threw his head on the steering wheel, and groaned, as if to say, "God, this woman is such a bother."

After the brain surgery, the doctor told us that my adrenal glands would be taxed. Back then I didn't know what that meant. I should have rested more in the hospital, but I could not avoid getting drawn into conversations. I counseled one nurse on starting an elderly daycare, another on Lyme disease, and still another whose mother had emotional problems. Besides, I was kept awake at night by the cacophony of hospital beeps, somebody's TV blaring, and a staff member outside my room banging on a stapler: *Bam! Bam!*

"Whaaaaaaayyying."

This was the gibberish that came out of my mouth a few weeks after the surgery when I tried to ask Bruce, "What are you doing?"

Soon thereafter, my neighbor Anne decided I should get out of the house and drove me around while she did errands. We looked at patio furniture and umbrellas without anything weird happening, until I tried to ask a clerk where the umbrellas were. "Mmuuuuuua!" was all that came out.

Now I was scared. When I got home, I called the doctor's office at Jefferson Hospital. The nurse directed us to "come on in and let us take a peek."

I spent almost an hour inside an MRI machine, my head stabilized by a vice as if my skull were about to be drilled. "Do not move," I was told. "Try not to yawn, blink, or scratch an itch." *Rat-a-tat, rat-a-tat!* boomed the machine. Then came the sloshing sound, and I pretended I was in my pool, with water slapping the sides.

Luckily no blockage could be found, and I did not speak gibberish again. Every year now I have to get a brain MRI to see if the coil is stable. I am given the image on a CD and Jefferson gets the report, but every year Jefferson calls for the CD again as if the report were not clear and they need to really scrutinize my arteries. Then I get a letter saying the coil is stable, with a prescription for next year's MRI.

Contrast dye was shot in my veins so many times that I became sensitized to it and my face, eyes, and mouth would swell up whenever they injected it. They tried giving me steroids instead, but I had the same reaction, so now I am spared the dye but have to declare an allergy on all medical forms.

My daughter has to go through this annual check as well. Aneurysms run in families. Reid was fine, but doctors discovered a six-millimeter bubble behind Sally's right eye. Surgery was not urgent. Still, if an aneurysm bursts, it can kill you.

Sally did have the surgery, however, right after she took the New York bar exam in 2002. Afterward, a neurosurgeon she knew told us he would not have recommended it, but as long as it worked for us, so much the better.

I still have two aneurysms, in my skull rather than in my brain, but the doctors say they're not an emergency. *Please, don't burst*, I tell my aneurysms when some stab of pain in my head sends me running to the mirror to see if my eye has turned bloodred.

Even while I was still recuperating in bed, I went back to living as if I'd make it to a thousand. I was asked to be board chair for Literacy Volunteers, which teaches adults reading and English as a second language. I received the Comeback Runner of the Year Award from my running club. In Washington, D.C., where Sally was interning, I ran the Lawyers Have Heart 10K in June. Then I won the August New Castle RRCA Championship Five Miler in my age group. Olympic Gold Medal Marathoner Frank Shorter and our then-Governor Mike Castle presented me with the award. When I told them I had just recently had brain surgery, Mike asked, "Are you all right?" *Not really*, I thought, but not because of the operation.

Chapter 15

NARCISSISM

As I recuperated from my 2002 brain surgery, my mysterious illness came back inexorably, as if misery could flow down from my head to my muscles and joints, like sand in a human hourglass.

Now I was getting anxious—make that sweating bullets. We undertook a cycle of grueling pilgrimages to Lyme doctors in Connecticut and Pennsylvania, always getting the same, fruitless remedy: more antibiotics. One memorable regimen involved a daily home injection of Biaxin. First I would lie on our massage table and brace myself for pain. Then Bruce would pierce my backside, compressing the plunger for nearly a full minute, until my glute was engorged with a prodigious dose. Meanwhile, I would dispatch my mind to the ski trails, as I had done for the presurgical angiogram, praying that the shot would be over before I slid to the end of my favorite trail. Then I'd stick a heat compress to my aching butt. Once I could run without pain, it was time for another shot, one every three days. My microbiome was annihilated. I didn't understand the damage to my gut at the time, and neither did most medical doctors. I wondered whether I would ever be well. Something was off with my health, and something was off with my husband.

My dear mother suffered from internal bleeding and a stroke on Valentine's Day, the anniversary of her engagement to Dad. She was in a coma for a week, and after a few days, Dad ceased to visit her bedside because he was overcome with stress and sadness. Keeping watch by her side, I felt as though I was united with her soul. With his bad sense of timing, Bruce showed up and interrupted the state of peace and calm that I had entered into as Mom was passing. Bruce directed me to the hospital lobby, where he called the funeral home, and then we both returned to Mom's room as she took her final breath.

A few months later, I experienced a couple of panic attacks and consulted with a therapist, Dr. Barbara Belford, since I had no idea what was happening to me. My cousin Lynda told me, "I wondered when the stress would catch up to you."

Early on in my sessions with Dr. Belford, I mentioned something about Bruce, and she let slip the word *narcissism*. What was this thing that might describe Bruce? I yearned for a name that would make sense of Bruce's peculiarity, so I scored two books on the subject: *Narcissism: Denial of the True Self*, by Alexander Lowen (1985), and an early edition of *Malignant Self Love: Narcissism Revisited*, by Sam Vaknin (2015). I madly highlighted the pages that reproduced Bruce's childhood in black and white. From Vaknin's shocking YouTube videos, I began to see myself, too, in full-color pixels, the victim of marriage to a narcissist. This was from the horse's mouth, since Vaknin himself was a narcissist and a brilliant communicator.

Then again, how could Bruce be a narcissist? They are the world's worst people. And I should run away, say all the experts. Still, just as I was not 100 percent sure about my chronic Lyme diagnosis, I had doubts that all these traits of narcissism would fit Bruce's mold, especially the grandiosity. Some psychologists spoke of covert traits, the insidious kind you can't put your finger on, which lack the bullying and cruelty of the overt narcissist but still make you doubt your own perceptions and undermine your self-esteem.

I began to wonder whether Bruce was a narcissist, overt or covert. At that time I was unaware of the narcissistic trait of being always on the move looking for supply, which would explain his continual absence. I was also unaware that he had another narcissistic trait of doling out information to me when he saw fit but keeping much of his life hidden. With the slip of the tongue, I found out years later that he had often been to a restaurant/bar that I had never visited until it was renovated. Andrew from the NARCDAILY podcast on YouTube now provides this insight about narcissism, but it was not available to me years ago.

Another slipup caused Bruce to be outed. The evening before a wedding for the son of close friends, he ran into town to pick up dinner from our favorite Greek restaurant. I was not feeling well and was distressed by the fact that I didn't think I would have the energy for the long ceremony at the church and also attend the reception. I fussed and agitated about it all night to Bruce, remarking how our mutual friends, the Smiths, often attend the same weddings and sit close holding hands and enjoying the romance of a wedding. It was quite upsetting for me to miss the ceremony, but I had no choice. When we arrived at the reception, I immediately saw Ms. Smith and another woman. "How was the ceremony?" I asked. Ms. Smith looked at me and said, "Didn't Bruce tell you when we saw him at the bar last night that we weren't going to the ceremony?" She was talking about a local Newark hangout. My blank, astonished expression alerted them to the fact that I was clueless. I had no response. To assuage my shock, she said, "He only had one beer!" Bruce could have alleviated my stress in a blink of an eye, but he chose to keep mum rather than expose his habit of stopping at a bar when he so helpfully offered to do takeout dinner errands. The women knew I was in the dark and quite thrown off-balance, so I was embarrassed as well as stunned. When I asked Bruce why he didn't tell me he had been at the bar and why he talked to the Smiths about the wedding and never mentioned a thing to me, he answered, "Did you expect me to sit in the parking lot?" *I'm sorry, I didn't realize you were so special. How about you just leave the house later to avoid the wait? Oh but then, I guess you can't socialize and drink at a bar.*

Dr. Abdul Saad of Vital Mind Psychology in Australia provides some clues about narcissism in his online lecture "The Childhood Origins of Narcissism." These people are damaged as children caught between abuse on one end and treatment as a little prince on the other. Essentially, says Dr. Saad, the parents reject the child's "spontaneous human expression" and require the child instead to live for their parents' status (Vital Mind Psychology 2016). In the melee of its developing mind, the child learns to survive by inventing a false self, exalted though fragile, which needs constant favor and praise or it crumbles.

I had felt sure Bruce had been a good child. But something went wrong. A few years ago, he told me matter-of-factly, "My mom used to hit me more than my dad." He said he deserved it, although I don't think a child should ever be hit. One time when his father came at him, his big hand ready to strike, Bruce toppled backward on a board and impaled his hand with a nail. That would have been traumatic for me; I can't imagine how much the fear and pain must have marred Bruce's child self.

His mother, Peggy, was never diagnosed with Asperger's syndrome, but I have come to wonder whether she was on the spectrum. Two of her brothers were engineers, and one was a bit distant and became estranged from the family. Bruce and Peg are both very social, not a common trait for aspies, but Peg did not communicate in a normal way. She confessed once that they never had conversations in the family. She joked that she had a memory like an elephant, but it was short. Like Bruce, she relied on lists and notes.

She had had a difficult time raising Bruce and his two younger brothers, especially since Bruce's dad, Ralph, did not pitch in with child-rearing. Peg agonized when the youngest would stand up in his highchair and she was powerless to get him to sit down when he refused. She confessed that she would be so upset with her boys that she would go into a closet and scream.

When I revealed this to Bruce, his answer was a flat "We didn't have closets in our house." I would have expected him to say something like "I didn't know she was so upset or stressed," or "I feel bad for her," or something that would have at least acknowledged his mother's pain.

Peg would often ask me, "Is Bruce okay?" She would be distressed and almost in tears. I had long thought Bruce was different, but he seemed okay in most regards. He wasn't depressed or upset about something, at least outwardly.

Then Peg said something telling: "I never let Bruce be a little boy."

Bruce had admitted to me that he had been "on his own" since fifth grade.

I wish I had known how to help her unravel all this, but it was way before I knew anything about narcissism or Asperger's, and at the time, I just wanted to ease her worries.

Bruce seemed to have taken over the role of the father and helped his mom, which added more wounds to his psyche. The "false self" he was constructing built up a strong defense. He could never tolerate being told he had made a mistake or bear any perceived criticism. That did not make him an easy person to live with. God forbid that I should inadvertently say the wrong thing, or he might fall into a narcissistic rage.

They say men marry their mothers, meaning that they transfer childhood feelings about their moms to their wives. I often felt that applied to us, and it has been a terrible burden. I would often tell Bruce, "I am not your mother; I am your friend, companion, lover, and wife." I tried to make him understand that this child-parent game between us was unhealthy for our marriage and that it was an impossible foundation for a relationship. When I learned of Asperger's syndrome, I asked my neighbor in Toledo what she might have noticed about Bruce's personality. She said, "He seemed to always be wanting to please you." A therapist once asked Bruce what he felt like when I was upset with him. Without hesitation, he responded, "I feel like I am a little boy getting into trouble."

I learned only recently that there had been a lot of yelling in his house between his parents. Eckert Tolle, the great spiritual teacher, was traumatized as a child because of his parents' fighting. Oprah Winfrey and Eckert produced a wonderful podcast series based on his book *A New Earth: Awakening to Your Life's Purpose*. In this series, Eckert describes what he calls the *pain-body*, an outgrowth of trauma that strives to "become you" and get its "food" through you (Tolle 2015). I could see how Bruce's pain-body demanded feeding the same way narcissism demands supply, and why, if Bruce did not get it, he would start his typical pattern of arguing and upset me. If only I had understood how to handle these attacks back then, instead of playing into that dynamic and creating my own stress.

When I came into Peg's life, I found her to be loving and kind, proud of her three sons and grandchildren, but she was a woman of contradictions. She was sociable but not conversational, a terrific grandma but a distant mother, educated but conventional in marriage. Her father sold insurance. Her mother, a Christian Scientist, died when Peg was young. After a few years of college, Peg left Minnesota for Sacramento, California, to work in a bank, where she met Ralph, a soldier stationed nearby. They married and set up a house back home in Minnesota. After her boys had grown up, she worked as a dietitian at the local hospital. She accumulated a huge social network comprising birthday groups, weight-loss counseling for Take Off Pounds Sensibly, Eastern Star, her church, and even a group that went for muffins and coffee after swimming at the YMCA. She loved to cook, peddled a bicycle all over town, and even rode a water ski wakeboard in her later years.

Ralph provided for his family by working at the local flour mill. He served as president of his local union, played softball, and bowled regularly. Apparently he liked to head out to the bar with his union brothers after a meeting. One Christmas Eve Ralph was out late, so Peg and her good friend Mary Ellen rode bicycles all over town to hunt him down—eventually homing in on him drinking Christmas spirits with his buddies at their usual bar. Ralph did not chat much. He would just sit in his La-Z-Boy chair in front of the TV, watching baseball, reading the newspaper, or teasing the grandkids and poking them with his cane.

One day I found myself alone with Ralph. He was reading an article in the paper about gun control, and we began to discuss it. I was shocked. Ralph was informed, articulate, and capable of an interesting exchange with me. I wondered whether he and I had something else in common. Perhaps we were both married to someone who had difficulties communicating and we had both similarly disengaged.

All the same, Peg and Ralph were great grandparents to their four grandchildren, taking them on trips and opening their houses as second homes to the working parents. And, oh man! Peg *loved* to take photos! She had tons of albums. They joined us on RV trips, and we all had great fun. Sally, as the only girl in the family at that point, grew close to her grandma Peggy. The grandfolks came all the way to Virginia for Sally's graduation at William and Mary. For Reid's graduation from law school, my parents and Peg and Ralph all stayed at Disney resorts. It was a blast. They had great chemistry together and got along famously.

Bruce and I felt another chemistry when we visited his home in Winona, Minnesota, along the Mississippi. Bruce was more reactive than usual when we were with his folks.

"Your parents are going to wonder why you married me," I told him. One of our fights got so intense that I fled the house and ran to the lake. He got me so frustrated that I threw a plastic souvenir cup from Epcot Center onto the pavement, where it cracked. When we packed up the RV to leave Minnesota, Peg was teary-eyed, and I felt sad for her. Blunt-hearted Bruce was humming and cheerful as we drove out of the driveway. Still fed up, I could not speak to him for most of our trip home and again considered ending our marriage.

My therapist surmised that Bruce was relieved to escape the stress in that house, a stress that had never been acknowledged or understood. I told Bruce that his parents had only done what they had known to do. It was the fifties, after all, and men did not help with housework or childcare. What I could not explain was that Peg had traits on the spectrum and that it was challenging for a woman with such traits to offer emotional support to her children, even as she does the best she can in practical ways.

Ralph suffered from Parkinson's in the latter part of his life. He passed away the day I had a breast biopsy, and though I was more tired than usual, we all flew to Minnesota for the funeral.

A few years later, Peggy succumbed to Alzheimer's, but I felt too unwell to make the trip, so I wrote a poem for the service entitled "Peg Had the Heart of Gold." And she did.

Regarding Ralph and Peggy's parenting, Dr. Saad explains narcissism as deriving from mixed good boy/bad boy messages. A consequent narcissistic trait is the need for reaffirmation of self-worth, what is called "supply" (Vital Mind Psychology 2016). Supply is the one nourishment narcissism demands, more than food, sex, or even love.

Everyday interactions with spouse and kids tend to be prosaic. Wives will ask their husbands to take out the trash, mow the lawn, walk the dog, remember to pick up the dry cleaning, and, while they are at it, buy some bread and milk. Kids will ask their dad to take them to their friend's house or fix their bicycle and then stare at the TV and refuse to clean their rooms. Not a gold mine full of narcissistic supply, for sure.

In an endless quest for supply, Bruce is compelled to abandon the confines of our household. Simply interacting at the bank or post office can give him a boost. Somebody says, "Hi, Bruce, howya doing?" and that opens his tank for more supply. He chats with everyone, and when we go on a trip or cruise, he discovers a smorgasbord of new people whom he can regale with tales of his illustrious life. It strikes my ears as "yabbering," which infuriates me because he hardly says a thing at home. Bruce often introduces me to some person that he has reason to encounter in his forays for supply, such as the nurse at the blood bank where he gives platelets. The nurse will exclaim, "I feel like I already know you. Bruce has told me so much about you!"

Who am I to these people but a character in his movie? One time I came up behind him at a party and heard him painting a scene that featured "my wife blah blah," and I startled him. "Oh," he said, in a dismissive third person, "here she is!"

Unfortunately for Bruce, he pocket-called me on his iPhone while he was on one of his forays. I tried to answer, "Hello? Hello!" but he didn't hear me. I heard him, however, my usually uncommunicative husband, playing Mr. Charming. He was telling a joke about how he eats dinner in the state of Maryland and showers in the state of Delaware, referring to the house that we built on the Mason Dixon Line. He was totally alive, and the guy he was talking to was guffing it up. So hilarious! This was my boring, hardly-mumbles-a-word-on-a-lunch-date-or-in-the-car husband. Two totally different personalities, and it was scary. I felt too insignificant for him to engage directly with me when, in reality, I simply did not provide narcissistic supply.

The kids and I decorate his life, as the song goes. We provide background and pulp for his conversation. We legitimize him. We make him normal, so people think of him as a caring father and husband. We integrate him into the outside world, a world that he would be unable to enter on his own. I forbade him to use us in this manner. I, whom he never talks to, will not be talked about for his own self-worth.

Discouraged by and fearful of Bruce's narcissistic tendencies, I began to have little hope that our marriage would ever be happy, at least for me. Bruce was fine with the way things were, especially if I left him to his own designs. We would continue stumbling along this uncertain path until someone actually listened to me.

Chapter 16

VERBAL ABUSE

"It sounds like verbal abuse to me," my sister-in-law, Cindy, mused. She knew I was going batty and couldn't figure out what was happening when most conversations with Bruce ended up in circular arguments. *Verbal abuse? What does that mean?* It sure sounded bad, but I was to learn it was worse than bad; it was scary and awful. It was a devastating diagnosis, but it was true. I knew it in my heart and felt it in my bones. Cindy heard Patricia Evans, author of *The Verbally Abusive Relationship*, on an Oprah Winfrey show and enabled this huge breakthrough by listening to me and not dismissing my feelings. I am forever grateful to her.

I learned from Evans' book that Bruce thought of me as the enemy and needed to have power over me. No way was he ever going to let us work out a problem or resolve an issue. The abuser "sees his partner as an adversary," explains Evans. "How dare she have a different view from his? He may choose to argue against her thoughts, her perceptions, or her experience of life itself." Accordingly, it "prevents all possibility of discussion" (Evans 1992, 89).

Bruce would use the tactics of verbal abuse, such as withholding, blocking, diverting, forgetting, countering, denying, trivializing, ordering, and—his favorite—blaming, to turn everything back on me. Whatever it was, it was my fault. If I was upset with something he did or said, he had standard answers: "You must be getting your period" or "You are just mad because I went golfing." At times, he acted like a true "asp-hole."

Bruce caused me to question my sanity. I was certain I knew the truth, but it seemed he would change the truth to fit his agenda.

Once, when I described this behavior to my therapist, she told me that Bruce wasn't forthright. To me it was a lie, sometimes a lie of omission. When I'd confront him with his lie, he would deny it. Perhaps it was just a defense mechanism: denial of some truth that was damaging to his ego. Another therapist said Bruce was deceptive. I would find out things he had done—which he either denied or said he had forgotten—and be shocked. He reminded me of a person testifying in Congress who claims, "I can't recall."

As Evans puts it, the categories of verbal abuse throw the victim off-balance and catch them off guard, causing them to feel disconnected, confused, and disoriented. Bruce could do this in the blink of an eye. It was a talent, and he was exceptionally skillful at it; I think he could probably do it in his sleep. When I tried to explain this to people, I was unable to repeat his abusive statements. It just wasn't in me. I had not needed to protect my psyche growing up, and I did not have a lifetime of practice.

Bruce often used the tactic of withholding. Evans hit the nail on Bruce's head: "The verbal abuser who chooses to withhold can add a variety of flourishes and camouflage to his withholding, such as pretending not to hear, picking up something to look at while his partner is sharing something, or watching television while saying 'go ahead, I am listening'" (Evans 1992, 87).

I often had to repeat what I said, even when I now know that he had heard me the first time. If he didn't have a prop like the newspaper on his lap, he would find something else to turn his attention to or mess with. If I asked what he was doing, he would answer, "Just straightening out the mail." He often coughed loudly. He claimed he had no control over his coughing, but I wondered if he repeatedly coughed when a client or friend was in the middle of a sentence, as he did with me. After a few minutes of this, I would be exhausted from having to retrace my thoughts and begin my sentence again. Often these stratagems worked, and I was silenced.

Therapists speak of "word salads," mixing up one's thoughts and words to such an extent that nothing one tries to say makes sense. Bruce's word salads would cause me such frustration that I would fall into despair.

Years later, after discovering that Bruce was on the spectrum with Asperger's syndrome and that his personality was rooted in narcissism, I began to correspond with Carole, another aspie wife, whom I met online.

"Carole," I said in one of our chats, "it only took me thirty-five years to realize when I try to talk to Bruce he has an immediate urge to pee. I would wait patiently, trying to collect my thoughts, until he emerged from the bathroom. That took the wind out of my sails."

"Ted does that, too!" Carole adamantly responded. "We lose our train of thought because we are thrown off-kilter with distractions."

That ploy doesn't work with me anymore. Bruce can pee down his leg if he has to, but he needs to listen to me before I let him escape to the bathroom. For years I was the fool to follow him around like a puppy dog, trying to talk to him as he walked away. It was beyond rude, and I was too deep into abuse for clarity. Verbal abuse is emotional abuse. I had always understood physical abuse, but becoming aware that verbal and emotional mistreatment is also abuse was a shock. What was I to do? This behavior was hidden behind closed doors, and I had no witnesses.

What I did was pull myself together, take a deep breath, and sit Bruce down by the fireplace for the second of our major talks. I laid it all out to him. He listened. I guess he knew he was doing that stuff, but I doubt he knew these tactics were identifiable and could be found explained in a book.

The only response he could come up with was, "April, you act like I know what I am doing."

"It hurts me just the same, Bruce, whether you do it on purpose or not. I don't like getting hurt. What if you had an uncontrollable tic with your arm shooting out randomly to bop me again and again? My body would be black and blue, like my feelings. You may not have meant to do it, but it still hurts."

He was outed and agreed to go to therapy. Would things finally change? At least he did not shut me down with "You aren't making any points with me" or run to the toilet. We were going into therapy blind, however, since we did not yet know that Bruce had Asperger's syndrome.

Before proceeding with therapy, it seemed wise to first consult Evans and get help straight from the expert. I would come to refer to her as Therapist Number One BD (Before Diagnosis), referring to the long, miserable delay before Bruce's diagnosis of high-functioning autism.

Since she lived in California, we met with Evans by telephone. The gist of what she said during those first sessions was that Bruce was verbally abusing me. In my first solo session with her, I told her the story of our harrowing ride to the beach in Virginia with toddler Reid in the car, when Bruce tore down winding two-lane roads at breakneck speeds and snarled at me when I begged him to slow down. Evans brought that up in our joint session.

"Why didn't it bother you," asked Evans, "that you were scaring your wife?"

He had no answer.

In retrospect, I understand how this may have been due to an Asperger's deficit of empathy. I do not mean that he was heartless, only that he was genuinely unaware that others have experiences of their own. If he thinks what he is doing is okay, then that should be enough.

Evans asked, "Bruce, how does it make you feel when April is upset?"

This is when he responded with, "Like I am a little boy getting into trouble."

She gave us an assignment to say two nurturing statements to each other every day. Bruce never came up with one, despite my suggestions: "April, are you feeling okay today?" Big fat "F" for failure.

After these telling sessions with Evans, Bruce and I decided to continue with therapy. Intuitively I felt that Bruce needed some dramatic change to his personality, and I didn't think normal cognitive behavioral therapy would be helpful. I wanted to get the "bad stuff" out of Bruce. Was it child abuse? Was it a forgotten, stressful event? Was it a personality disorder? Why did he feel stress building up inside? I went in search of a trauma therapist.

Since Bruce was new to the psychology scene, we found a therapist an hour away in Pennsylvania, eliminating any chance of his being spotted by local townspeople. His first session was on September 11, 2001, which complicated his plans for secrecy since from that day forward everyone would be sharing where they had been when the towers fell.

Therapist Number Two BD was a young woman trained in eye movement desensitization reprocessing (EMDR) therapy, which I vaguely understood as using blinking lights and movements that reprocess trauma. She erroneously decided Bruce was not a good candidate for this therapy, and it would be fifteen years before we returned to this modality. Following the therapist's instructions, Bruce learned to calm himself by picturing his favorite place by a stream in our nearby state park, where the water poured over a dam built of massive rocks and swirled in eddies below. He needed calming? That was a surprise to me.

However, Bruce and this therapist's failure to probe the roots of his behavior seemed to imply that I was a terrible person to live with, an unreasonable wife. What else would cause his outbursts of rage? Our everyday life was not stressful, so where was all this stress coming from? I spoke with this therapist on the phone and met with her in her office, but I could not seem to communicate our relationship problems with her. Cassandra Affective Deprivation Disorder symptoms were taking a toll. It was IMPOSSIBLE to have productive therapy without the Asperger's diagnosis, and I felt discouraged, distressed, and disheartened!

Giving up on Therapist Number Two BD, I found another who seemed promising. "Please," I pleaded to Bruce, "tell her how you might have narcissistic tendencies."

He returned less than two hours later and announced, "She said I am as narcissistic as she is."

Well, that didn't work out. I don't know what he says when he is in a session, but in hindsight, I know he is unable to describe our problems or his emotions—even if he actually tries. Therapist Number Three BD lasted all of one day. I then decided to join Bruce in therapy, where I would at least be privy to the sessions.

We went to couples therapy for six months—Therapist Number Four BD—and it was a disaster. The therapist was an attractive British woman, and after I learned about Asperger's, I felt sorry for her. She had the impossible task of trying to help our marriage with a huge clue missing. Bruce seemed to look forward to the sessions, but I hated them. We would blather on and on about some confusing conversation that had led to a fight. Very little came out of Bruce's mouth that applied to our situation. One time the therapist asked him what he would feel like if we were divorced.

"It would be weird to come home and nobody is there."

That was not exactly heartwarming, but he was just stating a fact, as he did in responding to another question: "What would you do if April cheated on you?"

"We would have to get divorced."

"Why, Bruce?" asked Therapist Number Four BD.

"That is what people do."

Boy, did I feel special.

We made no progress again. Bruce seemed to think he was doing something good and felt better, but I was frustrated. I would leave the sessions with my mind reeling and spend at least two days unable to sleep. *Am I not saying this right? How can I make her understand?* I don't remember who gave up on whom, but we discontinued the sessions with Therapist Number Four BD, and later I found out she went back to England, probably in search of more normal clients.

The next therapist that we found—Therapist Number Five BD—was a guy. Maybe he could figure out what was going on in Bruce's brain. But the sessions were so short that I barely got the problem du jour out of my mouth before he ushered us out of his office, his little clock going, "Bing!" The therapist seemed to question my motives, as if I were just trying to be a pain in the butt. All the same, the short-session therapist did provide us with one insight.

We were driving to New York for Thanksgiving dinner, via New Jersey, to check on a house my daughter and son-in-law were considering purchasing. My son and future daughter-in-law were along for the ride. We drove by the house and through the neighborhood, but Bruce missed a turn, and we found ourselves in a very run-down part of Newark, New Jersey. At stoplights, small groups of seedy characters ambled around our car. It was scary. It seemed like we could be easy prey for a carjacking or robbery. Everyone in the car was nervous and believed we were in danger. We needed to get out of there immediately. Bruce took no notice of the environment or our growing panic.

"Dad, get us out of here!" Reid shouted. "Turn around!"

Instead, Bruce pulled us into a gas station, where we were again the center of attention.

"Just a minute!" Bruce barked. He was still studying the map, which he balanced on the steering wheel. According to him, the map was wrong, not him; he was reading it correctly.

"We don't care," I pleaded. "Get us out of here and look at the damn map later!"

Finally, we drove off, soon finding the elusive turn to the main highway. As we breathed a sigh of relief, Reid said, "I saw some bad 'hoods in Miami when I was in law school, and this was worse."

Soon after this frightening episode, I had alone time with the short-session therapist. When I told him about our New Jersey experience, he said, "Bruce did not understand that the rest of you in the car were upset." *Right! Why didn't I think of that?* I could not imagine how he could not know that we were freaking out with fear. Now, after Bruce's diagnosis, I understand that he did not know because he lacks a theory of mind. He could not put himself in our shoes, and he was oblivious to his surroundings while he hyper-focused on the map.

After a few more short sessions, I gave up on Therapist Number Five BD. It would be eight more years before I would learn the cause of Bruce's peculiar and abusive behavior. When I finally did, I thought back to the wasted time, money, and frustration of all those counseling sessions and wondered how no one had picked up on the fact that Bruce had a personality disorder. It seemed to me that hearing his monotone, pedantic speech should have been a clue. Had none of them read Tony Attwood's *The Complete Guide to Asperger's Syndrome?*

We were having no luck with therapists, and our marriage was deteriorating fast. I was trapped because I was too weak and sick to think of leaving Bruce. *When I get better, I will go,* I often thought, but in a Catch-22, the stress of the relationship and having my feelings dismissed was only adding to my mysterious illness.

Chapter 17

TRY THE DU OR DO THE TRI

The moonlight reflected off Bruce's bare white behind as he swam laps in our swimming pool. His splashing had brought me to our second-floor bedroom window, and the sight below prompted me to break into song:

"There's . . . a . . . moon out, to-night/whoa ho-ho-hoo, let's go strol-lin'."

Bruce was alternating between the crawl and breaststroke, training for the quarter-mile swim in the upcoming Marathon Sports Sprint Triathlon, which took place each June at St. Andrew's School in Middletown, Delaware. That was where the movie *Dead Poet's Society* was filmed. It was a laid-back triathlon, and many local runners took part. A few were serious triathletes. Bruce did twenty of these fun races, beginning in 1991.

The swim stage for this triathlon was in the picturesque pond behind a stone school building set on a hill. The bike stage took a double loop through the rural neighborhood, and the run traversed the countryside through grassy fields and thick, green woods adjacent to the pond. As usual, I was Bruce's cheering section. Such a pastoral setting put me in a contemplative state of mind. I noticed that here, as well as in later triathlons I witnessed, there were very few women in their fifties competing. I was already becoming a more avid runner, and it occurred to me that if I were able to complete this kind of race, I would get a nice plaque, too. It was only swimming, biking, and running all smushed together. *How hard could that be?*

So began an incredible journey that I would rate as the most fun I have ever had, certainly the most exciting, and a bonding experience for Bruce and me to counter the stress of his Asperger's.

I climbed aboard my daughter's old Schwinn bike, and, with Bruce biking alongside and giving me instructions, I practiced shifting gears on inclines and straightaways. Then I practiced swimming distance in our pool, using a variety of strokes before jumping out for a short run. *Hey, maybe I can do this!* I bought the book *Total Immersion: The Revolutionary Way to Swim Better, Faster, and Easier* by Terry Laughlin and John Delves to learn swimming form and speed. I joined the YWCA to swim laps and work out. Then I plunged in, so to speak, and bought a 1970 racing bike with duct tape covering the handlebars; it had been high quality twenty years before, and it served my purpose. I practiced "bricks," where a combination of two of the three sports is used to train the body for the disorienting transitions. Switching smoothly from horizontal swim to vertical bike and bike to earthbound run can be critical in a competitive race.

When I felt sufficiently trained, I talked Bruce into doing the Karen Dudley Triathlon on April 12, 1997, at my daughter's college of William and Mary, where the swimming team sponsored a "tri" every year. There, Sally dragged herself out of bed at an early hour to watch us swim laps in the pool, run around the campus, and bike up a cobblestone hill three times to the finish, the run and bike segments being inverted.

"Mom," Sally said, "you did your first triathlon!"

We gave it another go on May 31 at the Bay Sprint Triathlon at Ft. Monroe in Norfolk, Virginia. This would be my first swim in open water, the ocean, and I was warned that it was different from a pool and that I should get a wetsuit. An acquaintance lent me a strange-looking, old-fashioned, long-sleeved, blue-and-yellow wetsuit. I looked like the flounder in *Little Mermaid*. Still, it kept me warm and buoyant when I first battled the waves and fierce currents. Big orange balls marked the course parallel to the beach, but every time I looked up to check on the direction, they seemed to slip behind a swell beyond my reach. I finally passed each one and let the waves carry my spent body to shore. I labored to put on my running shoes and was beginning to doubt whether I could continue when a young man putting on his shoes next to me said, "That was the hardest thing I ever did in my life!" *Thanks, kid, I feel better that it's not just me.*

When I finally finished, Bruce said, "Your run along the seawall was slow."

Gee thanks! I was just glad I made it to the finish line.

Later at lunch, I felt odd. I suspect this was the first inkling of my adrenals overworking.

Finally, the big day came to compete in the Marathon Sports Triathlon. I convinced a small group of friends and family to come out and cheer me on. The water was freezing, and I vowed to get my own wet suit as I kicked and pulled with numbing limbs. Emerging from the quarter-mile swim, I had to run up a hill to where the bikes were racked. I hopped on my saddle, wedged my toes into the baskets, and took off.

Bruce had worked on my brakes before the race, and I would have to apply them firmly to control my speed as I neared the bottom of an incline for the final stage. When I gave them a squeeze, they collapsed nearly to the handles and failed to appreciably slow me down. Bruce had made them too loose—aspergated! Swooping down a hill, I screamed at the volunteer to get out of the way. "My brakes aren't working! I can't slow down for the turn!" I was scared. How was I going to dismount at the transition area without crashing into people and smashing my vagina? I had already had that painful experience, not being used to the bar in men's bikes. I yelled to my friends, "I have no brakes!" Working those fool brakes as best I could, I managed to reduce my velocity enough to jump off without coming to a stop. I racked my bike, took off on foot, and finished the race faster than my anticipated goal. This time, I placed first in my age group and got the coveted plaque.

And after all that training, I was not going to make this the end of my triathlons. I was to earn six more plaques at St. Andrews, the final one on our wedding anniversary in 2004.

Traveling to triathlons in multiple states, we became friendly with several of the regular competitors. It was fun having triathlete friends, and I especially got close with a woman in my age group from Blackwood, New Jersey. Christine and her husband, Jack, also raced. She was a great cyclist, but I was a better runner, so if the bike course was long, she would beat me; if it was short, I would beat her. Christine and Jack came to Delaware for the Marathon Sports Sprint Triathlon at St. Andrew's. Driving to an early morning race one day, we spied the triathlon logos on their car ahead of us and pulled up alongside. Christine and I held up our goggles and made googly eyes at each other like little kids, thus relieving our prerace jitters.

Eventually we banded together as a team. With me as the runner and her as the cyclist, we competed together several times at the Lighter Than Air Biathlon in Lakewood, New Jersey. At the airbase where we raced, historic hangars rose above the concrete in the August heat, shimmering like pyramids. This was also the site of the Hindenburg crash. Christine and I were awarded Waterford crystal three times, beating out younger teams.

Bruce and I traveled to Cambridge, Maryland, to support Christine at the Black Water Eagle Man Triathlon, a half Ironman. This race included a 1.2-mile swim, 56-mile bike leg, and 13.1-mile (half-marathon) run. I ran beside her at each transition to cheer her on, and both of us were close to tears from the emotional weight of this grueling endeavor. We cried and hugged when she finished and was presented with an age group award.

As we raced in more triathlons, we began to upgrade our equipment. Bruce acquired a Soft Ride, one of these weird bikes with the seat floating on a single strut jutting back from the front post. Slightly more conventional, I bought a Cannondale. I also finally bought a wet suit so as not to freeze anymore and to help with my buoyancy at the same time. In the water, I plugged my nose and ears to avoid infection, stuffiness, and irritation.

The Lake Lenape Triathlon in New Jersey, occurring the weekend after the Fourth of July, was a fun one. There we met Christine and Jack and other competitors on the triathlon circuit each year. One fellow who was renowned for his speed and dedication was Ed Wright. Folks called him Mr. Triathlon. He came to all the triathlons in the tri-state area of New York, Pennsylvania, and New Jersey. He was in Bruce's age group, and they often raced each other, with Bruce beating him only occasionally. It was a big deal when Bruce beat Ed.

The run leg of the Lake Lenape Tri was through a pretty neighborhood adjacent to the lake: well-groomed lawns, abundant flower gardens, and underground sprinklers spraying rainbows in the sunshine. After the bike section of any triathlon, it is hard to get running legs going; they feel heavy or numb, and it seems as if you are moving in slow motion. That is why you have to practice those bricks. With about a mile of the three-mile course to go, I was moving along pretty well when Ed Wright (who had already finished, gathered his equipment, and loaded it into his car) jogged back to the race for food and awards. *Geez, I can't run with Ed Wright!* His jogging speed was as fast as I could go all out.

I was more worried about an elite runner in my age group from Pennsylvania, though. She rarely did triathlons, and her relatively slow swim time had her behind me, but now she was in her element.

I knew that Christine was ahead of me with another woman, so if I wanted a trophy it would have to be third place. But I'd have to beat that elite gal. Lake Lenape awarded pretty trophies, and I was determined to add one to my collection. Ed happened to be tall, while the woman coming up from behind was short and probably weighed less than a hundred pounds.

"Ed," I huffed to Mr. Triathlon. "Look behind me and see if you can spot a little woman. She is going to pass me!"

"I don't see anyone like that," Ed said after checking.

"She has to be there. She is tiny and wearing a white baseball hat!"

He glanced around again and said, "Oh, I see her now, but don't worry. She is two minutes back."

"I am telling you, Ed, she is a record-breaking runner. I have never seen her at a triathlon before, but she can catch me."

We ran along for a stretch, and I asked him to check again.

"She is one minute back," Ed reported, starting to get the picture.

He craned his neck every few seconds now, trying to keep an eye on her. "April! She is thirty seconds back."

He picked up his pace, prompting my legs to pick up as well. We rounded the corner to the finish, and he jumped off the course, yelling to me, "Fifteen seconds!"

I marshaled every bit of competitive spirit I could, sprinting harder and faster until I shot through the chute, and, a few seconds later, in cruised my tiny rival. I panted, "Hi. Good race!" I almost had a heart attack. Sprinting the last mile of a triathlon is not my style, but I got the trophy. Bruce collected one as well.

We decided to combine the Central Park Triathlon with moving our daughter into her room for her first year at NYU Law. The tri was the day after move-in. While Sally and Bruce carried her belongings into the building, I guarded the bikes on the sidewalk and got lots of attention from scary-looking people. I tried to ignore the questions I got: "Hey lady, these bikes yours? Are you selling them?" "What are you doing with those bikes?" "What do you *want* for those bikes?" *Are they thinking of bopping me on the head and grabbing the bikes?*

We mentioned to the NYU parking lot attendant that we would be competing in the Central Park Triathlon. He said, "You aren't going to swim in that dirty water, are you?" referring to the Parks and Rec pool.

"Yeah, I guess we are." What did we know about New York City pools?

Just then, the parking attendant driving my Cadillac swooped down the ramp and smashed right into a car driving up. The front hood was crumpled. *Oh my God! Will my car even be drivable?* We were all in a panic that we would be stuck at NYU with our two bikes and miss the race. Besides, I loved that car, especially the color of the paint: "gold diamond." Fortunately the damage was cosmetic. After some rushed paperwork for the insurance, we headed out.

We were told that it was likely someone would run up to us at a red light and steal our bikes by yanking them off the car, so we hurried through as many lights as possible on our way to our hotel. We wanted to pick up our numbers and shirts and find the location of the race that evening, so after parking alongside Central Park, it seemed logical to ride through the park on our bikes as the easier way. Unfortunately, we only had on our street clothes, making it hard to bike fast, and I was again getting scared as darkness descended on our trails in the depths of the park. We found the large public pool, picked up our packets, got the scoop, and biked back to the car as fast as possible. So far so good. No attacks or bike robberies. Rolling our bikes into the hotel was not much of a respite from the streets, however. We had to cram them into the elevator and then into the small room, where we were compelled to negotiate around them from bed to bathroom and back all night.

Arriving at the race the next morning, we found fellow triathletes racking their bikes and laying out their gear on blankets or towels like a picnic spread. There is never much room between bikes at triathlons, and everyone fights for space to place items such as helmets, bike shoes, sports drinks, gels, bike gloves, shirts, and sweatbands.

The water was very, very cold, having been drained and refilled the day before to clean out the biological detritus of public swimmers. When I jumped into the frigid water with my wave—the cohort of swimmers who started with me—it took my breath away. I was totally numb, and I struggled to make my limbs move. The pool was long, and the four laps seemed endless, but I got my blue body out as fast as possible and made a dash for my bike, where a photographer was kneeling on the pool deck shooting pictures of our feet. This was our contribution to New York City culture, but he robbed me of critical time in the transition.

Up and down hills, we biked for fifteen miles. Not having known that Central Park was hilly, I had not trained on hills. And I had not practiced dodging horse-drawn carriages full of tourists that made their sudden, mid-morning entrance. Because of the time I had lost due to that photographer, I was especially flustered by these obstacles.

More time slipped away as I struggled to rack my bike, since someone had taken my spot. Pretty soon I was running with it, and I finally slammed it down so that I could begin the run. I had never lost so much time transitioning from bike to run before. This run was five miles winding up and down hills, especially challenging after a freezing swim, a hard bike, and dodging more New Yorkers out jogging or taking a leisurely Sunday stroll. Worse, they pestered me with questions:

"What race are you doing?"
"Central Park Triathlon."
"How far is the run?"
"Five miles."

I had no energy to waste on small talk. Also, I was worried about getting lost and was trying to keep a few runners in sight. It was becoming increasingly challenging to pick out the racers in the crowd, but I did manage to keep a bead on a woman who looked to be in my age group. She seemed to be castigating herself, yakking out loud, shaking her head, and desperately checking her watch. Whatever she was saying to herself, she didn't like it. I thought she would not be easy to pass, but I was creeping up on her. Just when I was close on her heels, the course veered off the roadway, onto a narrow path, and down a long flight of steps. There was no way I could pass her without literally pushing her out of my way, so I was stuck five seconds behind her at the finish. She placed third, so that damn photographer had cost me my award. As I was complaining over the fact, I won a random gift certificate from a nearby bike shop. Folks sitting near me in the bleachers tried to cheer me up, saying my gift certificate was better than that trophy, anyway. Bruce, on the other hand, finished his race in second place, not having encountered interference by some artsy photographer taking pictures of people's feet in running shoes.

We did biathlons—or duathlons—in the spring and fall when it was too cold to swim. One early spring race was the Point Lookout Duathlon, held in St. Mary's, Maryland, and sponsored by an organization called Triathatlantic. We parked the RV at a campground with a great view of the Potomac River flowing out of its wooded banks and into the Chesapeake Bay. Nearby, we found a unique small restaurant where we could dine the night before the race.

We competed in the Point Lookout Duathlon several times, but this time it rained. As I completed the first run, I heard thunder and the rain began to pound. Lightning is usually the decisive factor in cancelling a race, but the lead bikers just came flying past. Then Bruce came by and I thought, *I am not a wimp*, so I jumped on my bike and took off.

I could hardly see as I peddled through the downpour and just tried to keep sight of the person biking ahead of me, even with rain all over my glasses. Cars started to show up on the road, and I worried that they could not see us. *Watch out for us goofy athletes on the road!*

I really wanted to beat this one woman who was a strong cyclist, so I prepared for the transition from bike to run by unzipping my jacket so I could tear it off faster. When I got near the bike dismount area, I forgot that I had already unzipped my jacket and unzipped my bike shirt, too. Unfortunately, my running shoes were so soaked that they swelled up, and I was unable to pull my foot out of the basket when I stopped, so I crashed to the ground. Several male volunteers stooped over me to ask if I was okay, which would not have been so bad if my shirt hadn't gaped wide open with my boobs splayed and completely visible through the white mesh bra. I scrambled to my feet, zipped up my bike shirt, racked my bike, and took off on the run. *Geez, that was embarrassing!*

I won first place in my age group, beating thunder thighs, but when I was called to get my plaque, I tried to hide from the volunteer guys.

Bruce participated in S.O.S., Survival of the Shawangunks, a grueling adventure race in New Paltz, New York. This ordeal comprised fifty miles of biking, running, swimming, running, swimming, running, swimming again, and running straight uphill to the finish. Bruce had to qualify by doing a half Ironman, which he did at the Blackwater Eagleman in Cambridge, Maryland.

At the start of an S.O.S, a small group of competitors gather on their bicycles at the base of the mountains in the early morning mist. All racers need a crew person to grab their bikes and rack them on cars when they finish the exhausting thirty-mile ride, the last five miles all uphill. I was Bruce's crew person and waited at the top of the hill to grab his bike and send him on his way.

Next, competitors run four and one-half miles to Lake Awosting, followed by a freezing one-and-one-tenth-mile swim. To meet Bruce at the lake that first year, I ran ten miles round trip through the trails. When volunteers asked me how I would get to the lake, I answered, "I am running!" I admit, the first time I ran alone through the woods was scary, but I figured out the trail marks and got to the shoreline in time to see the shivering swimmers crawl out of the frigid lake for a sip of hot tea and a snack. In later years, I enlisted Sally, Reid, and a friend whose wife was in the race to run with me.

Athletes had to carry all their equipment, so most did not wear a wet suit since it was hard to carry. They dragged their running shoes behind them in a waterproof bag. Bruce did pretty well because he had some fat on his bones, while the skinny guys sometimes quit, overcome with hypothermia. One time a young fellow was shaking so badly that I thought his teeth would fall out. He had to quit, and I saw him several times along the course with a red blanket wrapped over his shoulders. I called him Red Riding Hood, which seemed to cheer him up.

After the Awosting swim came a five-and-a-half-mile uphill run nicknamed "Little Godzilla." Views above were of the breathtaking Hudson Valley. These were the vistas that had inspired the Monumentalist Hudson River School art movement. The second swim, a half-mile, was across Lake Minnewaska, a few blessed degrees warmer than the first lake. I drove to the far end of the lake to cheer Bruce and others on and help a gal avoid a snake perched on a rock where she was trying to climb out. I snuck some swim shoes in my jacket for another woman who was unable to carry her entire load.

Soon the athletes were approaching the longest run, "Big Godzilla," an eight-mile stretch. The other spectators and I arrived at the Mohonk Mountain House, built by Albert and Alfred Smiley in 1870, to watch the final half-mile swim in Lake Mohonk. To reach the finish, the "Survivor Line," the athletes had to scramble straight uphill to Skytop Tower, where they were rewarded with another glorious vista, so high that I witnessed a small aircraft flying below us. Bruce reached the Survivor Line six different years, with times ranging from six and a half to eight and a half hours.

One year Sally took the weekend off from law school to attend the S.O.S. and watch her dad. We had another exciting time, and I was happy to have her run the trail with me through the woods to Lake Awosting. Someone took our picture, which I look at quite often. I am especially struck by the date: September 9, 2001.

Sally had taken the subway from the World Trade Center to meet us in New Jersey and again on her return on September 10. The next day, Sally was running on the Westside Highway and witnessed the first airplane hit the World Trade Center tower. Running in fear as fast as she could, she heard the other tower being hit. In shock, she called to tell me, "Mom, I just saw all those people die!" She and her roommate fled uptown to stay with a friend. We managed to get into the city a week later to see her and bring winter clothes. We smelled the terrible stench and beheld the hundreds of sad posters of missing family members on every tree and pole, so many loved ones never to be found.

Bruce's last S.O.S race in 2003 ended on a more positive note. During the race, Bruce stopped to aid a fellow participant who was hurting and lost. I was concerned when Bruce didn't show up when I expected, and I admonished him for losing so much time on his rescue mission, but Bruce had no regrets.

There was always a delicious feast and party after the awards ceremony, and one year we all trudged back up to the tower to witness a wedding. Two triathletes had chosen this setting for their matrimonial vows. They donned simple wedding attire, the bride in a blue sundress and holding a wildflower bouquet and the groom in an open white shirt and jeans. Lovely music by a guitarist resonated across the hills. We all got to partake of their huge wedding cake. A year later, the bride had to forgo the triathlon because she was nursing a baby.

Bruce and I did multisport races for ten years. One year we did eleven races. After each one, we would return home, laden with trophies or plaques, to soak in the whirlpool tub that overlooked our woods on Amaranth Drive, drink champagne in a froth of bath bubbles, and rehash the last race.

Training for triathlons might have been time-consuming and tiring, but it made our lives exciting. When we were not doing tris, we road-raced, which felt easy because all we needed were running clothes and shoes. Behind the scenes, meanwhile, our marriage was not so easy.

The last triathlon we were to do with Marathon Sports at Saint Andrew's fell on June 20, our wedding anniversary. Our friend, who owned the event, asked me, "What is your secret to staying married?"

How fast could I think up something? I was pooped out, and all I could utter was, "Drink a lot of wine."

It was a secret, all right.

Chapter 18

CASSANDRA

The outside world, the one that saw our races or attended our parties, has a vision of Bruce that contradicts my own. Fruitlessly trying to explain to everyone that something was wrong was almost as bad as our marital mayhem. No matter how I tried to explain a recent upset, I could not present the information in such a way that I was not left feeling dejected, exasperated, and alone. I imagine that anyone listening thought I was just a complainer, since the Bruce I was describing was not the Bruce they knew.

Cassandra Affective Deprivation Disorder (CADD) describes a condition experienced by women married to men with Asperger's syndrome. We know the truth and experience that truth, but we are not believed.

In Greek mythology, Cassandra was blessed with the gift of prophecy but cursed that no one believed her predictions. When she warned her fellow Trojans that armed Greeks were inside that giant horse, the Trojans threw a victory party, and the next day those armed Greeks burned Troy to the ground. Originally, Cassandra was cursed for not accepting the romantic advances of the god Apollo, whereas aspie wives are cursed for welcoming the advances of our husbands. Then we watch our marriages burn to the ground.

In her book *The Asperger Couple's Workbook*, Maxine Aston associates the symptoms of CADD with those of seasonal affective disorder and affective deprivation disorder. Symptoms of CADD may include low self-esteem, sadness, confusion and bewilderment, anger, guilt, depression, anxiety, post-traumatic stress, emotional breakdown, and physical illness.

My CADD began long before I ever learned about the phenomenon, when I started to feel that something was off early on in our marriage. My mother got it, but no one else did. In fact, they all loved telling me how wonderful Bruce was.

"Bruce is *soooo* nice!" a friend once said, dragging out her *o*'s to show how sure she was. Stunned, I stared at her blankly.

Placing her hand on my forearm and leaning in close to me, she repeated, "I mean it, April. He is *so* nice." Did she think I needed to be convinced?

Bruce was conscientious when dealing with clients in his law practice, and I regularly heard praise about how efficient, kind, and caring he was. During a dinner conversation with another couple, Bruce told a story of how he had helped an older client with dementia whom he had found wandering around the parking lot looking for tax assistance.

Our friend was impressed. "Bruce is a prince!" he exclaimed, and his wife nodded in agreement. "April, you are married to a prince!"

They did not know we had just left a stressful therapy session where I had railed about Bruce's insensitivities. Bruce slid his eyes to the side, connecting with mine—a mini-validation that he was aware of one of my Cassandra moments.

When I tried to explain to a friend how mean Bruce could be, I got the response, "Well, he has never been mean to me." Can't people understand that my experience with Bruce could be completely different behind closed doors?

"It's just a guy thing." This has been the go-to response for so many who have heard my complaints. It's not the only one, however; they are multitudinous:

"You are just being oversensitive."

"You are blowing things out of proportion."

"All husbands are like that."

"You have to pick your battles when you are married."

"At least you have things in common."

"Men are from Mars..."

Enough already!

Two Cassandra moments cut me to my core and stand out among the myriad I have experienced.

Bruce and I had been close friends with Chip and Doris for many years. When Doris's mother was on her deathbed, Doris sent me a heartbreaking email. I felt terrible for her, and I immediately shared it with Bruce. I did not expect Bruce to be excessively emotional, but I was shocked by his lack of any reaction at all. I felt terrible for Doris, while Bruce kept his eyes glued to the TV and barely grunted. I tried to nudge some sympathy out of him but gave up. *Well, this is Bruce.* The day Doris's mother passed, Bruce went over to her house to help with probate and estate administration.

A few days later, in the receiving line at the funeral, I was grieving for Doris's loss and waited to embrace her. When it was finally my turn, I reached out to hug her and express my condolences, but she physically pushed me aside to throw her arms around Bruce, who was next in line.

Doris gave a moving memorial to her mother. At the end, she tearfully regarded her husband in the front row pew and said, "Chip, I love you *so* much!"

If only I could say that in front of a crowd.

Then Doris turned her attention to Bruce: "I want to say a special thank you to my dear friend Bruce." She proceeded to declaim how helpful Bruce had been and how he had dropped everything to rush to her house.

Again, he's a prince!

Bruce will help people; that is not unusual. What surprised me was that he would rush over to Doris's house after his icy response when her mother was near the end. After the service, I asked Bruce why he had dropped everything to go over to Doris's so quickly.

"She asked me to," he replied. It was as simple as that. He follows instructions. I was hurt since I was the one who had responded empathetically while Bruce had required a prompt. He got the praise; I was pushed aside.

The second of my worst Cassandra experiences sprung up over a simple conversation:

"Do you want to have quinoa for dinner again?" I asked. "I know we had it last night."

"I didn't have any last night."

I said, "Yes, we did."

"No, I didn't," he shot back.

By now, I had gone from yellow to orange alert, and I was heading for red. "I know when I cook it and when we eat it." My voice was getting louder.

"Quinoa has never passed my lips," he replied.

What kind of goofy statement is that? Does he even know what he is saying?

As this pointless and nonsensical quinoa argument progressed, I tried to convince Bruce that we had, indeed, had quinoa for dinner the night before.

He was incapable of understanding why I was so emphatic, and he pushed on with crazier and crazier remarks. "I don't know why you're getting all upset. You're not gonna convince me that I ate it, because I didn't." His retorts were like little knives that he pulled from his brain to repeatedly stab me. My nerves were shot, my blood pressure was ballooning, and my heart was racing under my ribs with all this stress coursing through my veins. I hardly slept that night.

Unfortunately, this was the night before a 5K memorial race for a young man who had died of cancer. I had gotten to know the young man's mom, who was always happy to see me, as we ran this race year after year. This race would be arduous because I was especially sick from my mysterious illness.

We had planned to meet Bruce's younger friend and running mentor, Ray, at the race. Ray was involved in AA as a leader and sponsor, and at my insistence, Bruce had asked Ray to work with him on his drinking. Lately, however, whenever I saw Ray, I suspected that he held feelings of animosity toward me.

A few days before the race, I ran into Ray doing a training run and asked how it was going with Bruce.

"It's a process."

His tone told me he did not like me asking that question.

On the day of the race, I approached Ray in the parking lot while Bruce prepared to run. I confided that I was upset that Bruce and I had been fighting lately, and I thought his drinking had much to do with the problem. This process thing didn't seem to be doing much good.

"Why don't you just leave Bruce," he shot back angrily, "or go to Al-Anon and talk to other people with problems like yours?"

I was shocked and hurt. *Why am I the one who's supposed to leave my gardens, my cats, my home? And why should I join a support group full of people who don't know anything about Asperger's or what it's like to live with an aspie?*

I tried to calm down and focus on the race. First quinoa, then Ray, and I was feeling unwell. What next?

A mile or two in, I passed Bruce on the sidelines, sitting on a bench and holding a cup of coffee he had grabbed from the refreshment table.

He smiled and waved as I passed by. *What the hell?* I don't know how I finished, as emotionally and physically drained as I was.

After the race, Ray was even angrier with me. According to him, I had gotten Bruce so upset that he could not run. I countered that it seemed that Bruce was being manipulative, that he had just quit the race to rattle me.

Ray turned his back, yelling, "I don't wanna hear any more. Get away from me!"

Bruce could not offer me a reason for his actions. He said he didn't feel like running, and that is the only explanation he gave to Ray and me. I was dumbfounded, shaking with anger and exhaustion, and didn't want to get in the car with Bruce. I wanted to disappear into thin air.

"Take a bus," I implored, unwilling to be in the car with him, but I was too weak to make the forty-five-minute drive on the interstate alone.

On the way home, Bruce asked, "Could you explain to me what we were arguing about last night?"

He doesn't know? I was a few breaths away from a nervous collapse, and he did not have a clue.

I explained, "It started when I asked about the quinoa."

"You know I didn't eat any because it is what you have for breakfast."

It hit me then that he was thinking of amaranth, which he does not eat. He had gotten the two grains confused.

Good grief! Why didn't he mention that before? All that fighting for nothing!

No one not in my position understands what drives me off the rails except other aspie wives, like Carole.

She gets upset that aspie spouses suffer alone and that the attention given to the aspie in the relationship is so one-sided. I would not be surprised to find her standing in the park on a soapbox and shouting through a bullhorn, "Support aspie wives! Aspie wives need love!" I wholeheartedly agree.

How does one end up with an aspie husband in the first place, if he is so hard to live with once the knot is tied? How did we welcome our suitor's advances, unlike Cassandra of old? The answer is that we were fooled, duped, misled, and conned by the aspie's survival strategy of mimicking the neurotypical. They are acting. But they cannot keep up the charade forever and are forced to unmask. Remaining "on" all the time is as exhausting as an endless job interview.

Carole and I both experienced the switch to the autistic side when our marriages settled in. Carole once wrote in an email:

> They try so hard to win us over that they are perfect before getting married, but as soon as they win us and we are married, they can stop trying and just be themselves. I have often told Ted that the guy I married died years ago and now I live with someone else, someone that I never picked as my husband.

We have good reason to be angry about this initial deception. We were not forewarned that we were marrying a spouse with a disability. It was not obvious, as with someone who is blind, deaf, or using a wheelchair. If we had known, we would have had the option to weigh the odds and make an educated decision about our impending life commitment.

How deep the deception goes is a matter of debate. Are these guys aware that they are deceiving us by imitating the social mores of courtship? Granted, most people are on their best behavior during courtship, but rarely are they as extreme as in the cover-ups Carole and I experienced. Bruce has told me that he had not thought his condition would affect anyone else, and he hadn't been diagnosed. After all, his mother had always told him he was special. I don't think he intentionally set out to misrepresent himself to me, but I was tricked just the same.

Now that I understand Asperger's syndrome, I can see all the little red flags that should have caught my notice when Bruce and I were dating. But I did not know then what I know now, and I can see why so many people don't understand what I am talking about when I say that he is not who they think he is.

"How can we expect other people to believe us when they are experiencing the same thing we did at the beginning?" Carole once asked.

"Exactly," I answered.

There's a chameleon effect. I see it all the time. Bruce adjusts his personality based on what he thinks people want him to be—changing colors to reflect those around him. It goes beyond different speech registers, like how we all talk based on formal or informal situations.

"Ted can be on the phone laughing, talking, and being 'Mr. Charming,'" Carole said, "then hang up and be a completely different guy. It is infuriating."

I knew exactly what she meant. Bruce had his business voice for serious phone calls and a cooing, seductive voice for calls with women—even his mom.

One email from Carole typifies the feelings many aspie wives experience and why we suffer with Cassandra syndrome:

> Bruce is a man, but he is an Asperger man, and they are a totally different breed. None of my friends that I've tried to explain Asperger's[to] understand what I go through. Nobody will understand unless they live it. April, there are no words that can express the feelings that we feel living with our aspies. It is indescribable and nobody that has not been in our shoes could even imagine how hard it is or understand the depths of the syndrome.

Over the years, I have tried to refrain from mentioning Bruce's Asperger's to anyone because of the complexity of it all. But being a Cassandra is so difficult that sometimes I just blurt out the reality of my situation.

At a wedding shower for my niece, I sat and listened as women discussed recent divorces. My sister-in-law's cousin, a sharp gal, turned to me and said, "At least *you* got a good one!"

"No, I didn't!" I exclaimed. "He has Asperger's!"

At a small party we hosted in June of 2016, our friend John made a comment about how well Bruce and I seemed to be doing. I am not sure why he mentioned it at all, but I blurted out, "No, we aren't. He has Asperger's."

I was blown away that he understood. He had even picked up on the odd way Bruce speaks to me on the phone. "When we went on golf vacations, and Bruce called you from the motel room, he always sounded like he was making a business call," John said. He looked at me kindly, "You've really had it rough, haven't you?"

Wow! It was fantastic for this Cassandra to finally be understood!

Chapter 19

COMMUNICATION

Communication in my aspie marriage is a barrier higher than Mount Everest and more complicated than the Rubik's Cube. It is a mystery to me that the simplest of activities seem to overwhelm Bruce's brain and my nerves. This lack of cognition and understanding has been constantly irritating, like a patch of eczema that never heals, but there have been a few incidents that have left an especially aggravated patch in my memory.

Way too late in my marriage, I came to realize that Bruce and I actually communicated only about 20 percent of the time. Maybe signal flags, Morse code, sign language, drums, beeps, grunts, or a megaphone would have worked better than vocal cords. He never heard me except when I repeated myself several times, but even then there was no guarantee that he understood. I think the problem was a combination of lack of interest and his unusual way of comprehending words when they did reach his brain. My experience with human beings other than Bruce was that when I said something and they were three feet from me, they usually heard what I said. Even if there wasn't an immediate verbal response, it became evident later on that they knew and understood what I had said.

Bruce will not usually respond if I am chatting about something, such as when I think the cat has an ear infection again. *She keeps scratching her ears.* I will repeat this comment over and over, trying to elicit a response. Bruce's usual reply is, "Did you ask me a question?" He says this in an accusing manner, insinuating that I am not conversing accurately. Where did he learn that a response is only required as an answer to a question?

I pictured a scenario where my three-year-old grandson would understand me while Bruce would be confused: Pointing at the coffee table in my son's house, I would say, "Ethan, can you bring Grandma the book that is on the table?" Ethan would pick up the book and bring it to me. "Thank you, Ethan," I would say. Yet pointing at the table next to Bruce, I would say, "Bruce, can you bring me the book that is on the table?" And Bruce would have no response. I would repeat the question. "What?" Bruce would answer. I would again repeat the question. "What table?" Bruce would answer, his head swiveling around, looking all over the room. I would then say, "*That* table! You see the book on there? Can you grab it for me?" Then he would get the book, bring it over and ask me, "This book?" even if it was the only book on the table. It may be the fact that he consciously or unconsciously will not make anything easy for me, and by cooperating he loses control.

One of the most confusing communication incidents with Bruce happened during our attempt to redeem free ski passes to our favorite Poconos ski area, Blue Mountain. We obtained the passes when we purchased new ski jackets and, in my case, bibs on the last day of the winter season. It was a spring skiing day, and the crowd was in a festive mood, with big sales at the ski shop. In order to redeem the pass the next season, it had to remain intact and attached to the jacket. That was a good deal.

The next year, we donned our new outfits and drove up to Blue Mountain. I inadvertently cut my free pass, mistaking it for an old ticket from another ski area, but I hoped we could convince the ticket taker to honor it anyway. On the way up the mountain, I suggested to Bruce that we go to the lower mountain area to check in rather than the main lodge, bettering my chances of using the pass, but he drove right by the turn. *Okay, never mind.*

At the main lodge, we got in line, and Bruce went to the window and said, "I bought my ski clothes in Wilmington." *Say what?* I pushed him away and told the woman, "No, we got them here, and I am sorry I accidentally cut my pass. Can I please still use it?" She looked doubtful, probably thinking we were either lying or nutty. At any rate, I convinced her to honor the free passes, which, as anyone who has been on the slopes would know, are not cheap.

"Bruce, why on Earth did you tell her you bought your outfit in Wilmington?"

"Well, I bought the pants there." Vocal cords failed me again. Maybe I should have used a whiteboard and black marker or an Etch A Sketch! I understand now that texting works well to communicate with aspies, but that helpful tool did not exist back then.

We chalked up more communication failure at Amaranth Drive, where we had problems with the air conditioner kicking off due to an electrical overload that shut down the cooling system. Slowly, the house would get warmer, the air muggier, and our skin stickier. Bruce would just sit there, his forehead seeping tiny beads, and sip on a beer, utterly unaware of the heat.

"Bruce," I would finally say, "the house is getting warm. I think the air conditioner has shut down again."

Bruce would set down his beer, pull himself from his seat, trudge to the vent, and put his hand over the slots. "It is blowing," he would observe, "and I feel cool air."

"Bruce, air feels cooler when it is moving. That is why people fan themselves. The air is off!"

We had instructions from our electrician on how to remedy problems with the AC:

1. Go outside to check if the air-conditioning unit has stopped.
2. Turn off the house thermostat.
3. Go to the basement and flip the circuit breaker off for ten seconds.
4. Turn the house thermostat back on.
5. Go outside to see if the air-conditioning is back on.

After restarting the air conditioner dozens of times, with me taking him through the steps, Bruce still could not follow the simple sequence and restart the AC. In a fit, I grabbed an eight-by-ten piece of paper and practically broke a pencil as I forcefully scrawled the directions in big, dark letters and plopped it down in front of him. To him, it was as if it described how $E = mc^2$, and he never understood the procedure.

Judging by an unbearably warm trip we took in a new RV to Pensacola, Florida, in September 2014, these exercises did not make an impact on Bruce's understanding of air-conditioning. I had suspected that the RV's AC system was not all that effective when we first drove this unit, but Bruce insisted that we needed only to become acquainted with the new controls.

By the time we reached Alabama, however, we had the AC running full blast with no effect against the sweltering heat. Finally convinced by Florida's blazing sunshine, Bruce and I took the RV to a garage, where they found that the AC was not holding coolant but had no part to repair it. *Why do I let these things keep happening to me?* Fortunately, the mechanics were able to jerry-rig a repair and we made it home with slightly cooler air, if not cooler frames of mind.

Food preparation for an upcoming visit by my kids and grandkids was another communication hurdle with Bruce. On the menu was a special recipe of sandwiches made of chopped chicken breasts, saltine crackers, and chicken soup. I knew the sandwiches would be tasty but that my grandkids might reject the gooey concoction, claiming it looked like "somebody already ate it," as my dad was fond of saying. I was not sure we had enough chicken anyway.

"Do you think this will be enough?" I asked Bruce when he wandered into the kitchen.

"For who?" he asked.

This lack of awareness triggered my nerves, and I shrieked, "The queen of England, the mayor of Sheboygan, and all our neighbors!"

"How am I supposed to know?" he said.

Calming myself, I told him we needed ingredients for another batch, and he agreed to go to the grocery store for supplies and put it together himself, since I was behind schedule and rapidly wearing out.

When Bruce got home, I thought I could just peek down the hall to the kitchen and tell him to save some chicken for the kids. I had not considered that he cannot accept a simple request without a debate. "Please set aside three breasts for the kids."

"But I have to mix all the stuff with the chicken breasts," he answered.

"I think we will still have enough for the recipe," I explained.

He could not agree, do as I asked, or even comprehend what I wanted.

"But I have to put them in the casserole dish," he insisted.

"I know we are making the sandwich recipe, but do not cut up all the chicken. Save three breasts for the kids!"

Since my horrible, no-good sickness, I had become very thin. Nothing much fit, including my underwear. My bra swung loosely around my torso like a trapeze, barely capturing my deflated boobs. My panties were dollar store specials, and they were baggy. This pair was a mud mauve color and fit like a diaper. Now, as my old employee had put it, Bruce had tweaked my last nerve, and I became incensed, charging out of the bedroom in my sagging undies and yelling, "Can you *ever* make things easy? Save out three fucking chicken breasts for the kids!"

He acted confused and still would not agree, arguing that we needed all the breasts for the sandwiches. I must have looked like a hideous creature, my underwear drooping from my bones as I raged and ranted. The spectacle should have driven any neurotypical husband right out of his marriage, but it did not seem to affect Bruce in the slightest.

We had a large holly tree smack dab in the front of our house on Amaranth, and the Realtors convinced us to remove it for a quicker sale. The problem was that our neighbor, a nature lover and good friend for twenty years, loved the tree and said she would tie herself to it if we tried to cut it down. I wanted to find a solution. Bruce would not worry about such things and left the pondering to me, which I did for weeks, racking my brain and searching online for an answer. I even considered having it transplanted, a very expensive proposition.

One day I glanced out our window at the holly tree and perceived the outline of a smaller tree within the larger. Perhaps it could be trimmed, I thought, instead of destroying a magnificent specimen of Delaware's state tree. I found a good video online on how to do this and showed it to Bruce. It was very simple. We discussed it, and I assumed he understood my idea. Some prospective buyers would be looking at the house the next day, so I said, "Let's get the tree cut before they get here."

The next day, as we stood in the front yard, Bruce was flummoxed when I reminded him about the tree trimming project.

"Remember?" I asked, "the tree trimming video?"

"Well, I saw a video," he said. He kept repeating those words: "I saw a video," but he could not translate it to our particular situation.

"It was about this holly tree," I said. "Let's go to the neighbors and get the trimmers." It was not sinking in, so I tried to explain: "They have trimmers. Please get them, or I will."

We grabbed a couple trimmers from the neighbors' garage, and I proceeded to demonstrate our project, but the branches were too thick for me to cut through. I had to leave for a hair appointment, but I was shaking inside, my heart thumping and my mind whirling. *Why is this so hard? Why does he think we watched that video about trimming a holly tree?*

When I came back—surprise, surprise!—he had trimmed it, and it looked good. My neighbor came home from work and gave us a huge smile and hug. I didn't know how Bruce figured it out. I just knew that this was a hard way to live, and I was exhausted.

A raised stone, four feet deep, forty feet long, and five feet wide planter surrounded our new house. I had envisioned pink-and-white wave petunias cascading over the side, but first we needed a lot of soil. Before I could stay one step ahead of my aspie, Bruce dumped a massive load of some inky, smelly, filmy topsoil into the planter. I made him dig out as much of this muck as he could and pile it back into his pickup truck, but it left spatters of odorous black goo all along the front walk.

Bruce did not understand the difference between lightweight drainage soil for pots, garden soil for flower and vegetable gardens, and topsoil. This dirt discombobulation continued for a few years until I flipped out and said, "You know, when they build a new house, they scrape off all the soil, which has to be replaced to plant grass. The topsoil goes on top of all the dirt exposed during construction. That is why it's called topsoil! Garden soil is called that because it goes in gardens, and the fluffier potting soil goes in pots." A light bulb went on in Bruce's brain, and he finally got the soil types right.

But I am forever learning that he is oblivious to so much general knowledge that it shocks me, such as when he made a doctor appointment to have his sigmoid colon examined after a road race rather than before it. Remembering when he had previously had some polyps removed and had to rest for two weeks before running again, he stated, "I won't have to worry about not being able to run if I have a polyp removed."

"Bruce, it doesn't make any difference if they find a polyp before or after your race. The doctor's not going to just snip it off in his office. You have to take a ton of laxatives for a total purge and go to a sterile surgical center. They'll give you a general anesthetic, and you'll be in no shape for anything!"

Before we moved out of Amaranth, we looked for a getaway near a beach with water on both sides, because pollen and mold will blow out to sea and mold does not grow in sand. Long Beach Island, New Jersey, fit the bill as a barrier island between Little Egg Harbor and the Atlantic Ocean. Barnegat Lighthouse beams from the northern end, and small settlements with names such as Ship Bottom, Harvey Cedars, and Loveladies are sprinkled every few miles, terminating at a wildlife refuge at the southern tip. We spent a day surveying the area. Beach property is expensive, but we found one place with a stone yard across from a marina, and it looked to be a perfect refuge. Bruce said we could afford it, which seemed unlikely to me, but my spirits rose at the prospect—until he revealed that he was thinking of the refuge as a permanent residence!

I was shocked that we had been on such a different page the entire day. He was thinking of moving us out of our lovely house in our quaint college town of Newark and home state of Delaware to live all year round in this remote location. I was already feeling unwell physically, and now my mental state took a plunge. I wanted nothing more than to be instantly transported beneath the covers of my bed, preserving whatever bits of strength I had left. While I was thus enervated, Bruce asked if I wanted to go to a jewelry store that we had seen earlier and look at earrings. That we had miscommunicated and wasted an entire day had no effect on him. "No!" I said," I don't want to shop for earrings!" *For God's sake, I want to be heard and understood!*

Chapter 20

FAIRWAYS AND SLOPES

Running got Bruce and me a wall full of plaques, medals, and trophies, not to mention the camaraderie of great athletes. But two other sports helped bring us moments of near peace, one for its clear rules and rituals and the other for its exquisite pleasures.

Golf is an ideal sport for a neurotypical wife and aspie husband. Golf has parameters and clear-cut rules that reduce stressful communication challenges: Start on hole number one, hit your ball until it lands in the cup, and advance to the next hole, following numerical order until you arrive at the eighteenth hole. Discuss good shots and bad shots for an hour over drinks and dinner. Bruce and I don't fight on the golf course but focus instead on our own negative self-talk as we hook drives, lose balls, and miss short putts.

Even though fighting on the golf course was not our norm, one time we were swept up in the maelstrom of a nasty circular argument-in-process before we headed out to an evening couples league golf event. I was already fuming as we drove to the course. Unfortunately, the event was a couples' partner competition, not the usual pairing with another husband or wife. *Crap! I have to coordinate my play with him!* As we approached the first tee, we learned that the other couple in our foursome had bailed. *Double crap, I have to play with him alone! Can we please be excused?* We both dreaded the next two hours.

The format is alternating shots, and it requires cooperation and strategy. How about this for cooperation: "You go first, you asshole; your drive is longer than mine." I admit I left out the word "asshole" when giving this directive. Somehow we survived this bizarre matchup, and my only recollection is that we did not finish last. The evening was an example of the Hubbards' dual life. We should be con artists; we are so good at faking.

I was troubled about this duplicity and said so to my therapist Dr. Belford: "Bruce and I live a double life."

"A lot of people do," she replied.

Well, I don't like it, is all I know.

Bruce hawks for golf balls, which means that he gathers up any balls that were victims of errant shots. He sloshes through marshes, rustles through weeds, gets scratched by brambles, and disappears into trees, happily emerging with his bounty of formerly lost golf balls. He has perfected a bleach-and-water solution as a cleaning method and donates buckets of restored golf balls to charity shops and golf schools. Hundreds more of Bruce's bountiful harvests cram our garage like buckets of spherical clams. He doles out favorite brands to his golfing pals and gives me the pink-colored soft flights. Torture for Bruce is spotting an assortment of balls glinting under clear pond water just a few inches beyond the reach of his ball retriever. My son complains that I have taken up the hawking habit myself, which I confess has rubbed off on me.

During a holiday vacation in the mid-nineties, I convinced Bruce and the kids that we should all go to golf school in Florida to become expert golfers or, at the very least, less sucky golfers. The trip also provided an opportunity to visit friends and relatives, so with the RV resplendent in tacky Christmas decorations and a fiber-optic tree, we headed south with my dad, Andy, and Bebo the dog in tow. We spent Christmas Day with my cousin Lynda, who lived in Cocoa Beach at the time, and then Dad flew back while we RV-ed off to fine-tune our golf skills.

Our golf school, based in Sebring, Florida, had an imposing name: THE UNITED STATES SCHOOL OF GOLF. I liked to pronounce the name loudly while stiffening to attention and tendering a military salute. During the two days of instruction, Reid toned up his natural golf skills, which are considerable since he was on his high school's golf team. Sally learned that she had great "torque," an ability normally reserved for pro golfers. My feebleness and lack of oomph were pinpointed, but Bruce—well, he was a case study.

Over the years, he had invented a new and unimproved golf swing. My dad gave him golf lessons for Christmas every year, which Bruce either never took or, having taken them, completely ignored. Reid gave him tips, and I reviewed Tiger Woods' *How I Play Golf* with him often. If I had known about Asperger's then, I would have known it was a wasted effort. Instructions are for other people, not him.

When attempts to correct Bruce's swing failed by the usual means of demonstration and explanation, Nick, our young instructor, resorted to hauling out ropes, weights, and thick rubber bands, which he attached to Bruce's legs and ankles to stabilize the pirouette movements during his backswing. Good thing Bruce doesn't read social cues, so he was unaffected by the stares of the other golfers at the driving range. Sally and Reid kidded that Dad was into S&M. After our lessons, Nick headed to the bar for a beer, no doubt to calm his nerves after working with Bruce.

Bruce and I are often paired with strangers when golf courses are busy. I prefer cruising around in the cart by ourselves, but it can be fun to meet other golfers who we hope play at our less-than-talented skill level. Between shots, golfers become acquainted, and I have often witnessed a microcosm of the roller-coaster life I live with Bruce played out during the four hours of a golf round. Usually after introductions, which go reasonably well, Bruce will hit a normal shot, and everyone will relax. But then he will slam number two into the trees or out of bounds. I notice a worried look on the faces of the other pair, but Bruce is adept at rescue shots, so out he comes from the trees, and all is well again. His conversation is the same as his golf shots, sometimes on the fairway and sometimes in the rough. Usually, when the strangers find out he is an attorney, any apprehension about his eccentricity dissipates. *How come they don't ask me what I do for a living?* Bruce, however, knows it is not acceptable to just ask the guys, so he will bring up my or another woman's career if we are ignored.

During a trip to Myrtle Beach, South Carolina, home to approximately eighty golf courses, we were paired with two fellows who were married to sisters. Don and Daryl vacationed in Myrtle Beach each year. The brothers-in-law were our golfing partners one day, and we got along great, admiring each other's good shots and remaining reasonably quiet on a duff. We shook hands on the eighteenth hole and wished each other well.

The following day began without surprises. We jogged on the beach, ate lunch in the RV, and went shopping. I bought a tennis skirt to wear when I played with my friend Millie. We were not in any hurry and couldn't decide which golf course to play that afternoon. Bruce picked one at random, and we headed over and commenced our routine where he goes to the clubhouse, registers us, and brings the cart back to load up. I asked him to make sure we were not teamed up, as I didn't feel like indulging in the whole getting-acquainted ritual. He rumbled back with the cart and said he had good news and bad news.

"Tell me the bad news first," I said.

"We are teamed up with a pair of guys."

I started to complain: "I told you I didn't—"

He interrupted my rant with the good news: "It's Don and Daryl!"

"You are kidding me!" What are the odds, with eighty golf courses and tee times every ten minutes of the day at each, that we reconnected? Maybe that was the day to buy a lottery ticket.

When we met on the tee, we gave each other big hugs, enjoyed the round, and went to the clubhouse for a drink afterward. We corresponded for some time, but we never saw Don and Daryl again.

We became familiar with golf courses in the Virginia Beach area when Sally attended The College of William and Mary nearby and from travel to road races in the area. One day I was hoping to have a nice, relaxing game. As we arrived at the first tee, a good-looking, muscular young man trotted over and said the course pro had sent him out to join us. His name was Jack, and he was elated because he was a Mack Truck salesman and had sold two of those hundred-thousand-dollar-plus behemoths that morning. He figured he could afford to take the day off. *Well, I will try not to ruin his round.* Just as we were teeing off, another good-looking, muscular young man rushed over to us with a pull cart in tow. *Yipes, another one! This is going to be tense.*

On the first hole, we learned that the second guy was Jim and that he piloted F-14 fighter jets that are always thundering over and around the bases in Virginia Beach. *Somebody help me!* This was way past my comfort level. The two Adonises enjoyed each other's company and said, "Good ball!" every time I hit a decent shot. When I learned that they were young fathers with wives at home tending to their infants, I was reminded how little times had changed: guys on the golf courses, gals home with the babies.

It was fascinating to learn how Jim had earned his wings. He revealed that only one out of 100,000 applicants survives the formidable training, and he explained that F-14 pilots fly for only a year or two and then become instructors. I asked him what it felt like to fly a jet, and he said it was the biggest thrill imaginable and created a huge rush. I can't tell you how many delightful people we met on the fairways, but these two were top guns.

Jim said he was flying early the next morning and urged us to look for the arrows on the jet's tail; that would be his plane. The next day, the jets roared over our heads, and we jumped out of the RV to peer upward. We strained to see the arrows, but we were unable to spot them, though I know our golf partner was up there streaking through the morning sky, lit up in gold by the sunrise.

If you were to ask me at any given moment where I would like to be, I would answer, "On a ski trail, high on a snowy mountain." Whenever I was enduring any pain, I would take my mind out of my body to a ski trail for comfort. Born in Vermont, I was often on the slopes with my parents when I was a child. Later, I would cut classes at Green Mountain College to sneak off to Pico Peak, near Killington. My ski-bumming days in Stowe topped all my beach bumming days at the Jersey shore.

Bruce and I took mini ski trips to Vermont. We would take off in a flash after a big snowstorm, anxious to avail ourselves of the fresh powder. Our routine was to drive up and dine at a fine restaurant nestled in a hill by a river or in a quaint New England village. We would hit the slopes early in the morning and, after a full, invigorating day, relax by a fire at an après restaurant with other tired, pink-faced skiers. The next day we would reluctantly drag ourselves off the mountain in the early afternoon and head home, but not before grabbing a sub sandwich in Bennington, Vermont. Where did we get all that energy?

The ski slopes of Vermont (Mount Snow, Magic Mountain, Okemo, Bromley, and Sugarbush), New Hampshire (Mount Ascutney and Mount Sunapee), and Maine (Sunday River) are forever etched in my mind like a wondrous dream. Sometimes I will see a car with a bumper sticker that has a ski area logo and words like "Take me to the River—Sunday River," and I will fall into a reverie. My favorite one read, "Mad River Glen, ski it if you can!" The closest I got to that mountain, though, was partying at the base during my ski-bumming days.

On a return trip from visiting my uncle Glenn in California, we skied at Deer Valley in Park City, Utah, and both Vail and Aspen/Snowmass in Colorado. *Glorious* is an understatement! Traveling west to ski was limited because of my mysterious illness, and I regret that we didn't go more often—and how about Austria? That was a dream that never came true.

Parked at the bottom of Stratton Ski Resort in the RV one time, I looked way, way up the mountain, with snow swirling around the peaks and red flags blowing, and thought, *Do I really want to do this?* But we survived the elements, riding up in the gondola, trying not to fart with twelve people smashed together, and skiing my favorite trail, Gentle Ben, over and over until closing. I took the easy way back on the shuttle, if you call hanging on for dear life on the back of an open truck bed easy, and Bruce took the more challenging trail to the bottom. He spied me climbing off the shuttle and hurried over from the far end of the parking lot to carry my skis. His hand was behind his back, hiding a flower he had taken from a bouquet in the RV, and he presented it to me. It was one of the sweetest things he has ever done.

I love ski outfits and clunking around in the heavy boots. Try walking up and down stairs in those things! Riding a chairlift, swinging back and forth and silently floating up the mountain, is dreamy and calming to me, like snorkeling. Sometimes I would see chipmunks cavorting among the trees. The distant shouts of a skier or rider flying in ecstasy down a trail often echoed off the hills. *And how do these trees get decorated with bras?* That was left to the imagination, but they were as amusing to me as the sign that warned us to get off the lift by closing time was frightening: "These mountains will be as cold and lonely tonight as they were 200 years ago!"

Bruce and I did not fight on these trips. Usually, we would take the RV with our dog Bebo onboard. Horseshoe Acres Campground, close to the ski trails, plowed us a spot. Bebo loved the snow as much as I did. It was a frosty experience, trekking through snowdrifts with a towel and shampoo to get to the showers.

Bruce and I skied together, but he would eventually get sick of my fear of speed and head off by himself, which I didn't mind. I liked skiing alone. One early morning at Haystack Mountain, I was the first skier to reach a groomed slope that wound around the mountain. It was awesome to hear only my skis and the rustle of trees as I made the first tracks on the unblemished trail.

At the Greek Peak Ski Area in Cortland, New York, there had been an ice storm the night before. From the side of the ski trail, we heard tiny shards of ice crackling and tinkling as they broke from tree branches, scattering splinters of light as the sun came out. Diamonds falling from the sky by the thousands! I couldn't keep my eyes off the jeweled blue sky and would have danced around with my arms extended if I had not had five feet of board protruding from my feet. I was awestruck by the unique magic of the moment.

On many ski trips we took our kids along, and we all had a fantastic time. Sometimes Bruce's brother Doug and nephew Ross joined us on the slopes. One frigid winter, Sally came with us to Mount Snow. As we drew closer to the mountain, we watched the temperature drop lower and lower. *Oh my God, it's four below, seven below.* I still have the photo taken by a professional photographer on that mountain. We pulled off our face masks and gave him a big, warm smile, but I know how cold we really were.

Our trip to Breckenridge, Colorado, was our first experience skiing in the Rockies. Unfortunately, Sally missed the whole first day because she was suffering from altitude sickness. She vomited outside a ski shop in the fresh white snow, which I quickly attempted to cover up by kicking snow with my boots. That night, an overnight snowstorm blew through and made the place more beautiful and pristine.

The mountain was huge, and the view at the top was like being on top of the world. Sally and I lost Bruce and Reid for a whole afternoon while we attempted to interpret the trail map and figure out where they were. I can't read maps anyway, let alone a hundred and eighty-seven trails on five peaks covering twenty-nine hundred acres!

Reid had always been a natural skier. He took a gap year between college and law school to live in Lake Placid, New York, and ski on nearby White Face, known by the locals as Ice Face. Bruce, Sally, and I visited him there twice and experienced fun but challenging ski days. Lake Placid is a unique town and fun to tour, especially to visit previous Olympic sites. Reid and Bruce rumbled and rocked down the chute of an old bobsled course. Reid's friend convinced me to join the gang in a toboggan ride down an enormous slide that ended with us propelled across a frozen lake.

On another trip, we caught the X Games with Reid and Sally at Mount Snow, Vermont, cheering and shaking our bells as the athletes executed their daring runs. One ski weekend, we took the kids to ski at Mount Ascutney, Vermont, and then headed over to Mount Sunapee in New Hampshire.

Walkie-talkies had become popular then, but they had a glitch of sometimes picking up another family's frequency. (Those might have come in handy when I got lost on the peaks of Breckenridge.) When we got back to the RV, we heard a couple named Josh and Ellie gabbing on their channel. Reid devilishly cut in on their conversation, impersonating Josh and saying, "Ellie, I think we should break up!" We were the ones who broke up laughing.

After skiing, we drove the RV straight to Boston to join one of Reid's college friends for dinner. We arrived with an hour to spare, so Sally and I went shopping on Newbury Street. She bought a beautiful orange-red, off-the-shoulder gown for a formal dance. The next day we had lunch at the bar that was the model for the TV show *Cheers*. A massive snowstorm was forecasted, so we skedaddled out of town before it hit.

Now in my seventies, I ski for free in the Poconos and find I am having a hard time getting off and on the chairlifts. Who would have thought I could still swoop down a hill but have trouble negotiating a lift? I hope that does not end my skiing. My grandson Ethan is learning to ski and wants Grandma and Grandpa to accompany him on the magic carpet ride, the tricky conveyor belt that takes the kiddies up the bunny hill. We must board just as a yellow circle on the back of this animated snow creature arrives at the entrance and then balance ourselves while holding onto skis. The thing freaks me out, but Ethan is amused when Grandma cries, "Where do we step off? I am going to fall!"

Every time we go to Blue Mountain in the Poconos, where we brought Sally and her friends all through their high school years, I aim to conquer the Switchback Trail one more time. So far I have continued to make it to the bottom without wiping out, and I will typically plan my day around skiing that trail. *Don't be too tired but be warmed up.* When I get to the top, I take a deep breath and *Go! One-quarter down, one-half, the hardest turn, I see the bottom! Yippee!*

Chapter 21

JEKYLL AND HYDE

We were on our way back from the Disney marathon back in 2000, with the warm sun shining benevolently on the countryside. We had had a great week, I was happy, and Bruce seemed to be relaxed and enjoying himself. The weather was much too nice to go home, so why should we? In a trice, we made the decision to extend our trip. Off I-95, we veered to check out Jekyll Island, located about halfway between Jacksonville, Florida, and Savannah, Georgia.

We came to a small commercial enclave with shops and a restaurant where we could grab some lunch before hitting the beach. We took a seat on a cozy patio surrounded by flowers and ferns.

"You have a very nice haircut," remarked a fellow at the next table.

At first, I wasn't sure he was talking to me. "Oh, thanks," I said when it became clear that he was. He was sitting with a stylish female companion dressed in upscale artsy attire and creative jewelry. So began a long, stimulating conversation. They were a bit older than Bruce and me, and they had had quite a life. The fellow handed me a biological sketch, which was about his companion. She was his sister, Charlotte Gilbertson, a psychiatric nurse in World War II, an artist, a world traveler, and a champion in croquet and fencing. She had even worked for Andy Warhol. What a fascinating lunch this turned out to be! Gilbertson and I became regular correspondents until her passing in 2014.

After lunch, Bruce and I drove to a beach where we found clean white sand strewn with seashells, driftwood, and, best of all, no people. As we settled into our beach chairs, we felt lucky to be able to enjoy a sunny mid-summer-like day in January. I got to wear my new flowery blue-and-white bathing suit, purchased at Disney's Grand Floridian Hotel. Absentmindedly, I raised my arm and threw a seashell into the air, the universal signal for seagulls that it is time to eat.

High sand dunes paralleled the beach like a small mountain range, and in a matter of seconds, the sky filled with a huge flock of snow-white seagulls, their wings whirring and whooshing loudly, and they headed our way. We reflexively covered our heads and ducked as they softly settled around us.

"This is like the Hitchcock movie *The Birds*," I said to Bruce. "Don't move!"

The gulls, alarmed by my command, drifted back behind the dunes.

Feeling confident that we weren't going to get pecked to death, I said, "Wow! That was cool! Let's try it again."

"Do you want me to go get some bread?" asked Bruce, somewhat irritated.

"Great!"

He jogged back to the RV to get some bread, which we tore up in little pieces and tossed in the air. The undulating mass of seagulls came back over the dunes. After the bread had been snatched up, they disappeared.

"I want a picture of me feeding the gulls!" I said to Bruce.

"If you want the camera, I'll get it," he said, sounding miffed. "Do you want the camera?"

I was thinking, *Yeah, that is the best way to get a photo*, and said, "I will go back to the RV this time."

"I didn't say I wouldn't go." His tone was icy, as if he had just snapped into some dark, angry place in his soul.

This was his subtle aspie language, but I was still nine years away from learning his diagnosis. The interchange was not terrible, but it was not good. *Why aren't we gay and laughing?*

I mulled over how this should have gone. When I said, "I want a picture of me feeding the gulls!" it would have been nice for him to have cheerfully answered, "Sure, let me get the camera; it *would* make a good picture!" Enthusiasm and easy dialogue have rarely occurred in our thousands of exchanges. It made me feel a little deflated, but it didn't entirely ruin the moment. It was more like one insignificant penny clinking into a piggy bank full of hurts.

I stood in the sand, facing the dunes, and let her rip with more bread. I heard the whooshing sound before I saw them. As if on cue, I became surrounded by gulls. Bruce snapped the picture, which held a prominent place on our refrigerator for years, a lovely memory of dancing with the seagulls in my snazzy new bathing suit and great haircut. I held on to the memory, even though the vexation in Bruce's tone was troubling and presaged more bad stuff about to surface.

We decided to jog the trails and check out the fabulous cottages of J. P. Morgan, Rockefeller, and Goodyear. I can picture exactly where I was standing in front of the RV, ready to start running, when something seemed to snap with Bruce again, and there was that same dark and cold demeanor. Out of the blue, he was nasty and mean, exuding anger and hostility. Smackdown! Did he sense that I was having fun while he was losing control? I was shocked and crushed. What had I done to cause this narcissistic-type rage?

Another coin dropped into my piggy bank of hurts, which would get fuller episode by episode and year by year. Back then I had to let it go, or there would have been a fight, unresolved as usual, with Bruce denying that he had done anything untoward. Or, if he did admit it, he would claim that he'd had a good reason, probably based on something he'd claim that I had done to him.

As we ran through the woodland trails under Spanish moss, I tried to compose myself. Bruce acted like nothing had happened, and in his mind, I don't think he thought there was a thing wrong. Even though we ended the day with a nice dinner on the beautiful deck of the historic Jekyll Island Club, it took effort for me to enjoy the ocean view. My thoughts turned inward, and I brooded over my husband's Jekyll and Hyde personality. Some coins land with barely a clink; others are amplified by memorable events.

Chapter 22

SPIRIT-KILLING

Golf, triathlons, and marathons sustained me over the years and made life with Bruce tolerable. All the while, however, it felt like Bruce was clawing my self-esteem down with what I call "spirit-killing," which works like this:

In 2005, we drove the RV to California to visit my dad's cousin Glenn, who was like an uncle to me. Glenn had previewed the Rose Bowl floats and sent us pictures, but now I would see the parade in real life. I am so glad we went, since it was the last time that I saw my "uncle" and the parade was spectacular.

We hit Las Vegas on the way back and then headed to the ski areas of Utah and Colorado. The most remarkable day to me was when we skied in Deer Valley, Utah. The snow was so perfect and abundant, with layers of packed powder and fresh snow. The branches of the tall pine trees were piled with a foot of snow, just like in the cartoon movie *How the Grinch Stole Christmas*. It was the best ski day I ever had, even with the phone call we took on the side of the mountain from a doctor who agreed to administer the IV cocktail of vitamins and minerals that Dr. Ali had prescribed for my mysterious illness.

As darkness fell, we headed back to the RV, where I showered and dressed in my beautiful white cashmere sweater decorated with a white velvet ribbon, a gift from my daughter, and I put on my diamond stud earrings. Bruce was sporting a beard, as he had given up shaving for the trip, and he wore his fancy cowboy shirt with a bolo tie and turquoise clasp. We were ready to hit a restaurant in Park City, and Bruce was seated at a booth in the RV reading about restaurants in a travel brochure.

Curious to know where we were heading, I asked, "Have you found a restaurant yet?"

And then he snapped, using that cold, dark tone he has, "I'm still looking! Do you want to do it?"

I was hurt and dumbfounded. I wanted out of there. We were at the bottom of a dark mountain, 2,000 miles away from home, and I was stuck with no way out. I had to suck it up again. *Why does this happen?* I had been so happy and high on the gift of the beautiful day. *Perhaps he thought I was being critical*, I speculated, blaming myself a bit. Even though I was still rattled, we settled in for a delectable dinner in an upscale restaurant, where someone took our picture. It still looks fantastic sitting in our family room, but the piggy bank was getting heavier, and I knew my smile was fake.

Only after Bruce's diagnosis did we learn that aspies don't know how to manage their perceptions of criticism or modulate the tone and intensity of their voices. But there were more spirit-killing episodes ahead.

For example, the state of Delaware once proposed to drastically alter staff requirements for childcare centers and scheduled public hearings for input from childcare owners. It would have been a catastrophe for my staff, as many longtime employees would have to be let go if the new requirements were adopted. I interviewed my staff about the repercussions and wrote a speech for the hearing.

The meeting room was packed with many people I knew in the business, both professionals and parents. I was nervous about speaking in front of this crowd. When my time came, I focused on the purpose of protecting my employees by delivering my message of what a great job they were doing with children and their parents and that the regulations would put good workers out of a job. People frequently broke into applause with nods of encouragement while I spoke. I received great feedback, the speakers after me were complimentary, and most of them deferred to me and said, "I agree with Ms. Hubbard." One man who ran a large church preschool near Mother Hubbard Childcare Center said, "Now I know who Mother Hubbard is." It was an amazing, unexpected experience, and I felt obliged to acknowledge the applause with a nod and thank you when I left the podium for my seat.

As I walked through the parking lot to my car, I blurted out, "WOW!" I had discovered what it feels like to be an actor or speaker. More importantly, the state decided to grandfather in the rules, so my staff was saved.

I was eager to tell Bruce about my exciting experience, but when I got home and told him, he barely took his eyes off the TV. There was no, "Sounds fantastic. What did you say? How many people were there? Wow!" Crestfallen, I slunk off to bed. *Clink!*

One of our ski trips to Greek Peak in New York State also did not go well. I loved the lines of pine trees at the top of one ski lift, the way they cut into the blue sky from out of the snow. It was our usual photo op place, and we have several pictures from other visits, but this time, when I asked Bruce to snap a shot of me in the trees, he muttered, "Later," and just skied off. I didn't get it, but I tried not to let his grouchy mood dampen my spirits.

I was on my last ski run when a girl about ten years old came careening by, yelling, "Help! I can't stop!" She was out of control and about to crash. I dug in my poles and chased after her, shouting, "Make a snowplow!" I pushed out ahead of her and demonstrated with my own skis how to put the front of the skis together. Then I said, "Make a pizza!" meaning the pizza-slice shape of the snowplow, and she began to figure it out. I skied alongside her until she safely eased to the bottom of the trail.

Full of excitement, I rushed to tell Bruce, who was waiting in the lodge. He was seated at the table with a menu in his hands. As I took a breath to begin my story, he cut me off and said, "Hurry up and order, I want to get going." *Clink, clunk.*

As we drove past the ice-covered river and snowy fields, I felt that familiar sense of despair, confusion, and hopelessness. *What am I supposed to do? Get a divorce because I have a grouchy husband? Maybe, but I can't explain it to anyone. They won't understand.*

We spent New Year's Day 2009 at Rockefeller Center, waiting to take my daughter and our newborn granddaughter to Delaware while her husband worked on their apartment. I felt exuberant just being in New York City at Christmastime, hamming it up in front of big red Christmas balls and the huge Christmas tree. From the wide picture window in the restaurant where we were having lunch, we watched the skaters circle, spin, and skate *pas de deux*. Bruce was on a synchronized skating team at that time, and I suggested he take a turn on the ice. After a couple glasses of wine, I was emboldened to skate also, even though I hadn't been on the blades for a long time. Watching folks with limited skating skills hanging onto the rails convinced me I could do no worse.

It was not crowded, and we got on the rink in no time. The day was sunny and crisp, and Frank Sinatra was playing from the speakers. I soon got my sea legs back but was apparently too slow for Bruce, which was okay. What was not okay was that when I turned to say something to him, he was already off and gone. I couldn't even see him. Would it have been that hard to say, "April, if you are doing all right, I want to practice some of my moves, and I will be back in a few minutes, okay?" rather than just disappear? The pennies were piling in the bank, but I never said a thing. When I was taking off my skates alongside some other skaters, a woman next to me said, "You looked good out there." I had on a red fuzzy scarf that I had tried to wrap around my neck to look festive like the other skaters. Her remark meant more to me than she could ever know.

Sally worked for the Big Brothers Big Sisters of America program one summer, and she convinced me to volunteer. My Little Sister, Brianna, was nine years old when I met her, and our relationship continued until she was nineteen. I knew she and her family had it hard, and I was determined to enhance the quality of her life and expand her horizons. We planted trees and flowers, cooked apples from an apple tree, swam in the pool in the rain, made costumes for Halloween, shopped, and went to lunch. Bruce drove us to Rehoboth, where Brianna saw the ocean for the first time, and to New York City. I got to know her family as well. Years later I visited her at the hospital when she had her baby. One time, after I returned from the long drive from her house, I turned to Bruce and said, "I think I am making a big difference in Brianna's life."

His cold and cynical response was, "Everyone loves Santa Claus."

Bruce and I were enjoying our neighbor's son's wedding reception at Winterthur, one of the classy DuPont mansions in Wilmington, Delaware. I looked quite lovely in a silver-blue designer suit that my daughter had convinced me was the best buy in the Mall of America in Minnesota when we were touring that cavernous place while waiting for a flight home after visiting Bruce's parents.

The skirt was knee length, covered in lace tiers, and the jacket was a tuxedo wrap style with rhinestone and pearl-encrusted buttons. My itsy-bitsy shoes were silver heelless bejeweled pumps that matched my silver-sequined clutch purse. Diamond and pearl jewelry completed this elegant ensemble. Wow, was I sparkly and fancy! I was in my early sixties, and this was to be my peak fashion performance for the following decades. I have only a photo to remind myself that I was ever that glamorous.

Everyone at the reception was mingling and dancing to the lively wedding music band. Bruce and I were chatting with two fellows,

Jason and Drew, who were developers and Realtors. We had done business with them and agreed that they were movers and shakers in the community. The younger of the two guys, who was in his late thirties or early forties, asked me to dance. We rocked out to a fast dance and returned to Bruce and the other fellow when it was over, laughing and out of breath. He was a good dancer, and it was fun.

The following Monday, I got a call at the daycare from Jason. After a few pleasantries, the conversation went like this:

"Hey April, wasn't it funny what Bruce said at the reception?"

"Uh, I don't know what you mean," I stammered.

"You know, when you danced with Drew," he said.

"Okay?" I said.

"Your company must really want our listing!" He laughed.

Silence from my end.

By now, Jason knew he had said too much and cut short our conversation.

I called Bruce and asked him what this was all about. "It wasn't meant for your ears" was his only response.

I took that to mean that, even with all my sparkles, no one would have danced with me—the old crone—without an ulterior motive. To this day, I do not understand his making this joke at my expense instead of being proud that he had a stylish wife. Where was his heart?

Another spirit-killing smackdown. I have no idea what causes Bruce to speak so flippantly. I feel like it may have something to do with his fear of loss of control when I am free, lighthearted, and happy. Maybe he is just always repressing a smackdown or is merely a rude bastard. Whatever the case, he often managed to suck the joy out of me.

In June of 2005, our daughter was married in a loft in Manhattan overlooking the East River. She had a dual wedding, one American and one Indian, and it was exciting, beautiful, and memorable, as all who were there could attest. It was a very warm June evening, and we had cocktails on the rooftop of the building, with a view of the

Empire State Building, which was lit up at night with the same color as Sally's bridal gown: mauve. When the DJ played our song, I was hoping for a romantic dance with Bruce, but he was occupied drinking brandy with his middle brother, Doug. As the evening ended and guests were leaving, I suggested to Bruce that we make a trip back up to the roof with all the pretty lights and flowers and spend a moment celebrating the wonderful day. He did join me but then just stood there, silent, as I wished for an embrace, maybe some reflections on our sweet daughter being married, or remarks about the breathtaking view. But I got nothing. I was so disappointed that I vowed to myself that I would leave him. That damned piggy bank had banked its last cent. This last heartbreak was the last straw, and I vowed that I would tell him when we got home. But then his youngest brother, Glenn, came home with us, and our neighbor made us dinner, and the next day we golfed, and this spirit-killing life continued on its track.

Chapter 23

DEMONSTRATING

I am an activist and a demonstrator. I am not a person of color, LGBTQ, underprivileged, an animal being skinned alive for fur, a starving stray dog or cat, or a calf so constricted in a tiny container and heavily chained by the neck that its legs grow as stumps. It would be a lot easier to live "SOE-thinking," meaning Somebody Else's Problem, but beginning with the women's equality movement, my brain adopted a social conscience.

Abraham Lincoln said, "To sin by silence when they should protest makes cowards of men"—and women.

Maggie Kuhn, the organizer of the Gray Panthers, said, "Stand before the people you fear most and speak your mind—even if your voice shakes."

Life with Bruce has been mercurial. From the highs of our businesses, sports collaborations, and RV adventures, we plummet down the vicissitudes of Bruce's autism, my chronic illnesses, and the loneliness of suffering without validation. However, the world has a way of pulling you back into life, sometimes with its own tragedies. Our family was deeply affected by the attack of September 11, 2001, first with Sally's direct experience of the World Trade Center's destruction and second by our country's rush to war with Iraq.

The anti-Iraq vigil in our town took place every Friday between five and six o'clock. When the church bells chimed six times, we dispersed, only to reappear the next week (except when it rained, since the rain ruined our signs). We sweltered in the summer and froze in the winter. Even though we were demonstrating against a horrific war, the vigils were often interesting, exciting, and educational, albeit sometimes scary. People passing us had no idea of the intellectual conversations we generated as the most current of affairs were discussed and debated. The vigil lasted until Barack Obama was elected president of the United States.

We demonstrated on Newark's Main Street, opposite where another street ended at Main Street perpendicularly. A stoplight at the intersection gave riders time to read our signs and internalize their feelings. It always amazed me, after all the years that we protested, how many people would drive by with quizzical looks on their faces as if we had come from Mars. *Where have you people been? There is a war going on.*

Our goal was to get people to forget about happy hour, grocery shopping, or getting home on a Friday night for just one minute to reflect on our country's unjust and illegal war. But often, besides the thumbs-up and honks for peace, we got shouts of "Get a job!" or "Get a life!" Because I have demonstrated before, I was not a newbie to the process. Feeling strongly enough about something to put yourself out there is not easy, and I knew I needed to have a thick skin because of the opposition we encountered. One fellow had a sign "Honk for Peace," and we got more and more honks, waves, and thumbs-up as the years went by, but some people were really crude. I most objected to the driver reaching across the wife, child, or friend with their middle finger extended. It seemed to me that a mere thumbs-down or a shake of the head would have sufficed, but no, these were angry people. Sticking your middle finger in your child's face? What kind of example is that? After three years of people giving us the finger, I had had it and flipped the bird back to a big dude on a Harley, which created a gasp from my group of "peaceful" protesters. When one protester was hit by a snowball-throwing "patriot," he retaliated by chasing the guy down the street, which resulted in another communal peacenik gasp emanating behind him.

One of the biggest challenges to our restraint occurred when a red-faced, angry, pro-war, older white guy walked in front of each one of us. Eyes squinted, saliva sputtering, and index finger pointed in our faces, he bellowed short speeches and words of advice for each of us: "Do you have a soldier in Iraq?"

"Yes, we do, our cousin," answered two women from the university.

"Well, you are not supporting him! You should be ashamed!"

For the men in our group, his advice went along the lines of "Freedom isn't free!" whatever that means, or "You are not good enough to stand on the ground of this country!" or "You are not supporting our troops!"

To the contrary, we were totally committed to these Americans in uniform, who had been rushed into war poorly equipped and unprotected. "We are trying to keep them alive!"

He cursed and became more incensed as he passed in front of each of us. Frustrated and running out of clichés, he came to me and stopped, tongue-tied. It must have gone against his moral compass to holler at an older white woman. I guess I reminded him of his mother or grandmother. He stared at me and pointed, no words coming out of his mouth until, after some long seconds, he went to the next person, but his initial steam had petered out.

The steady honking of horns, rustling of signs, and waving of our hands with the peace sign was interrupted one evening by a deafening roar as a black monster pickup truck screeched to a halt at the red light directly in front of us. Two oversized American flags were snapping in the breeze on each side of the black-tinted windows, and a Dixie flag was emblazoned on the front license plate. *Yipes, the good ole boys have come to town.* "Everyone on my right dive to the right, and everyone on my left run to the left!" I yelled. He gunned his engine at the green light and drove right up to our line, but we stared him down. It reminded me of the 1971 movie *Duel*, starring Dennis Hopper. I guess he decided it was against his best interest to kill us, so he left us with his huge tailpipes doing the shouting for him as he laid rubber down the street.

International students attend the University of Delaware either full-time or part-time. With limited opportunity to be Americanized, many of them were interested in our vigils, taking lots of photos and asking questions such as, "What are you doing and why?"

We would answer, "There are a lot of people in the USA who don't agree with the Iraq War, and we are demonstrating against it." *Hopefully we don't occupy or bomb your country.* We didn't say the last part out loud. Some students told us that they would be arrested in their country for holding signs and peacefully assembling. We would answer, "This is America, and this is a democracy. We are a free country!" I don't know whether I was happy or sad to explain this fact to the young men and women, but you could feel they were really trying to figure all this out.

One summer evening, two male Chinese students on bikes stopped next to me where I was holding down the end of the line. One dismounted and propped his bike on a lamppost, and the other straddled his bike. They asked the usual question about what we were doing. One of the students was studying math and the other engineering. "Brainiacs" was written all over them. I explained the vigil, the protest, and that we are free, can go on the street in a peaceful way, and can complain if we think something is wrong with our government's policies or if we don't like a highway going through a park or the cost of bread. They focused intensely on me with unblinking eyes and did not move. I continued with my rant on freedom and democracy as long as they seemed interested to listen and uneager to continue their ride. I became uneasy with their silence but continued talking, adding, "You know, your country needs to do something about the terrible factory conditions and lack of labor laws. Chemicals from factories are polluting your air and sickening the population. And, by the way, the human rights situation is deplorable."

Am I pissing these guys off? I wondered. Finally, after about fifteen minutes, one fellow took his bike from the lamppost and said, "It was nice to meet an American woman who cares so much about the world!" They smiled and shook my hand, and off they pedaled. I felt drained after talking to them, but maybe I made an impact, a difference. I was dumbfounded at their reaction and have no idea if I even offered a response. I always get emotional when I think of that evening.

Bruce, as one of the town's attorneys, didn't think he should put himself out there politically, but eventually he started to attend more regularly. We went to peace marches and rallies in Washington, D.C., and New York City. We marched with Code Pink, holding pictures of men and women who had been killed in the war. We were there in 2005 when Cindy Sheehan, who lost her beloved son, Casey, early in the Iraq War, spoke in D.C. She asked Mr. Bush, "For what noble cause did my son die?" She never got an answer.

Driving back from that event, I realized there were no commonly sung peace songs these days, unlike during the Vietnam War, so I began writing lyrics. The title of my song is "America Cries." I hired a musician, and, with the help of two others, we created a CD and had more adventures selling or giving copies away at peace rallies. Bruce carried boxes of my CDs, tables, and display signs for many blocks in D.C. We also conscripted Reid to peddle my song at a New York City march.

Selling my song from a booth in both New York City and Washington, D.C., I hit it off with enthusiastic customers, often following up with emails. One educator, who was involved in a large youth program, told me he would use my words in his class for discussion. I signed autographs and had my picture taken.

College kids at our vigil played peace songs, and someone stuck mine in a CD player. "Sweet!" he exclaimed. *Wow! He likes it.* My song was played on WBAI radio in California. One lovely fellow who obviously had an ear for great lyrics and music bought it from CD Baby, which brokers songs online. I made a whole dollar in sales!

Not only was I a peace activist, but I was also engaged in the women's movement and Occupy Wall Street. At the Women's March of 2017, I bumped into a woman on Fifth Avenue in New York City who was wearing the same button I was from the 1976 March for Women's Lives in Washington, D.C. Even with half a million marchers, we spotted each other and bonded in our mutual, many-year journey for women's rights. Sadly, at a woman's march you can always expect the same facial sign: *I can't believe we are still doing this.*

While the Iraq War awakened us to resist military misadventure, the Great Recession awakened us to confront the greed of the One Percent.

Occupy Wall Street met the moment because the income divide in the United States was so vast. The middle class had shrunk, and the top One Percent of people seemed to have no limits to their avarice. At first it was hard to get a grip on the Occupy movement procedures and agenda. Still, the leaders were organized, sharp, and focused. Bruce and I visited Zuccotti Park in Manhattan as well as Freedom Plaza and McPherson Square in Washington, D.C. We also became involved with Occupy Delaware, located at Spencer Square in Wilmington and carrying the distinction of being the longest-lasting occupation in the country.

Each Occupy assemblage created a space for cooking and dispensing food, another for health, another for a place to meet, and one for business. Occupiers were not allowed bullhorns, so when pertinent information needed to be shared, someone would shout, "Mic check!"

"Mic check!" would come the response from all within earshot, who then kept shouting the information like a human megaphone to pass it to the rest of the crowd until everyone got the message.

When someone spoke, listeners responded with a set of hand signals. I liked the fluttering of the fingers. If people were enthusiastic about the content, they raised their hands high and waggled their fingers instead of applauding, which would have drowned out the message. If someone got too lengthy or repetitive, people rotated their hands, urging them to move on. No one could speak unless they had been put on a queue list called "the stack."

Celebrities often visited the parks. Bruce and I attended an exciting event in Wilmington, where Captain Ray Lewis, a retired Philadelphia police chief-turned-activist, and Lieutenant Dan Choi, an Iraq War veteran, spoke and signed autographs. I was particularly moved by what Lt. Choi wrote on my small sign, as he had come out as a gay man: "Love is worth fighting for."

During that time, my daughter worked for the New York Attorney General's office, located near Wall Street. On December 31, 2011, Bruce and I decided to take the subway from Brooklyn to Zuccotti Park to see the occupiers and to learn the route to Sally's office. I made a poster that read "Happy New Year Occupiers!" with the words "FREEDOM" and "DEMOCRACY" written on each side. When we arrived at the park, it was vacant except for a smattering of people holding signs that read "We are the 99 percent." I wished I had grabbed our same 99 percent sign for Bruce to hold.

A woman eyeing us as newcomers announced she had been at the park every day since the beginning on September 17, 2011. A nurse from National Nurses United, the largest nurses union in the country, was there with a sign advocating healthcare, good jobs, public education, and a healthy environment. A young man held a sign thanking unions for safe working conditions, workman's comp, overtime pay, and a forty-hour workweek. The first woman pointed behind us to the empty park, where two men paced around with phones to their ears. She said they were the leaders, making plans and probably talking with Chris Hedges or Micah White. Most Occupiers said there were no leaders, although a few people regularly served as "facilitators."

Leaderless or not, Occupy was to inspire a new generation of activists and leaders, now promoting climate action, Black Lives Matter, economic justice, peace, and human rights.

Meanwhile, we found ourselves at the center of attention for hundreds of tourists riding by on double-decker buses and taking pictures, looking for real American Occupiers and protesters. It was a warm end-of-December day, and we felt we needed to give them a show or at least something to take back to wherever they had come from since most seemed to be international tourists. We raised our fists in the power sign, held the signs high, smiled at the tourists, and posed for picture requests, rarely spoken in English. I only remember one guy giving us the finger. He must have been one of the top One Percent and had forgotten his limousine as he bounced around on the bus's upper deck.

A photographer with high-tech camera equipment strung over his neck showed up and introduced himself as Matthew Connors. He explained that he had photographed more than five hundred occupiers and would like to add us to his collection. I was wearing a black knit headband with a bow on the side and large gold peace earrings that my son had given me for my birthday. Matthew wanted a side shot of my earrings and took about thirty pictures of both of us. *Click, click, click.* The camera sounded like a toy cap gun as the photographer deftly positioned his body to capture different angles and instructed us to move along with him as if in a dance. I felt like a model, but mostly I felt kind of silly. Matthew sent us copies of the black-and-white photos, which I thought showed my wrinkles, but Bruce loves his and has assigned it as his obituary picture.

The dramatic collection of pictures was posted online and displayed at several museums worldwide, including the Fraenkel Gallery in San Francisco. We reconnected with Matthew in SoHo, Manhattan, one spring evening in 2012 to see the photographs projected one by one on the side of a building, which we thought was cool.

At Zuccotti Park, he told us he was a teacher at the Massachusetts College of Art and Design and chair of the photography department. We later learned he had received his MFA in photography from Yale University and his work was displayed in major art museums. After the Occupy project, he traveled to Egypt and captured photos of the dramatic events of the Egyptian Revolution for a book of photography and accompanying text titled *Fire in Cairo: The Berber Uprising*. We bought this remarkable book, and the last time I heard from Matthew he was heading to another dangerous part of the world; I think it was North Korea.

After our photo op session, another man approached our motley crew, which was still entertaining the slow-moving stream of tourists. He was also carrying a camera, but unlike Matthew's, it was a big one, a television camera! Standing in the background was a strikingly handsome man wearing a tailored tan linen suit and crisp white shirt. He was carrying a microphone. The cameraman looked pretty good himself. He smiled and asked the nurse and me if we would consent to an interview.

Mr. Handsome Reporter asked us about our position on the Occupy Movement. I have no recollection of my response, but I tried to be enthusiastic and make sense. He was Iranian, and I will never know whether a bunch of folks in Iran gathered around their TVs to watch the nightly news and saw my interview. It was a strange image to contemplate.

Our little trip to Zuccotti Park that New Year's Eve was more than we had bargained for: great photos of us by a gifted photographer, meeting a handsome Iranian journalist, being asked by loads of international tourists to have their picture taken with us, and learning the feel of international bonding. Bruce and I figured that hundreds of pictures of us would be on people's phones or photo albums all over the world. How strange it all felt. Worn out, we headed back to Brooklyn. I leaned on the door to Sally's brownstone apartment and pressed the call button. Our son-in-law, Bob, answered, "No protesters allowed!"

We had a nice New Year's Eve dinner there, just like ordinary people, but we had just had an extraordinary experience.

Chapter 24

STUDMUFFIN

"April, you're so lucky. Bruce is a studmuffin!" squealed my next-door neighbor, grasping my arm. Bruce was in a fashion show and had just made a dramatic entrance. This was uncharted territory for a person used to routine. The show was held in a local restaurant as a fundraiser for cancer survivors and sponsored by a retro clothing boutique. Bruce was asked to participate because at that time he had had the first of several melanomas removed and was a frequent customer of the shop, where he bought wide-brimmed hats for sun protection.

"I feel weird being in a fashion show." He frowned, contemplating the idea.

"How about going to a practice to see if you like it?" I suggested, wondering if he was capable of learning runway skills.

He agreed to give it a try, and apparently he was a quick study at the rehearsals, because you should have seen him strut around the tables at the show! He wore a royal-blue Nehru shirt under a white *Miami Vice* blazer, blue slacks, cordovan penny loafers, and provocative sunglasses. Such swagger and confidence! Working the crowd, he propped his sunglasses atop his head and spread both sides of his jacket with a flare. When he disappeared into another room, I heard a loud whoop and cheer! *Where did this guy come from?*

Bruce's looks were improving with age, or maybe other men with his years looked comparatively worse. I could not explain it. People regularly told me he was handsome. My guess was that lots of women in the restaurant thought he was a studmuffin. I was the one woman who felt that the "stud" in "studmuffin" had been vanquished by Asperger's.

As an aspie, Bruce misses the nonverbal cues we human animals give our mates to initiate some intimacy. Gentle touches, loving glances, hints, and teasing go unanswered by a man with Asperger's, who is likely to be averse to any touch. While we were dating, these difficulties were overcome by Bruce's twenty-year-old testosterone level. No red flags there. And I could understand his tendency to fall asleep when kissing me, because eight hours of the navy's language school, followed by bartending at night, was exhausting. When heavy breathing was replaced by snoring, I covered him with a comforter and left him on the couch. He woke up the next morning confused and dismayed by missed opportunities, but at least he was rested.

When we were in our early forties, I thought it would be fun to attempt a seductive ploy that Mom had created for Dad, designed to add spark to their love life. She taped pictures of arrows to the wall leading from the front door to the bedroom door. When Dad arrived home from work, she greeted him in a black negligee. I understand this scheme was a success, a critical factor being that Dad was an NT, or neurotypical. I figured, *If Mom can do it, I can do it.*

Prepared for a romantic evening, I waited for Bruce. When he walked in the door, I kissed him, pointed to the arrows, and flounced around in my alluring teddy. Well, maybe it wasn't a teddy, but I know I was wearing something sexy. With no response forthcoming from Bruce, I made some gestures and mumblings, trying to get his attention, but he just nudged me aside to do a few things and said he had to go somewhere. Well, I felt like an idiot and dejectedly changed my clothes and removed the arrow signs. I was so upset that I called Bruce's good friend, John, who lived in the neighborhood, and recounted what had happened. He came right over and sat with me at the kitchen table. All he could say was, "April, something is wrong! Something is wrong!" He was kind, but he was as confused as I was about Bruce's behavior and could offer no explanation except "Something is wrong." He shrugged his shoulders, gave me a hug, and went home. We never spoke to Bruce about that failed attempt at romance.

Well, something *was* wrong, big-time! I did not yet know that Bruce was an aspie! I could have run around the house stark naked, and he would not have noticed, or if he had, he might have thought I was hot, like feeling-too-warm hot. Now I know he lacked the facility to perceive, much less interpret, context clues. He just didn't get the hint!

There were other opportunities for romance. A few years later, we took a short ski vacation to Vermont. It was picture-perfect as we relaxed in a cozy inn while snow flurries swirled outside. Our room was decorated with floral wallpaper, lace curtains, and a four-poster bed covered by a patchwork quilt. Embers glowed from a small fireplace in one corner, and a television tuned to a football game glowed in the other corner. I snuggled in bed with a glass of wine and watched Bruce watch the game. This was boring and a waste of *ambiance*, I decided, so I took action. First I threw my sweater on the floor where he was sitting and then proceeded to discard my clothes until they were scattered around him like Friday's dirty laundry. Unable to break his focus on the game, I threw my bra on his head. *Hello, there is a bra on your head! Some breasts in this room are now bare!*

"What are you doing?" he finally asked.

"Uh, nothing," I sighed. "Getting dressed for dinner?" I knew the question was too subtle. As Gilda Radnor's *Saturday Night Live* character Emily Litella would say, "NEVER MIND!"

"Hooray, hooray for the eighth of May, outdoor intercourse starts today!" Bruce liked the story of how a friend, my cousin, and I chanted this ditty as we barhopped in Stowe, Vermont, with paper daisies attached to wires stuck in our hair. It was 1966, and we had worked through the cold winter and were celebrating spring skiing. Bruce and I decided this ditty could be taken literally when we moved to a house with a secluded yard. Bruce liked to be outside and didn't like wearing clothes, so it seemed like a win-win situation. We continued this fresh-air tradition for many years, weather permitting, with only one snag—when my son dropped by unexpectedly. Bruce threw on his shorts and scrambled across the yard to meet him at the driveway gate. The sight of his mom lying in the grass wrapped in a blanket might have been TMI regarding his parents' love life.

In addition to the "eighth of May," we were able to create some of our elusive husband-wife closeness with intimate jokes. For instance, Bruce was in charge of cleaning our big pool, which was a level down from our bedroom. If I happened to be coming out of a shower or changing clothes, I tapped on the window to get his attention. When he looked up, I mashed my naked body against the picture window and waved. He seemed tickled by my antics, and we both laughed as I made faces and clowned around.

He turned the tables on me when we rolled around the golf course in the cart, his aspie tension usually at a minimum. Bruce was always the driver and thought it funny to place his hand, palm open, on my empty seat. He was sneaky, and my concentration was on my last shot, so I yelped with surprise when I sat on his hand and he copped a feel. When it was time for true action, however, it was another story.

"April, I am always ready!" he would insist, pulling his head out from behind his newspaper and then ducking it back in. "I am always ready," he would say, as if he were continually dosed with Viagra and walked around with a twenty-four-seven erection. With this little statement, "I am always ready," he freed himself of responsibility in the bedroom. I attempted to explain to him that couples need to have some level of intimacy in their everyday lives, which then leads to sex as a natural outcome, not as some break between sections of the news.

I began to imagine how I might get him to be more intimate:

First, you could be physically present once in a while. I guess we could try phone sex, but it would not be the same.

Second, you actually have to talk to me. You know, I say words and you say words back or vice versa—share your thoughts, feelings, hopes, and dreams. Merely stating, "I am taking out the garbage" or "I'm gonna wash the car" doesn't qualify as sharing thoughts and feelings. Terms of endearment were not part of Bruce's vocabulary, but they would have been icing on the cake. I was just hoping for conversation.

Third, you have to touch me. That is a biggie. It can be a hug or kiss or love pat. I am not particular. When we were first married, I would wrap my arm around Bruce when we sat on the couch in front of the TV until my arm got numb. I figured newlyweds were supposed to have contact, and I am a touchy-feely person. It took me twenty years to realize that his body stiffened when I hugged him. Note: *I hugged him*. I don't remember him hugging me. What could possibly be the reason he was uncomfortable with hugs? He would extricate himself from my embrace as soon as possible. Aspies, I understand now, often have sensory overload. Hugs can feel uncomfortable or be overwhelming. Snuggling in bed causes sweaty skin, so no spooning is allowed either.

For years, I assumed he was only uncomfortable showing affection in public, but I had to face facts: he was also not affectionate in private. While we both enjoyed dances and parties, Bruce would hold me on the dance floor like sixth graders at a mixer. What about dancing cheek to cheek or gazing into each other's eyes? On New Year's Eve, I got better kisses from other husbands than the quick obligatory peck from Bruce.

I became obsessed with watching other couples' displays of affection. I felt like a voyeur, intruding into the private lives of strangers and sneaking peeks at couples on the street, in the shopping mall, and at restaurants. During a party at a friend's house, I noticed how one husband reached over and took his wife's hand just like that, for no apparent reason, except that maybe he loved her and felt a need for closeness. I saw a man in a restaurant put his hands on his wife's shoulders and kiss the top of her head as she headed to the restroom. *She is just going to the bathroom, for crying out loud! Man, these women are lucky.*

I sat Bruce down and told him, "Bruce, you are not physically affectionate. Affection is missing in our marriage." This was the first of a series of *serious talks* I had with Bruce.

The best I got from this was that Bruce would at least plan to hold my hand, but that's about as far as he would get.

"I was going to hold your hand today," he said, "but you walked with other people."

"I am glad you are thinking about it," I told him.

As years passed, the difficulties, fights, misunderstandings, and resentment would often overpower romantic inclinations. Even when things were going smoothly, Bruce seldom initiated sex. It was easier for him to be "always ready."

Sex was not enveloped by intimacy before or after. Soon after sex, Bruce would disappear into himself, and I would feel particularly vulnerable to his cool attitude and aspie meltdowns. I began detaching emotionally from Bruce to protect myself from being hurt, and sex became an even more remote possibility. My long illnesses were also a problem. Who wants to have sex when they feel like they have the flu? We were battling an invisible foe, and I was tired. People outside the world of Asperger's would be surprised to know how many aspie marriages are platonic. My mother-in-law would declare that when a problem cannot be easily resolved, it is a "situation." Bruce and I were dealing with a sexual "situation," although few of his friends would doubt his sexual prowess.

"The Mystery of the Missing Black Lingerie" forever sealed Bruce's reputation in the brains of our men friends as a passionate, sexual god. I was telling two couples in our circle how I had lost the robe of a black peignoir set. It was a mystery why it was missing. Well, this stirred the men's imagination for sure, especially when told how I found it a year later on top of our wooden canopy bed. I guess I don't dust much.

Their dirty minds were just bursting with fantasies. It was true that I had been wearing the peignoir with the lace bodice and matching robe. It was true that we had had a fire in the fireplace in our bedroom and a chilled bottle of champagne sitting on the mantel. It is not true that Bruce appeared with a rose in his teeth, tangoed me around the room, planted a passionate kiss on my lips, tore off my nightgown, and flung the robe way up on the top of the canopy. This is an oft-repeated story, and I always fail to dispel their illusions.

"It wasn't really like that, guys," I argue.

"Oh yeah, April, right, sure, uh-huh. Eh, Bruce?" Wink-wink. "We know what happened!" I will never know how the robe got to the top of the canopy, but I know I didn't toss it up there. Possibly Bruce saw the dog nestling in the soft material and stuck it up there for safekeeping. He is forgetful and taller than me, so I think that is the best-case scenario for resolving the mystery.

Even though he has never been unfaithful, Bruce has pulled some nasty stunts with other women. While he was in law school and I was eight months pregnant, he got the bright idea to go to a payphone and call an old girlfriend. Why he even told me after using a payphone on the sly and not our house phone, I have no idea. His only explanation was that he had been thinking about her and wondering how she was doing. I was astounded by his actions and felt betrayed, but what was I going to do, waddling around with my huge belly, far from home?

When the kids were little, we went to a small wedding for one of my employees and gathered at her apartment for a modest reception. I hung around with other guests while the kids played and watched the bride open gifts. Bruce was sitting on a barstool in the kitchen area, talking to a woman. I didn't care, thinking he was bored with the festivities. Later I learned that she knew him from his law office.

After I gathered the kids together to walk home, I leaned over next to him and said in his ear, "We're going home now."

"Home?" He gulped loudly.

"Yeah, home, like our house. It is time to leave. The reception is over."

Finally, he caught up with me and the kids. Apparently the woman wanted him to go to a party with her. "She thought it would be neat to walk in with a lawyer on her arm," he told me.

"Say what?" I asked. "Are you out of your freakin' mind, Bruce? Why did you lead her on?"

He couldn't tell me. I guess he liked the attention. I figured he was surprised to be caught in a situation a little beyond his control—hence the weird gulping sound.

During a party at a friend's house, Bruce sat next to a woman at a bar and never got up the whole night. I think he knew her from the real estate world since he was a real estate lawyer. I tried several times to disengage him, but it never worked.

"Bruce, I have to run out and pick up our daughter and take her home." I thought, *OUR DAUGHTER! Remember her? We are married and have children, in case anyone cares.*

"Okay," he said, not budging.

I was able to dislodge him for only a few minutes to go to the phone and speak to a mutual friend who was in the hospital, but he immediately went back to his seat at the bar. I guess he was having a nice little intimate conversation while I wandered around trying to socialize like a fifth wheel.

At one New Year's Eve party, after we had been happily chatting with our neighbors, Bruce started playing pool and ignored me all night. When I talked to him, he would not respond. I tried to forget it, socializing with the rest of the guests, but I was unnerved, confused, and hurt. He has done that several times. Even though I now know about the Asperger's diagnosis, I still cannot accept any reason for this behavior.

As odd as it is when I cannot get answers from him, it is even odder that he will not explain himself later or give me a straight answer. If I were to ask him about it the next week, he would say that he did not remember. What if the shoe were on the other foot?

Running a daycare with all women employees, and with mostly moms rather than dads coming to get their kids, I was left with few opportunities for extracurricular activities with men. My employees seemed to be swinging, new boyfriends and pregnancies just a matter of course. *How do they manage this stuff?* I wondered. My director, who was privy to this information, claimed that they routinely hit the bar scene. And I didn't. Guess that was my problem.

The only time I noticed a guy checking me out at a bar was when I was with Bruce. We were sitting on one side of a horseshoe bar in our local tavern when a group of motorcyclists clambered in to claim the opposite side of the horseshoe. They were taking a break from a Sunday spring ride and were in a boisterous, talkative mood. It was easy to follow their conversation and hear their names. One guy, Peter, kept looking at me. He was tan and fit with light brown hair, sexy in his black leather jacket. After a few minutes, I realized he was looking at me as if flirting. He would chat for a while with his buddies, who seemed to defer to him, and then he would glance back at me. I was eating a bowl of fruit, thinking, *How do you suck on strawberries in a sexy way, like in the movies, and catch his eye?* This idea tickled me, and I had to stifle the urge to giggle. A blind person could have picked up on our exchanges, but Bruce was completely oblivious as he concentrated on his lunch.

Bruce made a trip to the restroom, and I wished he wouldn't come back to the bar. When he returned, I wished he would fall through a hole in the floor. *Excuse me, dear, I am going for a ride on a motorcycle; don't hold dinner.* After Bruce paid the bill, I reluctantly tagged along behind him. *Crap, I will never see this guy again.* And I never did see him again, even though I still think of him, especially when I spy a row of Harleys lined up outside the tavern on Sunday afternoons.

When Bruce was in law school, our house was located a block away from Toledo Hospital. One rainy day, while a friend was trying to beautify my hair with highlights, I heard a knock on the door, opened it, and set my eyes on a Robert Redford look-alike. *Yipes!* The resemblance was amazing. He wore a tan raincoat with the collar turned up and had sandy wavy hair, damp from the rain. He was adorable.

"Is it okay if I park in front of your house to go visit someone in the hospital?" he asked.

"Sure, no problem," I said. *Oh crap.* My hair was sticking out all over and I had a towel around my shoulders. Well, it's not like Robert Redford would be interested in me. I stood at the doorway for a minute after he left, trying to fix his image in my memory bank. I walked back to my friend, who was waiting in the kitchen.

"Sandy," I said breathlessly, "My zipless fuck was just at the door!"
"Your what?"
"'Zipless fuck,' like in Erica Jong's novel *Fear of Flying*."
A quote from Jong will clarify:

> The zipless fuck is absolutely pure. It is free of ulterior motives. There is no power game. The man is not "taking" and the woman is not "giving." No one is attempting to cuckold a husband or humiliate a wife. No one is trying to prove anything or get anything out of anyone. The zipless fuck is the purest thing there is. And it is rarer than the unicorn. And I have never had one (Jong 1973, 13).

We peered out the window, hoping for another sight of this dreamy creature, speculating who could be the object of his attention. However, during the break from our vigil, his car disappeared.

Years later, at the Delaware Women's Conference, Erica Jong was the keynote speaker. She autographed a copy of *Fear of Flying* that I had purchased for my daughter. She said, "Didn't we raise the best daughters?"

"We early feminists sure did," I agreed. We were the transition generation from the old to the new. It seemed to be in poor taste to inquire whether she had ever managed to have a "zipless fuck," but I was curious.

If my marriage with Bruce were defunct or if I were defunct, women would be all over Bruce like flies on honey. When I tell him this, he shrugs off my remark, declaring he isn't interested in other women. But with the shortage of other eligible older men, Bruce's status in the community as a retired lawyer as well as his studmuffin looks—which are fading now with age—would be a call to action for the mature single lady. Probably he would eventually not be able to resist her advances if he could decipher the signals. How long would it take for another woman to know something was wrong? I imagine that she would not catch on to the subtleties of Asperger's for some time. When she finally did, we could compare notes.

How's Asperger's working out for ya?

Chapter 25

SUPERMAN

I guess when you are sure you will die of old age, as Bruce always believed, there is no need to fret about health or safety precautions. The only exception he admitted to beyond a geriatric demise was a fear of an airplane crashing into his car, which was highly improbable. He never related the origin of this lone fear to me. Was it perhaps a childhood nightmare?

Our frequent drive to the Delaware beaches takes us past Dover Air Force Base, home to the enormous C-5 Super Galaxy and the C-17 Globemaster airplanes, which often pass overhead like giant roaring blimps as they practice taking off and landing.

I am known to make a snarky comment as I see the big gray bird floating above our path: "Look out! We are going to die!"

To which Bruce once responded, "No, it has to hit us from the back."

We would be squashed like a bug and blown to smithereens whichever way it hit us, but so far so good on all our trips scooting past the dangerous flying machines.

Bruce had no reason to doubt his virtual invincibility, as he was rarely sick, except for a couple of head colds and one bout of strep throat, which sidelined him only for a short afternoon of bed rest. Germs were meaningless to him, and I had to be constantly vigilant about his passing an illness on to me. When I took over driving the RV at a fuel stop, he often made me tea or brought me food, and I finally realized that he habitually handled money and the gas pump without washing his hands. Now I check on him, but initially he told me, "It's only the gas pump."

We visited a friend in the hospital, and when we left, I said that we should use the disinfectant we kept in the car. Again, his response was, "I only touched the doorknobs." I guess Bruce thought he was the only person who opened doors, or maybe he could get germs only if he stuck his hand in a recently used bedpan!

He has reformed, somewhat, after COVID-19 converted almost everyone into a clean freak. Still, I often remind him to wash his hands after doing errands.

All his cuts from thorny briars and brambles while searching for golf balls, his falls on the running paths from roots and rocks, his bike crashes, and his injuries while working on projects around our house and his rental properties yielded enough blood to keep transfusion bags full. Bruce covered in blood was a regular sight, which the kids and I became accustomed to and which he was unbothered by as he licked his sore spots like a wounded animal, slapped on Band-Aids, and went on with his day. He never got infections, so why worry?

One of the most gruesome sights of Bruce and his bloody accidents was when he ran the Waffle Ten-Mile trail race in our state park, a race sponsored by our local restaurant Caffe Gelato. At one point, Bruce fell hard on his knees but finished the race. Runners and spectators were aghast at the sight of blood flowing in rivulets down his shins and soaking his sweaty white socks till they turned a sickly pink.

There was a huge after-race feast at the restaurant, but Bruce had to go home to change, clean, and apply antiseptic and bandages. I took a photo to gross out the kids and grandkids.

(He routinely donates platelets to our local blood bank, absorbing my responsibility, since I do not like the sight of blood, neither mine nor his.)

Bruce has a vast tolerance for liquor and doesn't seem to mind if he is tipsy or drunk. He drops into a dead sleep and wakes up as if he had been on the wagon and not a binge. The problem with such hangover resistance is that he lacks any motivation to self-limit. Even if it doesn't bother *him*, unfortunately, it bothers his *body*. Years ago our family doctor warned, "It isn't if, but when heavy drinking will take you down." For much of his Superman stay on planet Earth, Bruce has cruised through life in a semi-fog of rum, gin, or beer.

Never someone to worry if he got his eight hours of shut-eye, Bruce rarely napped after a night shift while in the navy, and off we would go to the ocean or some other pursuit without his having rested. The day we moved our belongings from Virginia to Delaware before heading to law school in Ohio, he packed a rental truck and drove five hours after working all night. A bad night's rest for me was usually followed by a bad day. Bruce, however, ignored sleep deprivation and forged ahead, which was an asset as he ground away at the University of Toledo, often studying late into the night after working all day and attending evening classes.

This stamina also came in handy when we RV-ed across the country; all of our trips were made easier because he could drive for long hours at a time. When I took over the driving, he would rest on the bed or lean back in the front seat for only a few minutes of shut-eye to recharge his batteries. Just as he would set his mind on a long-distance run, he would set his mind on a long drive and relentlessly pursue his destination.

Sidewalks in our town needed to be cleared of snow for pedestrians, or else the owner of the property could be fined. After one snowstorm, Bruce worked diligently, shoveling and shoveling the sidewalk of four rental units. The snow was two feet thick with a layer of ice in the middle. The tonnage, which he calculated at the time, was enough to send him to the hospital for a double hernia repair a few weeks later.

After a hurricane, Bruce decided to use a chain saw on broken tree branches behind his office. Standing under the limbs, he yanked the starter cable, revved up the chain, and sawed off one of the limbs dangling overhead. This created a chain reaction that brought another heavy limb down on his chest and knocked him to the ground. Though bystanders who witnessed the violence of the accident urged him to seek medical attention, he finished the job and then came home, where I was ready for us to head out and play golf. He collapsed on the bed and said he could still go, but only to chip and putt. I knew something was wrong, so I dragged him to our local emergency room, where they took an X-ray of his sternum. "Do not move!" the white-faced doctor said to Bruce. "Lie down and do not move!"

Bruce's sternum was broken, and there was the danger that a splintered bone could poke a hole in a lung or even his heart. Off he went in an ambulance with me following in pursuit, and he was immediately seen by a trauma doctor.

"Well," said the doc, looking at Bruce in amazement, "you're not dead, so I guess you are going to make it."

The doctor was astounded when Bruce asked him whether he could fly to Minnesota with his friend Buzz to run the Twins Cities Marathon in two weeks. The X-rays showed that he was not in mortal danger, but he was in agony. A week later, when another X-ray showed he was healing well, the doc told him, "Go ahead, if you can bear the pain." Bruce's finisher medal for completing the marathon on October 6, 2003, should have additional engraving: "Completed with a Broken Sternum."

Bruce liked to bicycle all over the county, usually without mishap, but one day the law of averages caught up with him. He cut too suddenly into his parking lot, slid on a patch of sand, and pitched onto his head, leaving him dazed and cut up. As usual, he shrugged off my suggestions of medical help or checking for a concussion.

Once when he was biking on the left side of his friend alongside a Newark park, his buddy called, "Turn left!" Bruce turned right, smashing directly into his partner and sprawling them both on the pavement. No doubt sore, they remounted and made it to Delaware City.

I can't blame the following bicycle accident on Bruce, however; it was a "reverse-aspergate," where *I* caused *him* harm. Always a nervous cyclist, I was fearful of taking my hands off the handlebars to grab my water bottle out of the cage affixed to the frame. Often I would miss and drop it on the road. I did this while training for a biathlon one time, and Bruce's front tire hit my bottle on the road, throwing him into a muddy ditch. Covered in grime and leaves, he crawled out, handed me the bottle, and off we went.

Sally was competing in a biathlon with us when I did the same thing, and when she rode past the bottle in the road, she told the woman biking next to her, "I bet that is my mom's bottle." It certainly was, and I biked back to retrieve it. Luckily Bruce was ahead of me that time.

Bruce had the bright idea to join Reid on a trail ride and purchased a new mountain bike. *What can go wrong now?* I wondered. *He ain't no spring chicken.* Reid had to make a short drive back home because he forgot his biking socks, unaware that Bruce and Reid's friend would not wait for his return. Before Reid could show him how to manage his new mountain bike, Bruce was flying down a forest trail and crashed head-on into a rock. This time he was wearing a helmet; it saved his skull but not his neck, which remained painfully dislocated despite years of physical therapy.

While Bruce could not be blamed for his ignorance regarding the unique characteristics of a mountain bike, he certainly knew never to mix ammonia with bleach, didn't he? Nope. I discovered him working with this toxic combination in the house, dizzy and with eyes burning. I wish I had been forewarned about this cleaning attempt, but Bruce is not forthcoming. He goes about his projects in his own world, never asking for help or advice. If it's given, it's not taken.

At one of our races, I was complaining to a running friend of ours, who was an ER doctor: "Bruce has been wheezing badly for days."

"What happened?" our friend asked.

"I guess it was the lye I used to clean out some sewage in the basement of our apartment building," Bruce said.

"He inhaled the fumes!" I cried. I did not mention that he'd been wading in college student poo.

The doctor immediately prescribed steroids to treat Bruce's damaged lungs, and he was good to go.

Being out in the fresh air, however, was not necessarily safe. With the intent of conjuring up business for one of my daycare centers, we hired a couple of my kids' friends to pass out pamphlets in a nearby neighborhood. We transported everyone to the site in our motor home, and Bruce decided to get a bird's-eye survey of the neighborhood to offer guidance. When I returned after a foray for more pamphlets, Bruce was climbing down from the top of the RV and gave me a serious look. He calmly informed me that he could not pass out pamphlets and had to leave. Then I saw his hand, blood seeping through his fingers. Bruce had snagged his ring finger on the ladder as he descended from the top of the RV, and it was cut badly. *Did he really have to look at the neighborhood from up there?*

The task at hand forgotten, Bruce went to the ER. He refused a pain-killing injection for the stitches because he was told his finger would swell and they would need to cut off his wedding ring. He decided to save the ring by enduring the pain, and his ring was left intact. It was a nice gesture, but I was left with the kids, the RV, and one less helper.

During an ice storm in 2018, Bruce decided to put kitty litter on the driveway. I assumed he was going to cover a few areas at the top and on our walk from the garage. While I was making dinner and listening to a radio show, it dawned on me that he had been out there for quite a while and should have accomplished his task. I opened the door and shouted, "Bruce, are you okay?" He was stumbling around and muttering incoherently, having taken a bad fall. Later we realized that he may have been stunned and possibly unconscious for a time. It was so slippery that I had to crawl on my hands and knees to talk to him, and I found out later that Bruce had been daringly traipsing up and down the glazed driveway.

I called Reid, who dragged his dad off to the hospital while I babysat Ethan, our grandson. I was tired because I had run a hilly subzero race the day before and had planned on crashing after dinner. Later, Reid told me the story:

"Why are you here?" they had asked at the hospital emergency room.

"I fell. Har-har. Guess a lot of people are falling tonight."

Reid had filled in the medical details: "He is 72, on Xarelto, and hit his head on the ice!"

They rushed Bruce in for observation. He was discharged around midnight, apparently none the worse for the fall. Again, his hard head had saved the day. He always said his head would look ugly if he went bald since it is covered with indentations, scars, and bulges.

Bruce's strong constitution also served him well with difficult physical tasks, such as when he unloaded Sally's furniture in Manhattan.

In 2002, Sally and two other recent law school graduates leased a small apartment in Manhattan with jobs awaiting. She instructed us on what furniture to pack in a U-Haul truck, which got fuller by the minute. A minor glitch was that there were three of us and the truck only held two passengers. Never worrying about safety, Bruce suggested that I sit on the floor in front, wedged next to the gear shift. Who worries about seat belts or getting impaled on the gear shift? I took the bus instead.

Parking a truck in Manhattan is next to impossible, but we found a spot across the street from Sally's apartment building. Unfortunately, it was not a legal spot and was marked by cones and signs indicating that it was a nightclub gathering area, but we took it anyway. Sally was the director, Bruce was the mover, and I was the lookout. Bruce was indeed Superman that afternoon, never pausing for a breath as he unloaded the truck, hauling the heavy bed frame, headboard, dressers, boxes, lamps, and chairs. I briefly left my post to help with a load but hurried back, in dread that tough New York City cops would order us to move.

Sally had drawn the short straw and gotten the basement bedroom, adding to the harshness of this project, because Bruce had to lug everything down a steep flight of stairs. He stomped up and down, I paced, and Sally organized. Finally, we kissed our new member of the New York State Bar Association goodbye.

It had been a long day, and I was exhausted, with my illness sapping my strength. But the job was done, and I was anxious to get on the road and get home to bed. Traffic was slow, and as we approached the Holland Tunnel, police waved us away. Recent security laws instituted after the attack on the World Trade Towers forbade truck traffic through there, so we had to head north to the Lincoln Tunnel, which would add another hour to the three-hour drive ahead.

I fell completely apart, wailing that it was too much to bear. "We should have known this rule and headed north in the first place!" I cried.

"We have no control over this, and stressing just makes it worse," Bruce said. "It is useless to worry about something that we can do nothing about." This gave me a glimpse into his live-and-let-live philosophy of life, which most likely had an impact on his strong constitution, impregnable immune system, and astonishing resilience after injury.

Chapter 26

THANK YOU VERY MUCH

Bruce gave me many lovely gifts during our half century of holidays and birthdays, especially in the jewelry department, but some of the gifts left me scratching my head.

Many times, the gifts were simply a little off. He could not quite "make the connection," as he often admits. For instance, once I showed him a lightweight black headband and told him I wanted more of them for running since I kept losing them. When I subsequently opened his package to me, I found a heavy wool one. *Huh?* Or I asked for a bathrobe and instead got a Jones New York black lingerie set, like the one where the robe got tossed on top of the canopy bed in "The Mystery of the Missing Black Lingerie." I didn't need two of those. When I mentioned this, he said, "It's a robe, isn't it?" *Yeah, a nonfunctional robe with full sleeves decorated with flocking to dip in the dishpan.*

One winter I was in dire need of running tights, so I brought out my old stretched, torn, and thin black ones to show Bruce. It seemed like a good Christmas gift idea, but when the day arrived, no tights for me under the tree. It was no big deal, but Bruce had no memory of me showing him my old tights. If he would have said, "I am sorry, I looked for tights but was not sure what to get," or "I couldn't find your size," or "Here is a gift certificate so you can buy the ones you want," I would have been fine, but apparently my demonstration of raggedy tights had been a futile effort.

Early in our marriage, Bruce was into mechanical devices. Electric curlers may be practical, but I felt they lacked romance as a gift. One year he gave me a handheld body massager, which, although primitive compared with high-tech massagers today, came with several attachments. None of them helped my tension headaches, however, because no way could they release the knots in my neck, especially when I only created more muscle tension by trying to hold the massager in place. My mom could release the knots and cure my headaches with an old-fashioned hands-on neck massage, but I guess that kind of human massage was too much touching or work for Bruce when he reluctantly made the effort. *I wish he would ask me how I am feeling rather than complain that his thumbs hurt and shove me away.*

Years later, Bruce made a massage about-face and hired my sports massage therapist to teach us how to give each other massages. It was expensive, costing $200, plus another hundred or so for a nice massage table. This was my birthday present, but I was perfectly happy going to the young sports massage guy for my piriformis muscle pain. When I had an appointment, I made the joke, "I am going to get a twenty-year-old guy to rub my butt!" even though I wore my running shorts for privacy. Where did Bruce get this idea to take over massages? We tried it only a couple of times because it was too much work to fit into our busy schedules. When we did give each other massages, Bruce did not follow the important instruction of not pushing on the spinal column when he massaged my back, creating more stress than was relieved. The table, unfortunately, was to become my torture venue for Lyme-treatment injections.

One year early on, Bruce and I were seated around a coffee table at my parents' house, munching snacks and hors d'oeuvres and trying to create a cheery birthday for me, but it wasn't happening. The October weather was dreary, and Mom must have been ill, because Bruce and I were planning to go to dinner alone. I opened some nice gifts from my parents but began to wonder where additional pretty wrapped birthday boxes—such as from Bruce and the kids (although they were too young to shop alone at the time)—might be hiding. Finally, Bruce sat up in his chair, folded his hands, and made an announcement: "April, you can have a waterbed!" *Wow.* I was both stunned and deflated. For one thing, we couldn't afford a waterbed. For another, if I had wanted one, we could have figured it out and bought one together, especially since we were still sleeping in the same bed back then. That evening, when the new restaurant we tried out was dreadful, I wanted a birthday do-over. But we did eventually buy a waterbed.

I am only one and a half years older than he is, but Bruce talks about "your age," as if I were a dowager. When I turned fifty, I was eligible for the Delaware Senior Olympics, so I decided to compete in a 5K race in both regular and senior categories. It was my first experience with the Senior Olympics, and I had to swallow the fact that I was a "senior." My running friends who were far short of senior status were tickled that one of the giveaways was a water bottle that advertised a funeral home. *Yipes, they cut to the chase!* I won in my age group for both categories and got a bunch of nice prizes. Still, there was no need to further advertise my age.

Nonetheless, as a Christmas gift, Bruce gave me a vanity license plate he had gotten emblazoned with "Senior Olympics." I was only fifty, for cryin' out loud. I was not on the board of the Senior Olympics, and I had no reason to alert drivers in my wake that I was *old*. I never put it on my car, and I still don't know how he came up with the idea. I felt like it was a hidden put-down. I would like to see him put it on his car!

For my sixtieth birthday, my daughter and her fiancé drove down from New York City to join Bruce, Reid, and me for a round of golf, gifts, and dinner. The next day we tailgated with friends at a University of Delaware football game. Everyone was acting as if they were in on something, and I was not in the loop. Soon, I learned what they knew. Appearing over the bleachers, an airplane towed an enormous banner over the stadium. The banner read, "Happy 60th April ♥ BRUCE." How many women want their age announced to a whole town? When I tried to explain this to Bruce, he reasoned that race times were printed in the newspaper by age groups, which meant that anyone could see what age group I belonged in.

"Bruce, the whole town does not read the running section of the paper!"

Some people thought it was sweet, but one woman said she would kill her husband if he pulled a stunt like that. I did not know how to take it or what to make of it. *Was he praising himself? Was it a bid for narcissistic supply?* He had to include "♥ BRUCE." As payback, I put a huge sign on the door to his office when *he* turned sixty, a year and a half later, but it did not have the same effect as unknown motorists zoomed past in their cars, with not so much as a glance.

When it came to the art of receiving gifts, Bruce needed some coaching. After he opened a gift, he would look at it quizzically and hold it up for inspection while the family waited with bated breath for a comment. Maybe his delayed response was a lack of childhood training in gratitude or just plain confusion, but a sweater is a sweater. His repeatedly anemic reactions to presents prompted us to fill in the blanks for him, wherein he would eventually mutter a tardy thank you. Eventually I learned to give him a crash course on gift appreciation before his birthday or Christmas.

Part of the problem was that he had no need for gifts because everything he wanted he bought for himself. He liked to wander around stores, and luckily he was cheap, so Goodwill Industries and other thrift shops were his favorite hangouts. I never knew what his latest purchase had been until he appeared wearing new clothing or whatever else he fancied. This behavior was so opposite to my inclination, which was to model a new dress or drag my latest purchases out of a shopping bag when I got home, just to share my enjoyment of the new acquisition. I purposely didn't buy myself things just before my birthday or Christmas so that it would be easier to come up with a wish list when the family asked for one.

Now that Bruce and I are older and in the shedding rather than gathering stage, Bruce declares that he doesn't want anyone to give him anything. Buying gifts for Dad is the family challenge, but I explain to him that the kids find joy in giving their father presents, so please accept them graciously.

When we lived in Caravel Farms, Bruce's secret shopping habit extended to car buying. One car he showed up in looked like it belonged in an army caravan, as it was greenish-brown and boxy. It was some kind of Ford and had the acceleration power of a snail. We almost rolled back down one of the Green Mountains in it during a trip to Vermont. Besides, it was ugly.

That unfortunate purchase was bad enough. However, I felt compelled to set boundaries on Bruce's impromptu car shopping when he arrived home one evening in a vehicle better suited for interplanetary travel than driving to the law office or school sporting events. I was so flabbergasted and appalled that I could hardly speak. I don't know how he came across this unexpected "deal" or where our current automobile had gone, but this car was either a 1980s Lincoln Continental or Lincoln Town Car. It was blue, with the back section of the roof a white soft top, lots of chrome, and a front end that would arrive at the grocery store before the back end left the driveway. Unless we had a chauffeur or were "Driving Miss Daisy," it was completely unacceptable as a family car.

"Oh my Lord, Bruce, this looks like a pimp car or a car that belongs to a drug dealer! You can't really think we are going to be seen driving that behemoth!"

But Bruce insisted that we would be an instant success in it and that in time it would grow on me. Unfortunately, before we could ditch the monstrosity, we had to drive it the next day to the grand Wilmington Country Club for my mother's wealthy and very classy friend's birthday party. I think it was our one and only foray to a social gathering at this esteemed establishment.

I was embarrassed as we floated like a blue cloud under the front portico of the country club, and I hung my head as I dashed out the door, hoping the parking valet wouldn't think Bruce was my "john." The young man must have thought it a hoot driving that thing and probably thought it unusual that Mrs. Cranston had friends from South Philly.

Car ownership in the Hubbard household drastically changed from that day on. We got rid of the pimp car, and I made sure I was consulted before we bought a replacement vehicle. While we were at it, I upgraded my status from the owner of the crappy second car to the owner of a vehicle just as nice as the one we purchased for Bruce.

Wrapping holiday gifts fell to me because Bruce was often at a University of Delaware football playoff game or otherwise occupied. Whereas my dad was a beautiful gift wrapper, and my mom happily relinquished the chore to him, I was the head wrapper in our family. The only problem with this was when Bruce would postpone wrapping my gifts until Christmas Eve and then ensconce himself in the basement for the evening. Even though we had dinner with my parents on Christmas Eve and opened some gifts with them, when we got back to our house, I would complain that it was lonely for me to be sitting by myself after the kids had been tucked into bed. So we would argue and I wouldn't sleep well. Eventually Bruce solved the problem by changing his last-minute wrapping.

Not too long ago, I was overwhelmed with the number of gifts to be wrapped and solicited Bruce's help. We trudged to the family room in the basement and hauled out all the boxes, bags, wrapping paper, tags, and ribbon, much of which was from charities that I donate to and quite pretty. Bruce began rapidly working on his boxes, but I didn't give him instructions, so the blue paper covered with penguins was matched not with the blue penguin tag but with the children over the world tag, the paper with the bear wearing a Christmas scarf and skating on the pond was paired with the blue penguin tag, and so on. I let him proceed until he stuck a curly purple ribbon on a red-and-silver package. He actually got the hang of it when I pointed out the system, and we ended up with very nicely wrapped presents—until our cat Voter chewed all the bows off anyway.

Chapter 27

CRAZY-MAKING

When at her wit's end, one of my childcare employees—who was originally from West Virginia—would say, "He has just tweaked my last nerve!" My employee would then be in full freak-out mode. This state might be sustainable for a short time when a person has to cope with a difficult situation, but no one could continue in freak-out mode day after day, month after month, and year after year. In my marriage to Bruce, I had to pick and choose my freak-out moments, but the never-ending stress and strain took a big toll. Rarely did I go out in the world when I was not in a frazzled state, which made me appear negative, scatterbrained, or confused. Cartoon drawings of a person standing in front of a huge gong, which someone had gleefully banged, were popular years ago. The poor soul's eyeballs would be going in circles, and little squiggly lines would depict the shock waves that rattled his body.

That's how it was when I tried to communicate with Bruce: like a gong resounding in my brain.

Pointing at the wall, my therapist Dr. Belford said, "Talking to a person with Asperger's is like talking to a wall."

Here's another take:

"It makes you want to shoot your brains out." Dr. Kathy Marshack credits her daughter with this phrase in her book titled, appropriately, *Life with a Partner or Spouse with Asperger Syndrome: Going over the Edge? Practical Steps to Saving You and Your Relationship* (Marshack 2009, 171).

Dr. Belford and I discussed this problem. "Do you think he doesn't hear me," I asked her, "or the words don't register, or he forgets what I say?"

The problem, we decided, was that my words did not register, meaning that Bruce did not process them into his short-term memory. But that's not quite it. I believe that he habitually doesn't even hear my words in the first place, as he is so easily distracted. He might hear the first words I say but not listen to the rest of the sentence, especially if it is more than just a few words. For example, once I said, "Let's go to McDonald's." Then I quickly changed my mind and said, "Forget McDonald's. I like the fish sandwich at Burger King." Bruce then pulled into the McDonald's while I gazed longingly at the Burger King across the highway.

If I had asked him why he hadn't gone to the Burger King, he would have insisted, "You only said go to McDonald's." *Arggh! Are we speaking the same language?*

Recovering from my hysterectomy in 1994, I asked Bruce to pick up some videos to lift my spirits. He brought me *Angela's Ashes* and *Cider House Rules*, real joyrides. *I'm already physically ill; now I'm a mental case.*

One of his most annoying habits is interrupting me mid-sentence when he thinks he knows what I am going to say. I get flustered and end up responding to whatever he has interrupted with, which is usually irrelevant to my initial subject. Then I am forced to collect my thoughts and start over from the beginning, which is both frustrating *and* exhausting. His usual excuse is that he didn't know I was still talking. *Hey, Bruce, my mouth is moving, and there is sound coming out. When my mouth is shut and no sound emerges, then it's your time to talk.*

I wonder whether others see how much I have to guide Bruce's conversation in social settings. I fell into this guiding behavior years ago. I've read that it's a sign of codependency to help a grown man speak correctly. He doesn't seem to know when to wrap up a conversation and may veer off point or say things that I would never say—insulting things, embarrassing and inaccurate things—leaving me to get us back on the proper track.

For example, we were touring a college and standing with other parents in a group when Bruce made a joke. The joke was good, as far as that goes, and the parents smiled in amusement. But then he insisted on looking each couple in the eyes to see if they were laughing. "Heh-heh," he snickered at the first couple, and then he turned his head to the next couple. "Heh-heh," he repeated. The third time around, the parents were beginning to give him weird looks, and I had to move him on.

He will sometimes blurt out facts in situations where it would be better to hold one's peace. We were standing at an educational display booth, listening to two presenters proudly talk about the reclaimed marsh and river in our nearby town. There was even a ribbon-cutting event planned to celebrate the recent renovations. Bruce and I had just run a 5K through the area, and we had both noticed that some of the water looked oily, but I wasn't going to point out that fact to the scientists. Bruce did. They became defensive and explained that it was a natural byproduct of the marsh.

When the children were young, a lot of information came out about the carcinogenic effects of red, yellow, and orange dye in food. I read Bruce several articles on the topic and asked him not to buy Kool-Aid or any other food with dye, but for years he continued to buy Christmas candy that I had to throw out. I assumed he didn't want to do something when my wishes were constantly ignored.

On a trip in the RV to a wedding in Idaho with my in-laws, Bruce stopped for gas and came back to the RV with a big pack of popsicles full of red, yellow, and blue dye.

"Bruce, I really don't want the kids to have this!" I said.

He angrily threw the box on the table and said, "I'll eat 'em, then."

Again I tried to make all the arguments against consuming the dyes. It did no good; he could not generalize that all food with red dye was bad, not just Kool-Aid, and he would not admit to being wrong. I just wanted him to say, "Oh no, I forgot. I will take them back or throw them away." It could have been so easy, but Bruce makes a mountain out of a molehill, setting everyone, including his mom, on edge. Worse, everyone in the RV looked at me like I was a troublemaker.

Years later, our cats were throwing up after eating cat food. I checked the cans, and they had dye in them, so I asked him not to get that kind. Finally, after repeated requests, he looked at me quizzically and said, "You think the cats are going to get cancer?"

As these situations continued, one would think that I would have given up on presenting Bruce with explanations or examples, but I was still unaware that I was not dealing with a person who could listen to or understand my points—or give a damn even if he did understand. For example, I hated it when he pulled the RV over to the shoulder on the highway to make a quick stop. It was dangerous to sit a few feet from semi-trucks that roared by and made the RV shake as if struck by an 8.0-magnitude earthquake. My pulse would quicken, and my stomach would tie into a knot. I tried to hammer home my point by showing him reports of officers or other drivers being plowed into while parked on the side of the road. My friend had been witness to such an accident, which I described to Bruce in the grisliest of terms. But trip after trip, Bruce would persist in his careless behavior. To him, it was not dangerous, and that was that. He wasn't worried about cars and trucks, only airplanes, I guess.

I was never so angry in my life as when Bruce drove my car from a party to pick up his car, which we had left at the daycare center. He drove right by the center.

"What are you doing?" I cried. "You missed the turn!"

Bruce pulled my car to the side of the highway while ignoring my protests. Why bother turning onto the service road where the daycare center is located when he can dash across a four-lane highway in the dark of night? I tried to stop him from leaving me in such a vulnerable situation. I was terrified of his intent to sprint across four lanes of highway with a fifty-mile-per-hour speed limit.

"There aren't any cars coming! I'm not stupid!" he yelled, slamming the door and taking off.

I climbed into the driver's seat of my car and checked the rearview mirror to see a big semi bearing down on me. I was close to a heart attack with outrage at Bruce's arrogant, know-it-all behavior, and I could scarcely drive. When I got home, I raced into the house and exploded with anger. He offered not the slightest apology or indication that he even understood the situation. To add insult to injury, we had just enjoyed a wonderful beach weekend with our daughter after her brain surgery. As the anger dissipated, it was replaced with depression.

I imagined the uncomprehending remarks of friends: *You want a divorce because he gives the kids food with red dye or parks on the side of the highway?* How could I handle this? Who would understand?

"I would have shot him if I had had a gun!" I said to Carole during one of our venting phone conversations.

"Same with me, absolutely," she answered.

"Bruce has gotten me so enraged over the years that I am sure at times I was temporarily insane."

"No judge or jury would believe what they do to us," Carole said.

"We would be sentenced to several lifetimes in prison, a lethal injection, or the electric chair," I said. "The prosecution would present a string of witnesses testifying that our husbands were such 'nice guys.'"

"It would be the Cassandra syndrome at the highest level," she agreed.

"But the verbal abuse is crazy-making!" I said. "Throughout our marriage, I threatened Bruce that I would leave him on the grounds of mental cruelty. I felt like a fool when my therapist asked me why I put up with it all these years."

"We didn't know what was happening!" we said in unison.

"It is not our fault," I added. "Remember, it is called *crazy*-making, and it was all we could do to keep our sanity. No matter the intent, these husbands of ours are pros at scrambling our brains and emotions."

"Sometimes I think I am really becoming crazy dealing with Ted all these years."

"You sound okay to me," I said, tucking the phone under my neck. "I have not heard you say anything to indicate you have a mental instability. We have to trust ourselves on this. But maybe we are getting crazy from crazy-making? People who live with sick people become sick themselves."

"Maybe we are so crazy that we can't tell anymore," Carole said.

"We can't think straight if we are stressed all the time either," I reasoned. "Having our words repeatedly twisted doesn't exactly lend itself to focused, coherent thinking. And the often-weird behavior makes me feel like Commissioner Dreyfus in the *Pink Panther* movies who was driven over the edge by Inspector Clouseau."

"Today I think I have lost it and am crazy for sure," Carole said, trying to get a grip. "I can't think straight."

"Jeez, Carole, stop thinking that. *You* are making *me* crazy! Keep saying to yourself, 'I am not crazy, I am not crazy. My husband is an aspie.'"

Chapter 28

SENSITIVITIES

When a potential marriage partner says he doesn't like pudding, would that be a red flag that something is suspect? The same as when a guy says he wants ten kids and believes his wife should stay home, his favorite website is about conspiracy theories, his friends have prison records, or his apartment is jammed and cluttered like a hoarder's? I mean, it is just pudding, right? Wrong. It is not the taste of pudding he cannot stand but its feel; it is too slimy, too soft, or something similar. And Bruce is not only hypersensitive to pudding but to body lotion, even suntan lotion. Spray-on sun protection is now available, but it was not in time to spare him several melanomas and basal cell anomalies. Toothpaste also fits into this category of intolerability.

Ever since Bruce escaped his parents' supervision, he has avoided brushing his teeth. He developed severe gingivitis during the first year of law school and needed surgery to remove the top layer of his infected gums. The day Bruce was undergoing this nasty and painful procedure, two-year-old Reid and I were walking on a sidewalk behind the dental office. Through the window, we saw Bruce tipped back in the dental chair with blood splattered all over his mouth, face, teeth, and bib. At this gory sight, I felt my own blood drain from my head and my stomach start to churn. *I can't let Reid see his father like this!* I quickly hustled us down the walk. Good thing this butchery was on the navy's tab.

How could anyone endure this misery again? Bruce would surely join the rest of us teeth brushers now. No such luck! He has never brushed his teeth regularly. The extent of his dental care consists of flossing with pics, which he carries around in his car in the drink holder cup. I admit I do chuckle with him when he tells me that the dentist compliments him on his oral hygiene after his checkups. Bruce also claims that brushing his teeth in the morning ruins the taste of his coffee. At least I have never had to complain about the toothpaste tube being squeezed from the middle.

Apparently Bruce does not feel the cold and, so far, has not died of hypothermia. I know his body is cold because the area around his mouth turns purple, making him look like Fred Flintstone. He sometimes runs a winter race in nothing but a singlet. When he golfs in cold weather, he often wears shorts. Everyone else is layered up, but he does not notice or care. "What the hell is it with this guy?" the looks on others' faces say.

Neighbors around our townhouse nicknamed him "Nanook of the North" for his habit of walking barefoot in the snow to get the morning paper. He did make some progress, wearing slippers to get the paper when it was down the long driveways of our Amaranth Street and Mason Drive houses.

If we had lived on a tropical island, I might not have known how much Bruce hates the feel of clothes. The fewer the clothes the better.

Bruce sleeps naked, and when he is up and about, he prefers to "go commando," which refers to the practice of dressing without underpants. No tighty-whities or baggy boxers for him, just hanging free and loose, like a wind chime on the back porch. As far as I know, his clients at the law office had no inkling of these bare-assed inclinations, nor did his friends and family. When a level of decorum was required, he was forced to keep his pants on, so to speak. All other times, he went commando. One asset to this practice was that he seldom needed new underwear. Around the house he wore blue, black, or gray sweatpants or flannel shorts with an elastic band at the waist. If he was standing near me, I habitually grabbed the waist, pulled it out a few inches to peek and ask, "How's your peter doing?" and snapped it back. He never answered the question, but he gave me a stupid grin and claimed this game was one of the reasons he didn't wear underwear, even though I know he would have gone commando anyway.

One day he volunteered to make a quick run to the grocery store. He dashed into the bedroom, slipped on a pair of clunky loafers, grabbed his car keys, and headed for the door, the family jewels floating freely and flopping against his shorts.

"You can't go to the store like that!" I said.

"Why not?" he asked.

"First of all, the clunky shoes do not go with the short shorts—flip-flops would look better—but mostly because I can see your balls and penis!"

"No one will notice," he shot back. "Who is looking at my crotch anyway!"

"People don't mean to look, Bruce, but it will catch their eye. What if they are bending down to get something on a lower shelf?"

"I don't care!" he retorted, getting upset because he hates any change of plans or detour from his intended action.

"You are the one who wears a suit to funerals because you feel it is fitting for a small-town attorney. Now you are going to go to the store flashing your junk? Besides, the senior bus is there on Mondays. You want to give some old lady a heart attack?"

He stomped back into the bedroom and changed his shorts, still probably without underwear, but they were heavy denim cutoffs.

A few days later, he was floating free and loose in his gray flannel shorts again.

"I want you to know I didn't go to the store like this," he said.

That's a relief!

Loud noises bother Bruce almost as much as underwear, and he seems to have become even more sensitive to them over time. A restaurant with bad acoustics will agitate him. I once asked my son how Bruce stood the noise at those University of Delaware football games, and he said that sometimes Bruce covers his ears. Still, Bruce blares his ever-present fifties and sixties music in his car, which I can hear even before I see him coming up the driveway, so it must depend on the source.

Bruce's visual senses are also easily overwhelmed. After we discovered that he has Asperger's, he opened up to me about how he notices so many things at once. Sitting at a restaurant one time, he pointed out the formation of the ceiling tiles, the arrangement and number of decorations, and how high the lights were hung. Everything for him shares the center of attention; for me, that stuff is just peripheral. I think this explains one of his problems with driving; he is too hyper-focused on details to differentiate choices. E-Z Pass or cash lane? Exit 21A or 21B? Here it comes, there it goes.

Like others with autism, Bruce experiences sensory stimulation at a higher level than neurotypicals do. Lights are brighter, noises are louder, and physical touch can be more intense. I have craved contact since we were newlyweds in Chesapeake, Virginia, when I had to scoot over from the far end of the couch and make my arm numb trying to embrace him. For a long time, I thought I was imagining it when I would hug him and his body would stiffen like a board.

An old video shows us gathered at a cookout with my parents. Bruce is watching the kids play and enjoying his drink. When I try several times to hug and kiss him, he keeps turning away. At the time I thought he was just teasing, even though some other gal's guy might have camped it up and given his wife a big hug and a smooch. Something was off, though, and I had no idea what it was.

Chapter 29

FUNGUS AMONG US

I have always been the woman you would see hauling briefcases, childcare supplies, golf bags, racing gear, downhill skis, and protest banners in pursuit of prosperity, health, a full life, and justice. That is not who Bruce saw as he pulled the car up to the curb on the Upper West Side of Manhattan, where I was waiting. This time I was hauling a heavy bag of needles, vitamins, and mineral supplements. Dr. Ali, a specialist in integrative medicine, was trying to keep me alive, but I was getting sicker—and poorer—with each $600 bag. My poor behind was sore as well, branded like livestock with scar tissue from the injections. We had spent more than a hundred grand on my recurring infirmities by that point in 2006. Now I had the long drive home to endure, including an hour-long crawl through New York traffic just to get to the Lincoln Tunnel. The Tioga Bike Shop, where I had once won biking gloves from the Central Park Triathlon, was along the way to the tunnel, and I stared at it gloomily as we inched by.

During the late summer and early fall, when I was sickest, I would seek out the restorative benefits of sea air at the beach. I might stay in a motel or in a campground in our RV, or, when we had a condo, I would go there. One time I was so weak, I just stood with my head against the window in our bedroom at Amaranth, unable to move, think, or act. Bruce tossed a few clothes in an athletic bag, grabbed some food, and threw me in the car to head for the motel. My gardens were in full bloom after months of hard work, and I liked nothing better than to float in my pool, sit under the umbrella, read, and soak up the beautiful, peaceful surroundings. Alternately, I would cuddle with my pets, play golf in my league, run local road races, or have lunch with my girlfriends. Still, I knew instinctively that I needed to leave.

Friends thought I was lucky to laze at the beach. *Not when you are sick and alone.* It was then an "exile," as a more perceptive friend aptly named my time away. I sat on the beach if I had the energy, but often I was just too damned tired and instead lay in the motel bed, eyes fixed on the white swirls of acoustic tile overhead. I tried to add some cheer with a little bouquet of zinnias from my garden set on the dresser, but then I'd watch them droop and fade, like me, as the days faltered by. From the privacy of the little balcony at my hotel, I could observe happy vacationers heading for the restaurant next door. During rainstorms, I would sit under the eaves and watch the water drip dolefully from a spout.

Coincidentally, the course of a road race we still run winds right by the resort motel that had been my old house of exile. When we run past it, I do not know whether to turn away or look, to cheer for being back in the race or cry for what I have undergone. "Bruce," I say afterward, "look, there's that balcony!" *Was it all just a nightmare? And is it really over?*

I was not merely too sick to run, however; I was becoming unable to operate my childcare businesses. I was missing things, like the

$150,000 that I finally discovered had been embezzled by a longtime, trusted employee.

Hence we were selling off my centers, and one of the buyers would often call me for staffing advice while I was still in exile. Ironically, she provided me with a vital clue about my illness. One day she mentioned that her daughter had suffered an environmental illness and advised me to call an "environmentalist." Not sure what she meant, we called a company named Indoor Air Solutions. After measuring mold inside and out to the tune of $3,000, the company's scientist advised me to consult a mold and environmental doctor.

I went into action with renewed vigor, first making an appointment with such a doctor and then tediously copying my voluminous medical records, using the copier in Bruce's office. Right in the middle of my task, the environmentalist called to report that we had an exorbitant amount of outdoor mold, but the house was clear. *How does this help me?*

Bruce was exultant and said, "Let's go for a drink!"

Indoor Solutions was not a solution, so I had to check my husband: "This is not good news, Bruce. We still don't know what the hell is wrong with me!"

I stacked a pile of medical records on my car's front seat and drove out of the parking lot. The first time I hit the brakes, the pile of papers flew all over the floor. Driving with my left hand, I frantically tried to organize my records on the seat with my right hand, becoming more and more infuriated as they kept slipping and sliding. I began throwing all the records around crazily, crunching the papers and mixing them up all the more. Proceeding down our crowded main street in this maniacal mode, I could have easily had an accident. *Officer, I was just flipping out over being sick for twenty years. Sorry about that.*

My anger and frustration escalated with each mile, and I arrived home in a frenzy, Bruce following close behind. *He's getting the picture now*, I thought. *He cannot just dismiss me and think we'll be sitting by the fireplace having a relaxing drink tonight.* Crying and swearing, I yelled, "I can't take this anymore! I can't take this anymore!"

I took a cold pack I had been using to treat an injured knee and slammed it against the dining room wall over and over—*Wap! Wap!*—until the sticky goo broke from the plastic and stuck to the wall. We never did get all the goo off that spot, and I am sure it is there today. It takes a lot to get Bruce's attention, but I was so hysterical that he had to respond. At least he did not slap my face to bring me out of the trance, as they do in the movies, but he did shake my shoulders to bring me back to the real world. I collapsed in a sobbing heap.

"I will call the guy back," Bruce said.

Luckily, the fellow couldn't fit us into his busy schedule, so Bruce called another company. They also had no time for us but gave us a referral.

Driven beyond all composure, I was tormented by the idea that Bruce had not thought to call this company seventeen years ago when we had moved to Amaranth and I had first gotten sick! I remembered when an allergist had told me that something around my house didn't agree with me, and I had been anxious to tell Bruce, but he had blown me off. That would have been a good time to find an "environmentalist" instead of ignoring this provocative remark and leaving me dejected at his lack of action all these years.

After Bruce contacted Cogent Diagnostics, a mold remediation company, I was in the parking lot of yet another doctor when the owner, Frank Peter, called me and said, clear as a sunny day, those words that saved my life:

"I don't think the problem is outside your house. I think it is inside." I will never, ever forget those words! I was stunned!

Frank and his assistant, Bob, came to our house, brandishing an instrument that detected temperature behind walls. It enabled him to determine that we had a lot of cool walls, which might indicate water.

"Look at Bob," he said, waving the thing around. "His body is warm, and the screen is red. Now look at this wall. The screen is blue, meaning it's cool." Frank had just purchased this instrument for

$10,000 and was excited about using it. I thought it was neat also, but what did this all mean?

I decided to sit at the computer and calm my nerves while fretting that this might be another wild-goose chase. The guys came into the office and asked to remove a tile from our floor. They would do it by the heat vent to cause as little damage as possible.

Bob pried up the tile and set it gently aside. There on the exposed surface, we saw little black spots—spots of mold. They asked permission to stick a moisture meter into the wall.

"What the heck, be my guest," I said.

As soon as they poked their probe through the drywall, the dial swung into the danger zone and beeped like a forklift backing up. I grew to fear that beeping sound; it predicted trouble and expense. Every time it beeped, a wall had to be torn out.

Oops! I think Frank knows he has a new client.

It was January 2007 when Frank and a crew arrived for further investigation of the "hot spots" or places that seemed suspect for water damage. Dressed in white hazmat suits, respirators, goggles, and gloves, they descended on our house like doctors protecting themselves from the novel coronavirus. Bruce was at work, and Frank thought it was best if I also made myself scarce, so I went to lunch with my girlfriend Millie.

When I returned, plastic was draped over a wall in the living room like a huge circus tent. A colossal air filter was roaring, sucking air through a wide tube from the covered area to a window. Frank was anxious to show me pictures he had taken from inside the walls. The photos showed that the wallboard and insulation were black, a sharp contrast to the off-white paint and white furniture in our bright cathedral-ceilinged living room. In shock, I put my head in my hands. Frank gently placed his hand on my shoulder and said, "Now you know you are not crazy."

All these years, my own beautiful house had been killing me! Whenever I had been exhausted and gone home to rest, I had been getting sicker. Every breath I had taken in that house had been slowly destroying my health.

The remediation project was huge, costly, and time-consuming. Removing the stucco was the first project, and it sounded like a hundred jackhammers going at once. My poor cats ran away, fearful of the racket. The builder, we learned, had neglected to install flashing under the stucco, which would have diverted rainwater. Frank's crew found a regular menagerie of molds, including *Penicillium/Aspergillus, Fusarium, Alternaria, Stachybotryschartarum, Chaetomium*, and, in our poorly ventilated attic, *Cladosporium*. No wonder I felt chest pains whenever I spent time up there.

Each day a caravan of various construction trucks crowded around our little cul-de-sac. A massive dumpster sat in the driveway to collect the rotten wood, previously known as the walls of our house. It was unsettling to see guys roaming around in hazmat suits, respirators, and goggles. Clearly, *they* didn't want to breathe the air in my house. Our kitchen, which was intact, became the control center. There, sweaty workers would doff their masks, rest, and then return to their tasks with renewed determination and vigor.

The time required to complete this remediation looked to rival that of building the Brooklyn Bridge or Great Wall of China. There was no way we could place our cats and all our necessaries in some temporary domicile while the work dragged on, so we decided to stay home and endure the hassles. Rooms were shrouded in translucent plastic, and the fans of huge filters roared throughout our house as we burrowed from room to room like moles. Every time I heard the beep of that moisture meter, it meant another wall had been found to be contaminated. Our front foyer was so rotted that the whole room had to be demolished. It hurt to watch them jackhammer my lovely ceramic floor tile.

We took a trip to Florida to get away from it and returned to find all the stone in front of the house removed. Bob, who worked the moisture meter and counted the mold particles, had decided not to break the news to us about the rot underneath the stones so that we could enjoy our trip. Removing and replacing the stones was hugely expensive. *Jeez, cut us a break already.*

Everything in the house had to be removed and either cleaned with a mold killer or thrown out. I mean everything! Think of the contents of an entire household all cocooned in black plastic bags in the garage.

Each Christmas at Amaranth Drive, I decorated the foyer with three special things. One was a Christmas doll that I sat on a chair after adjusting her pretty dress, blonde ringlets, and cap. She came out only for the holidays before I lovingly arranged her in a box in the attic until the next year. The second was a beautiful latch hook rug depicting Santa going down the chimney that Bruce's mom, Peg, made for us. Since it was large, the inside front door was a perfect place to display it. Peg had finished the back of the rug with green satin, and it was a favorite piece of mine. The third decoration was a lovely wreath of artificial poinsettias, greens, and twigs that was a gift from our friend Buzz. I hung it on the wall facing the front door, as it made for a wonderful greeting piece.

During the mold remediation, Bruce—in his hurried, robotic manner—disastrously grabbed the box with my foyer decorations and threw it in a dumpster when I was occupied elsewhere. I did not realize this sad fact until a year later when I searched in vain for the box. My heart is broken when I am reminded of Peg's creation, my sweet Christmas doll, and Buzz's wreath all heaped in a landfill with the rotten, moldy wood removed from the house.

One day during this same time I went golfing while Reid, Bruce, and Bob wiped down all the silver with the antifungal cleaner Sporicidin. When they were done, the silver was all stripped away. It had only needed to be washed with soap and water. When Bruce dunked my clothes in the same cleaner, a lot of my best outfits shrunk. Bob cleaned my large pile of race bib numbers, which I had saved throughout my many years of running. I can still picture him sitting on the floor, wiping each one down assiduously. It was a special thing to do for me.

My granddaughter, Amelia, was born in July of 2007 amid the renovations. We drove to New York City for the joyful occasion of our first grandchild, but I felt sick, and it was difficult. *Well, I should be better soon.*

Finally, it was time to put everything back. The blue plastic cover that cloaked our lovely house was removed. I often joked that a burglar could break into our home with only a box cutter. The crews worked twelve hours a day, standing on scaffolding in the burning sun, and installed our new yellow siding. We called it the "House of Sunshine."

One early morning Frank came for his last inspection. We thought it would be funny to sit on our bench on the front stoop and greet him in outlandish morning attire. Bruce wore his bathrobe and held the newspaper and a cup of coffee, and I put on a flowery lingerie outfit and stuck pink curlers in my hair. We all laughed. We said a fond farewell to Frank and later to his assistant, Bob, whom I nicknamed "Particle-Counter Bob." Frank and Bob said we handled the construction well, all things considered.

Insurance declined to cover our disaster, and we got only a pittance from our builder. The savings from my career in daycare went down the drain or into a dumpster, but I endured a year of this misery with high hopes that I would finally feel good again, as I had so many years before.

In the summer of 2008, we threw a "decontamination party" and invited Bob, Frank, Joanne—the daycare buyer who had first suggested an environmentalist—and all our friends and family. I designed invitations with pictures of mold and painted white roses black for table decorations. A garland of white face masks hung around the outside of the deck, and I posted pictures in each room of the mold that had been found there. The whole family, even our one-year-old granddaughter, wore black-and-gray-spotted outfits in keeping with the mold theme. It was a beautiful day outside our House of Sunshine, but inside my body things were not so beautiful.

I had been trying to work with a mold and environmental doctor, but I could not handle his detoxification protocol, the long drive to his office, his personality, and having twenty-three vials of blood drawn at one sitting. And I didn't improve. My immune system had been on overdrive, trying to protect my body for seventeen years, and I had become highly reactive to many substances, an inflammatory sensitivity sometimes called "universal reactive syndrome."

Keeping away from mold, my top priority, was not that easy. For example, the next summer after remediation, we went to Fire Island with my daughter and family. When I walked into the house they were renting, I immediately smelled the mold, which I was becoming an expert at identifying. I called Frank for advice, and he said to stay outside as much as possible. It would only be two days, but it caused a setback to my health, and I became sicker than usual until the first frost. I often had to change hotel rooms or leave restaurants after sensing the presence of mold.

I remained hypersensitive to Bruce's role in all of my misery as well as to mold. Some years later, Bruce neglected to properly repair the plumbing in our Brooklyn condo's kitchen sink. Again our lovely tiles had to be destroyed. I sent a piece of the subflooring to our favorite lab in Florida. The results: high mold. When a leak from an air conditioner in the condo above us dribbled through the ceiling, we had to replace some hardwood flooring.

We traveled in a Winnebago Minnie Winnie for many years after the house remediation. My energy had still not returned to normal, but we continued our ski trips and vacations. A few days into each trip, I would feel unwell. This was mysterious and scary. Taking the Minnie to Santa Fe to visit yet another doctor, we had to travel across the Texas Panhandle in heavy winds. I was driving when we heard a terrible sound of tearing from the front roof. I screeched to a halt and pulled over. We jumped out and saw the outer skin above the windshield flapping in the wind. We only got a split-second look, but what we saw underneath was unmistakable: black mold! Bruce climbed up the ladder and got on the roof. Cars and trucks were whizzing by at 80 miles per hour, and the RV started to drift into the road. *Holy crap! I forgot to put the RV in park!*

I jumped in the Minnie and hit the brakes, simultaneously realizing that Bruce would be thrown off by the force of inertia. Expecting to see him cartwheeling to the ground, I braced for a terrible accident, but he had the sense to hang on. This potential calamity was another reverse-aspergate, like the time I dropped my water bottle in the path of Bruce's bike wheel, causing him to land in a ditch.

We limped to an exit, which was luckily only a few miles away. Usually they were few and far between in this desolate area. The decrepit gas station/garage we pulled into was creepy, and the seedy-looking employees reluctantly dragged out a ladder from a storage area. Bruce taped and stapled the top back on. The Winnebago company was to discontinue the front window overhang in that model due to the high incidence of water damage. At least I now knew why I had felt ill on RV trips. As we had been blowing down the highway, mold had been pelting my face like trillions of minuscule toxic darts.

We traded in the Minnie Winnie when we reached Albuquerque and continued swinging haphazardly between the good life and bad luck.

Chapter 30

OBAMABAGO

In 2008, Bruce and I decided to collaborate with each other in Barack Obama's presidential campaign. Since our state of Delaware is blue, we needed to travel to swing states. We thought it'd be a great idea to decorate the Winnebago with pictures of Barack Obama and Joe Biden, campaign bumper stickers, and Americana window clings. A poster board sign lettered with the word "OBAMABAGO" affixed across the windshield overhang completed the transformation from vacation vehicle to *seriously mean campaign machine*. I thought we looked very patriotic and hoped we would not raise any unnecessary ire from passing vehicles. I value my friends of all political persuasions. Fortunately, the Obamabago was most often welcomed on the road.

The Obama campaign website posted events needing volunteers. We decided to help staff the Democratic Party table at a county fair about three hours west of Philadelphia in a red part of the state. Pretty, green mountains encircled the fairgrounds, but we couldn't let the pastoral setting fool us. Pickup trucks and trailers displaying McCain-Palin and NRA stickers told us we were in a red county.

After parking the Obamabago in a rutted, dusty field, Bruce donned his blue jeans and red-white-and-blue collared shirt emblazoned with stars and stripes and a picture of Mt. Rushmore. I wore blue jeans, a red race T-shirt imprinted with the American flag, and red-white-and-blue beaded jewelry, which, by the way, I had designed myself.

Inside one of the big tents was our little card table covered with a white cloth, Obama signs taped across the front and campaign and voting information stacked on the top. "I guess this is it," I said. And then, "I wonder where anyone is?" We sat down, open for business.

Bruce whispered, "Don't look now, but the competition is a few tables over."

Glancing surreptitiously to the right, I saw a huge, newly constructed wooden booth looming over us in all its grandiose glory. It was big enough to be a bar in a local beer joint and decorated to the hilt. It was the combined sheriff and McCain-Palin campaign booth.

Oh boy, this is going to be fun, I thought.

The sheriff looked imposing with his big Stetson and shiny badge. We knew what kind of officer he was by the BIG sign at his BIG booth. In my mind I read *JOHN WAYNE FOR SHERIFF!* Our little table felt like an apple cart next to the Walmart. Throughout the afternoon and evening, the sheriff and his posse took turns smirking, staring, and pointing at us. They didn't believe in being subtle and tried to ruffle anyone coming to our table for information. Mysteriously, anti-Obama propaganda would show up at our table if we left it unattended for a few minutes. Obama's secretive plans detailing how he was going to take your guns away seemed to be the favorite theme. *Do folks really believe this nonsense?* I toyed with the idea of approaching their booth with a smile to say, "I think these papers belong to you." It was hard to hold my tongue, but it didn't seem prudent to mess with the sheriff, especially if later we found ourselves sharing the same remote country road.

Eventually, reinforcements arrived in the form of two young women who worked with the local Democratic Party and had volunteered for this gig. We learned that they had deep roots in this part of the country, their families having run a nearby farm for generations, and they knew most of the visitors who stopped by our table, including a group of college students who had just registered to vote. The kids were excited, and we took turns high-fiving and praising their commitment to democracy. Unfortunately, we got a lot of mean looks and comments from people heading to the BIG booth.

A few weeks after that experience, we packed the RV for another trip, this time to friendlier territory: the home of Mel and Judy Barwinske in North Washington, Pennsylvania, an hour north of Pittsburg. They had transformed their house into a staging area, augmenting the local field office and home base for the plenitude of local volunteers. The Obamabago was a welcome sight in their large driveway. The Barwinskes received instructions each day from the local field office, run by a young man named Eric, a bright, dedicated young guy with law school in his future. After each day of canvassing, we met back at the Barwinskes' house to share experiences and review strategies for the next day.

Canvassing is a challenging experience and not for the faint of heart. We were cold-calling and needed to be ready for whoever answered the door. We had had practice in the primary election and local Delaware elections, but there was no way I was going near a scratched-up door with a torn screen and a vicious growling dog. I felt it wise to skip any domain with motorcycles parked out front and curtains closed. *I am not waking those dudes!* Most people are nice, but you never know when a nasty one will open the door.

However, I got a charge out of a lady who answered her door in a flowered kimono and fluffy slippers. "Hello," I said. "I am with the Obama campaign."

"That's too bad," she answered and slammed the door in my face. *Wrong house!*

We were supposed to canvas only Democratic voters, but registration information changes, so it was always possible that we might inadvertently knock on the wrong door. I relied on Bruce to navigate streets and houses, numbers being his forte. He would take the odd numbers, and I would take the even numbers, always keeping an eye on each other for safety. One time, Eric dropped us off in a small town. "A word of caution," he warned. "These folks are heavy gun owners."

I was amazed at how modest the homes were in that rural area, but none were lacking in showy displays of Halloween decorations and favorite football teams. I talked to one man named George who thought all politicians were corrupt and didn't have his interests at heart, so he was not going to vote. I pleaded with him not to give up: "Even if we are not rich and powerful, we have one-person, one-vote and need to honor the people who died for this privilege."

One man invited me to sit on the red-white-and-blue bench in front of his small, one-story duplex while I gave my spiel. Crafty Americana ornamentation adorned both sides of the red door, and an American flag fluttered over our heads. This man was a patriot, but he was a poverty-stricken patriot, having recently been laid off from his paving job. He was fearful of not being able to pay his rent and being evicted from his home. He insisted I tour his lovingly tended vegetable garden. His bush beans were his pride and joy, and I left with a bag of seeds that he wanted to share.

A gray, weathered Victorian house stood on a hill at the end of a street. It looked like the famous house from *Psycho*, with exceptionally ghoulish Halloween decorations adding to the creepiness. I thought about skipping it but decided to inch my way up the dirt driveway. Suddenly a black cat jumped out of the bushes in front of me. *Are you kidding me?* I climbed up the creaky steps, tossed the flyers on the porch, and scurried back to the street below.

I knocked on the door of a pretty white cottage surrounded by a white picket fence, a beautiful flower garden, and a rose trellis on the side lawn. This was a welcome change from the *Psycho* house. An older woman answered and invited me inside, where her mother was sitting at the kitchen table. They were happy to have a visitor and proceeded to show me family pictures. At least they were eager to hear about the Obama platform, but I finally made my excuses to extricate myself and get back on the street. Bruce rushed up to me. "Where were you? I couldn't see you anywhere!"

He had become fearful when I was out of sight for so long. This behavior was unusual for him. People often asked me what Bruce thought about my being in vulnerable situations, such as running in the park at night, and I always gave the same answer: "Nothing!" Maybe his concern now was because he had just talked to a citizen who firmly believed Obama was a Muslim, plus there was that pesky gun thing.

We returned home for a couple of weeks and then went back out in the Obamabago, bound for Portsmouth in southern Ohio, the childhood home of Bruce's dad. Portsmouth is a low-income but picturesque area located on the Ohio River adjacent to the state of Kentucky. The volunteers were expecting us at the field office and deserted their posts to check out the RV. Too pooped to canvass, we stuffed packets of policy information and then enjoyed dinner with two of Bruce's cousins. The next day we jogged by the old Hubbard homestead. It was vacant and sat solitary in a wedge of state roads. We paused in a reflective state, picturing the bygone days of Jesse and Daisy and their kids and grandkids running around chasing chickens and swimming in the quarry.

We ended our canvassing stint in time for the Democratic rally in the town square. Hundreds of small American flags and campaign signs for local elections lined the sidewalks, and bunting hung on the gazebo, which was the makeshift stage. Delicious baked goods and jars of homemade jams were offered for sale. A band was playing, and our field director, another aspiring attorney, was coaxed up onto the stage, where he played guitar and sang "This Land is Your Land." It was a great experience to be there in this small, middle-American community, where people are as real as they can get. I called my kids and held up the phone so that they could hear the music. Our hearts were full that day.

We headed back to the Barwinskes' staging house in Pennsylvania for the final push a few days before the election. It seemed like old-home week, since I was beginning to feel familiar with this community, bonding with the voters on repeat visits. Even the *Psycho* house seemed less scary in the sunny autumn air.

The second day there, we gathered in the Barwinskes' basement, fueling up with food and drink provided by volunteers. We had picked up our canvassing assignments and were going over them when Judy got a call from Eric, the field director, to wait for him. He arrived in short order, carrying batches of door hangers and voting directions. We stood in a group waiting for him to speak. Word had just come in from the head office in Chicago: No more canvassing. We were going to start the Get Out the Vote today.

A hush went through the crowd, and a chill went down my spine. We set our pens and clipboards down. *Oh my God, this is it! All the work is finished!* It was in the hands of the people (or was supposed to be).

I say "supposed to be" because Bruce and I had witnessed voter intimidation and suppression attempts in the 2004 presidential election. We had enlisted in the bipartisan group Election Protection with the purpose of helping people when they arrived at their polling place. We trained for two days, and each monitoring group comprised three people: an attorney, a person who could speak Spanish, and a layperson.

We were assigned to a poor neighborhood in Philadelphia, Pennsylvania. Wearing our "You Have the Right to Vote" T-shirts, we set out with optimism, which quickly turned to dismay as we witnessed all sorts of voter intimidation. Big black SUVs with D.C. plates pulled up, and tall, muscular, Secret Service-types jumped out and stood at attention in suits and sunglasses. Even I was afraid of them. We were told to take photos until our attorneys working the polls showed up. As soon as our guys left, the big bruisers came back. This went on all day.

Sometimes the bruisers actually went into the polling place and leaned over the voters as they signed their cards. I saw one of the guys slip cash to a homeless, flannel-shirted, toothless soul who lied to us that he had been hired a week earlier as per law and was a valid poll worker. He kept sidling up to people, mumbling and making the voting process as unpleasant as possible. Needless to say, I was upset that this was allowed to happen in the United States of America. To this day, my heart is broken and my confidence in democracy shattered. All the same, before we left Philly, we took a gray tiger cat off the street and named her *Voter* in honor of our Election Protection work. She stayed with us for sixteen years.

"Make sure you put the correct hangers in the corresponding districts," Eric said, "or we could be accused of voter fraud." Apparently some volunteers in Indiana had neglected to do just that. The rush I got from the big transition was interrupted by another thought: *I don't want to be responsible for people going to the wrong polling place!*

We became acquainted with a retired police officer, Ted, and his wife, Penney, a retired teacher, and teamed up with them to pass out the voting instructions in their quaint historic river town of Avonmore. We were efficient with Ted driving and the three of us checking the addresses, taking turns jumping out of the car, jogging to the front doors, depositing the information, and climbing back in our seats. *There is a lot of exercise involved in volunteering!*

When we stopped for gas on the way home, a man filling up next to us offered to help pay for the gas because he liked the Obamabago. When we got home, however, our anti-Obama next-door neighbor repeatedly joked that he was going to slit our tires, thus thwarting our campaigning efforts. Its glory days finished, our Obamabago once more became the Minnie Winnebago. Bruce and I received many thank you letters, commendations, voting results, photos, and news clippings from the Ohio and Pennsylvania field offices, which I collected in a scrapbook. The Barwinskes were rewarded for their efforts with an invitation to the Obama White House for a reception on the South Lawn.

Hurrah! In working together on this project, Bruce and I had enjoyed a respite from our troubles. We continued to support political candidates we thought would help the country, and this enabled us to meet famous people, greet big donors, and check out high-end apartments in cities like Philadelphia and New York. My favorite cocktail fundraiser was in the Upper West Side of Manhattan where Gloria Steinem was the featured speaker. Maybe the marriage could last a little longer.

Chapter 31

DRIVING DISASTERS

Imagine what it's like for me to drive with Bruce, a man as easily distracted as a cat is by a catnip mouse. Anything off the side of the road will grab his attention and hold it, whereas I might simply glance at it, take note, and stay focused ahead. For example, I might see a cop and quickly note, "Somebody's getting a speeding ticket," and that's it. Bruce will stare at the cop, rotating his head like a feline following a bird as we cruise by and he processes the information. It's the same with runners: he will look long and hard with widening pupils to see if he knows them, even if we are way out of town where we don't know anybody. If Bruce gets it into his head that he needs a snack, or perhaps his sunglasses, he will twist around and obsessively fumble in the console, glove box, or back seat, even in heavy traffic.

I wonder what he was doing the time he sideswiped a car on the Delaware Memorial Bridge. He had kept that to himself, but when the insurance company called him while I was in the car, the jig was up. "The guy was in my blind spot," he explained. The latest cars have blinking lights on the side-view mirrors, which would help—if he would use them.

I do not know what makes him blow through red lights and stop signs. Sometimes as he closes fast on a red light, I have to scream "Stop!" while jamming my foot into an imaginary brake.

"I was just about to slow down," he will claim, although I will not have felt the slightest drag of deceleration.

Sometimes he will run through the same stop sign both coming and going. On the way to see Ethan play baseball and then driving back, Bruce ran through the same red octagon both times.

"You missed that stop sign again!" I will burst out for the umpteenth time. "Why do you do that?"

And for the umpteenth time, Bruce will answer with some variation of, "Didn't see it, didn't expect it, it shouldn't have been there," as if any of those would be a reasonable explanation.

"Tell that to the cop!"

And he does not understand why I am continually screaming, "Stop!"

When we drove down the mountain from a skiing trip in Pennsylvania, he made a last-second left turn, careening right through a red light on a dual highway.

"The light was red!" I cried. "What are you doing?"

He must have been focused on the Sheetz gas station on the corner, all red, white, and pretty. He pumped gas and got coffee while I practiced deep-breathing exercises.

Pretty things almost got us killed again when we exited a campground near Santa Fe, New Mexico, and he again ran a red light.

"You ran a red light!" I shrieked. "Didn't you see it?"

"I was concentrating on the designs on the back of that truck up ahead," he replied.

Of course! Who wouldn't?

He would have totaled a Mercedes sports car that we were following in Fort Myers, Florida, if I had not screamed. He explained that his eyes had been captured by the red, orange, and yellow shingles on a house roof. Those Mercedes passengers had no idea how close they came to being slammed into while Bruce admired pretty things. Even he was unnerved by that incident. We might have ended up spinning donuts in the yard of that house with the fancy shingles.

When Bruce was backing up the RV in a restaurant parking lot in Vermont—CRRRUNCH! "It's just a snowdrift," he said. *If only!* Nope, it was some New Jersey guy's Trans Am. Bruce left a note and made a new acquaintance in Jersey while working out details regarding the deductible and insurance payment.

Bruce backed out of my son's driveway one Thanksgiving and smashed the neighbor's car parked on the street. It was a little dicey to knock on the neighbor's door on Turkey Day only to tell them that their car now sported a new dent. I'm not sure Reid's turkey, green beans, and mashed potatoes were worth the $1,000 we paid out in compensation.

To make a little extra change, Bruce decided to rent out spaces in the parking lot of his law office to students, but after he backed into one of his customers' cars, there went the gain from his parking lot project.

A backup accident was not only inconvenient, costly, and embarrassing, but it could also be dangerous, as when we were working for the Obama campaign. We had campaign signs in all the windows of our RV and "OBAMABAGO" written in big letters across the overhead window. I was scared shitless of stopping in rural nowhere or in tough city neighborhoods. Who knew what could happen? Bruce never seemed to notice the tenor of the locale.

In one incident, for example, we stopped at some *Deliverance*-style backwater full of good ole boys driving pickup trucks with rifles on the back racks, and Bruce backed into some guy's truck. I almost fainted, and I began desperately pulling our posters down. I hoped the guy couldn't read, or at least could not read fast. Bruce got out and talked to the vehicle owner and several other tough-looking characters who had gathered to check out the action. After a few dire minutes of muted conversation, all was hunky-dory. I think Bruce's childlike manner, some energy field surrounding him, or maybe his Minnesota accent makes him appear so nonthreatening that he gets out of these jams. The same amiable Dr. Jekyll that fools everyone at home takes over. Mr. Hyde would get us all killed, I am sure. In this instance, the RV had a mark but not the good ole boy's huge truck. While Bruce was settling matters cool as a cucumber, I was a quaking aspen.

To be fair, I do not do well backing up my big Lexus SUV. I have backed into Reid's car, a minivan, and a state park tree, each time deepening the same dent on the left side rear.

Keeping track of the gas meter has not been Bruce's forte, ever since that portentous event of running dry after passing his bar exam. On a typical trip once, Bruce was at the helm of the RV when I noticed the gas gauge slipping below the quarter mark. "Bruce, we may run out of gas."

Bruce checked the gauge. "We still have a hundred miles."

"What if we run into construction," I pleaded, "a crash, a ten-mile backup?"

"We'll still have ninety miles."

"I don't care if we have a million miles left. I am not standing on the side of the highway waiting for service. And we need to find a gas station that's cheap." An RV guzzles gas like a football team guzzles Gatorade.

Sure enough, taillights soon lit up and traffic slowed to a crawl. Bruce started messing with the mapping app on his phone. "Looks like only a mile or two," he said, eyes off the road and on the little screen. "Looks like it'll break up by the next exit."

"Looks like you are swerving into the next lane!" I shrieked. "Give me the phone!"

I tried to reason with Bruce that the threat of running out of gas far exceeded the hassle of stopping more often and keeping a minimum reserve in the tank. Such advice always falls on deaf ears, especially if I don't stay one step ahead of my aspie and check. But sometimes I forget, especially when we trade cars at home and I head out somewhere and casually check the gas meter. *Oh shit!*

Somehow, on one trip, we found ourselves on a long, lonely stretch of flat road in South Dakota, praying for a gas station to emerge on the horizon like an oasis. My father-in-law, mother-in-law, and two kids were in the RV with us, and we hadn't paid attention to a sign that said, "Last gas station for a lot of miles," if there had been one. Now I was in another situation of stress-caused cortisol running rampant in my veins. We all peered through the windshield, eyes darting back and forth from gas gauge to empty road. Just as the needle edged past the empty line, a town smaller than a penny stamp arose where the road met the sky, and we were saved from hours stranded on a dusty roadside.

One time, though, we *did* run out of gas. I've blocked most of that RV trip from my brain, or possibly I just remain afflicted with stress-induced amnesia about it. All I remember is that we were on empty, and it was all over but for the shouting and a frantic call for assistance. Then, lo and behold, way down a slight decline appeared gasoline price signs, towering like palms in the desert. We coasted in, with just enough force to slide next to a pump.

The biggest gas-gauging mistake I made occurred on the crowded northeast corridor heading to Maine one summer for my niece's wedding. It was my first time driving our huge Chevy Suburban and pulling a thirty-four-foot trailer—all in all, around sixty feet of moving metal. I was nervous, but we found a long, straight stretch of clear highway where I could take over. It didn't seem that difficult, so I let my nerves subside just a little as I got the hang of managing the braking and trailer movements. By now we were in New Haven or New Hope—I am not sure which—but it was basically one long urban stretch through Connecticut. I began to feel uneasy because my brother had called and warned us that we were cutting it close for my niece's rehearsal party. I glanced at the gas meter: not even a quarter of a tank left. Worse, traffic was bumper-to-bumper, and construction barriers and orange barrels barred us from using the shoulder if we had a mishap—like running out of gas.

I started pounding the steering wheel with my hand and yelling every cuss word I knew before shouting, "Bruce, we cannot let this huge contraption stop in the middle of the highway! We'll cause a ten-to-twenty-mile backup. People will be so inconvenienced—forget that they'll be pissed—and anyone with a gun'll probably shoot us. Not to mention the cops will give us a ticket and a humiliating tongue-lashing. It'll be a freaking A1 disaster!"

My heart was pounding as we crept ten to twenty miles per hour in this bumper-to-bumper turtle parade. There were no gas stations on interstate overpasses, and there was no way to get off an exit and drag that thing through town if there were any exits, which there weren't.

Peering ahead as I inched along, we spotted a Sam's Club gas station. It was hard for me to pull our big rig into the small station, and I was about ready to pee my pants. Unfortunately, it was a no-go. We weren't members, so—no gas for us. I pleaded with them to help us. "Them's the rules, lady." However, down the road, Mr. Anal told us, we would run into another gas station that would serve us. Fortunately, it turned out to be on a service road and not the kind of place where we could get shot or arrested if we stopped.

With the tank finally full, Bruce took over the driving. Still, by the time we arrived at my niece's rehearsal dinner party, I was mentally and physically shot. My son-in-law, Bob, delivered me a plate from the picked-over buffet, and I gulped down several glasses of wine. I hardly slept that night and woke to an unwelcome hangover.

Gas is not the only thing needed to keep a big diesel RV running. Two years before the Sam's Club fiasco, we'd driven our brand-new Navion RV to Florida to meet my daughter and family. When we pulled into the first campground, I was feeling terrible. Something was wrong, and I thought it must be some chemical reaction. By the time we got to Disney World, I felt even sicker, and Bruce was having asthma attacks.

We went to Epcot with the family and stopped for lunch. It so happens that on the bus ride over there, I had chatted with a nice woman about our mutual health problems, and she had mentioned having a rescue inhaler. During lunch, when Bruce had a bad attack and we headed to the door for air, serendipitously there was the woman from the bus seated near the door of the same restaurant, and she let Bruce use her inhaler. He was able to breathe again. Oh, the days before COVID-19!

I'd get better when we stayed at the campground and worse when we drove to meet friends. Then I'd get better again at another campground. By now, I had begun researching diesel fuel, which was the only difference in this RV from others we'd owned. It seemed reasonable that diesel fumes might cause a reaction. Reid's later research confirmed our suspicions. We were so sure at the time that the problem was the diesel, we stopped at a dealership, looking to trade in the Navion. It shaped up to be too much hassle, so we pushed on home and hoped for the best.

To change drivers, we had to park the RV in a truck lot, where trucks keep their diesel engines running in a cacophonous symphony. North of Jacksonville, we stopped to switch seats while situated between two huge semis spewing exhaust. When I tried to start the engine, there was nothing. Nada. *Oh my God, what is wrong with this thing? It is brand new!* My heart skipped a beat as I kept twisting the key. *Oh, my adrenals! C'mon baby, START!* It was the day before Easter Sunday, and we were far from any towns.

Bruce pored through the manual, flipping pages back and forth to figure out what was wrong. We finally contacted a service company, and I sat on a bench for hours, waiting for their truck to arrive. When it did, we were told the battery was fine, although I had known that it wasn't the darn battery in the first place.

When Bruce at last connected with Navion's emergency service, we learned the secret. It turns out that a warning light Bruce thought meant low window-washing fluid was really a warning that we needed an additive called AdBlue. You have to reload an AdBlue reservoir next to the gas tank every so often to control nitrous oxide emissions. If the reservoir is empty, the diesel engine won't start. I always left RV maintenance up to Bruce and had never thought to check something like that. Because it was Easter weekend, nobody selling AdBlue was open within forty miles. Bruce finally found us an Easter angel who was willing to drive an hour to bring us the additive. I watched the time pass, feeling sicker and sicker and seesawing between anger and despair.

When we finally got the precious AdBlue, I said, "Bruce, great. Get it in the tank and let's get the hell away from these diesel trucks and on our way."

But no-o-o-o! The spout from the can did not fit the pipe to our tank. It looked like a no-go, but after an hour of angling, spilling, and tipping, the additive was in the tank, and the RV started. We gave our angel a huge tip and thanked him profusely for his act of kindness. When we pulled into a campground that evening, the clerk told us how her truck-driving son had also gotten ill from diesel fumes.

Still, the trip home was hell, especially since we had to add another day due to the AdBlue fiasco. Easter traffic held us to a thirty-five-mile-per-hour crawl from Richmond to Delaware, all while Bruce's asthma got worse and I suffered from body aches, sinus problems, blurred vision, and an overall feeling that I had been poisoned.

Once home, we took the RV to a shop. They gave it the once-over and discovered a design flaw. It turns out that there was a vent to the kitchen oven just over the exhaust pipe. Suspecting that the gas fumes were coming in that way, we did experiments with fans and incense: the smell came right inside the RV. Once aware of the design flaw, we wrote to Winnebago for compensation. We wanted only to return the Navion and get our money back, but we lost the appeal and took a $30,000 bath in selling it cut-rate to a dealer.

We lose a lot of time when Bruce blows past exits to destinations, even if we have been there before. It took me years to recognize that this is habitual. Coming back from the Neptune Festival Race in Virginia Beach, near our old navy station, we were on our way to the Chesapeake Bay Bridge-Tunnel. We had taken it at least fifty times previously, but this time Bruce cruised right past the exit. I had been focused on my knitting, trusting Bruce to know this familiar route.

Absolutely baffled, I asked, "How could you miss that turn?"

"I thought it was the second turn," he answered.

"Why didn't you read the sign that says 'Chesapeake Bay Bridge-Tunnel'"?

"I thought it was the second turn," he repeated.

We immediately got stuck in the heavy traffic for Virginia Beach, and it seemed to take forever to turn around. "It was only twenty minutes," Bruce claimed.

"I don't care how long or how far it is. I am tired and feel lousy, and I don't like it."

Even with today's GPS and cell phone apps, Bruce messes up by putting in the wrong destination. His biggest flub was when we tried to pick up our daughter at the Baltimore train station to take her with us to my niece's bridal shower. He put Amtrak in the GPS, and we found ourselves an hour out of town, in a bad section, where the trains were stored. My poor daughter was stranded at the train station waiting for us, we missed half of the shower, and, as you might imagine, I was a stressed-out mess.

Since I no longer have the stamina and energy for nerve-racking road trips, I try to keep them to a minimum. I made Bruce buy a Honda with brake assist and lane warnings, but I fear that the assisted braking would still not be much protection from a crash.

Bruce drives a 2003 limited-edition, white Chrysler PT Cruiser, called a "woody" for its decorative wooden panels on the back and sides. My son drove with him to New Jersey to buy it from a guy who owned a bar called Woody's. It is so old now that Bruce periodically replaces the wood panels with stick-on, shelf-type appliqués.

The exterior is covered with stickers of all kinds: gay rights, animal rights, political statements, peace messages, triathlons, road race distances like 26.2, the Boston Marathon, and a neat surfboard sticker from the original owner. A hula dancer sways on the inside dash, along with tiny matchbox-type PT Cruisers. Cloth dice and a metal peace sign dangle from the rearview mirror. His vanity license plate is WUDEE, indicating both his type of car and the YoUDee mascot of the University of Delaware (UD) football team. At one point I had to convince him to remove a sign he had around the rear plate. He could light it up from the front when someone drove too close. It said "BACK OFF." How did he think that would go over?

The front passenger seat is kept in a down position; instead of a passenger, the spot holds all of his sunglasses, drink glasses, golf clubs, mail, snacks, cozies, towels, and shoes. The steering wheel is overlaid by, and the driver seat is covered with, a road race design throw. To me, his car smells musty, and it is definitely permeated with dust. My breathing suffers if I have to spend one minute in that vehicle, as when I have to move it. I worry that Bruce's asthma might be aggravated by it, but he has no such worries, wheeling around town with the windows always open and sixties music blaring.

Ironically, I once had a glorious experience riding with Bruce, but it took a blizzard.

We were visiting our daughter in Brooklyn when the snow advisory was announced. Soon cars would not be allowed on the New Jersey Turnpike. If we stayed, we could be snowed in for days. We have seen what happens when the city is blasted by heavy snow and the plows just bury the cars, as they did to my daughter's in one storm.

She and her husband were unable to exhume it from its snowy tomb for an entire month.

The blizzard was coming up from the south and we would be heading right toward it, but we thought we should be able to beat it home. Halfway home, with an hour and a half to go, a big snowflake hit the windshield: splat! Soon we were in a whiteout: heavy, blinding snow and wind. Well, being from Minnesota and Vermont, we knew snow and how to drive in it.

All other citizens were off the road as instructed, so it was just us, cops, and plows. I was waiting to get a citation, but the few cop cars that we encountered ignored us. Following two tire tracks, we inched along. At one point, we pulled into a rest stop, where there was not one car marring the accumulating snow in the lot. It was a strange feeling not seeing a soul as we ran into the restrooms and back out into the storm.

I loved that blizzard. It was the safest I have ever felt driving with Bruce. No cars to rear-end. Nothing to take his attention off the road. No speeding. And I love snow. When we finally got to the twin spans of the Delaware Memorial Bridge, we felt we had made it home without being arrested or getting stuck in a snowbank. As we floated over the arched span, snow swirled all around us, causing halos to glow in the bridge lights. We could not see above, below, or around us. No city of Wilmington, no Delaware River, no factories, no nothing. It was fantastic, like coasting in a spaceship. It was times like these when our individual idiosyncrasies matched.

Chapter 32

ASS WHAT?

Why am I holding my hands over my ears, shaking, my stomach in knots, and telling Bruce to stop—please stop—asking so many questions? I have answered his thousands of questions for thirty-eight years, but today, Memorial Day 2009, my long-overworked patience has expired. Today I can no longer formulate answers to his questions. The subject is not rocket science; it is mulching the garden, the same garden we have mulched for twenty years.

Bruce hoisted the handles of a wheelbarrow piled high with mulch and trudged straight toward me. "Where do you want me to put this?" he asked.

"Here, where we are working in the garden," I responded, and turned to pick up my garden tools.

"Where do you mean?" Now Bruce's wheelbarrow was right up to me.

"Just spread it where it needs it."

"Over here?"

"Yes, put some in the zinnia garden and then some out front."

He backed the wheelbarrow up, scooted it to the edge of the garden, and asked, "How much?"

I was getting nowhere, I had work to do, and I did not want to take him by the hand and show him each step. "Just one or two inches thick."

"The whole load?" Bruce's questions were coming at me like freight cars.

"Whatever it takes!"

After dumping the mulch, he headed to the front and then turned back at the gate. "Which garden out front?"

"Around the shrubs where we put it last year," I answered, getting agitated.

"How many loads do you think I need?"

"I don't know how to explain it to you anymore! Mulch goes in the garden! Put in one inch or two inches, up to our knees! I don't know! What we always do."

I was exhausted from giving endless directions to Bruce in addition to being principal manager of the house, the kids, our social life, and all aspects of married coexistence, and that day I collapsed from the mental load. Bruce was incapable of executive function, and my own executive functioning skills were not functioning. I was functioned out! I was questioned out! I resolved to return to Dr. Belford, who had been my Therapist Number One BD. We had given up on counseling for eight years after Therapist Number Five BD, the short-session therapist. Luckily, Dr. Belford had a cancellation, and I got in the next day, Bruce's persistent interrogations buzzing like bees in my brain.

"Doctor Belford," I wailed, "Bruce asks a lot of questions! All the time! I get tired because he usually does not understand my answers. He doesn't seem to know what is going on."

I saw a sixty-five-watt light bulb going off in Dr. Belford's brain. She leaned over and pulled out a reference book from a shelf and thumbed through it, until she stopped on a page and read it intently. Suddenly she thumped the page with her fingertip.

Looking at me, she declared, "Asperger's!"

"Ass what?" I didn't understand the word. "Ass-burgers?"

"No, Asperger's," she explained, reading from the book, "'a form of autism named after Dutchman Hans Asperger, who discovered the condition in 1947.' Asking a lot of questions is a common trait for a person with Asperger's syndrome."

A few days later, I was back on the couch in Dr. Belford's office. Opening my file, she said, "I knew you were on to something when you called right away because you always take something and run with it."

"I am 99 percent sure that Asperger's syndrome is the problem," I declared. More discussion about the characteristics seemed to cement this theory in which, finally, the pieces of our mixed-up marriage fit together.

I had been validated! I wasn't crazy, or, as a British aspie wife would say, "Now I know I am not mad!" I had *not* been imagining things. I *knew* there was something wrong! Rays of sun burst through the dark clouds of confusion, hurt, and pain, and I was ready to go running down our main street, shouting the news to the townspeople. I was relieved and excited when I left Dr. Belford's office, but what was I going to do with this information?

I had to tell Bruce.

Now I had a name for what drove me crazy, like a secret weapon to defend my sanity. Unfortunately, Bruce might disarm me by not listening to my explanation. He might get upset or deny any possibility that he had Asperger's. I did not know how he would react when I told him he had a form of autism.

After work, Bruce usually followed me around the yard or house, seeking instruction for plans or projects, but not tonight. I sat by our pool, with notes and a prepared speech stashed in the pages of my novel. Bruce was working on something in the garage, so I got up and wandered to the vacationing neighbors' house to visit their cat. Bruce would usually join me on their deck for a drink, but not tonight. I heard noises in our backyard and wondered what he was doing.

Did he suspect something was up? Dinner prepared, I sat on the bench in front of our house with a glass of wine. Waiting for Bruce to arrive, I clutched my book and held my breath.

Before long, the food was overcooked, and darkness was falling. *What the hell is he doing?* Rarely did he putt around and work on a project by himself. Determined to tackle this problem that night, I called him to come and sit down. I strove to avoid announcing a "talk," as the last two talks had been about his lack of affection and verbal abuse.

He reluctantly joined me, knowing something was up and that it probably wasn't good. At this point, I had extracted the notes from my book. Bruce eyed them nervously.

Nonchalantly, I said, "Bruce, I think I know the reason for the difficulties in our marriage. Dr. Belford came up with an idea the other day, and it seems to fit our particular problem. It is a condition called Asperger's syndrome, and it is—"

Predictably, Bruce interrupted without letting me finish. "Like the guy on *Boston Legal*! He rubs the tops of his thighs like this." Bruce stood up and demonstrated the motion, which is called "stimming." "He has Asperger's." He identified with the character and was eager to tell me about him.

Holy shit! Bruce already knew about Asperger's from a TV show!

Excitedly, I read more of my research. One example described the reaction of a person with Asperger's who had witnessed a car crash. It said that he would note the vehicle's make, its license number, the state where it was registered, and how many times it rolled over, without any feeling for the people getting maimed or killed.

Coincidentally, the previous Saturday, while driving back from the beach, we had experienced almost the same phenomenon.

"Look, there is a huge whirlwind in that field," I said, pointing to the right of the highway.

"It's a car," said Bruce. An SUV was flying and flipping through the soybean field, barely visible through the swirling dust.

Bruce hit the RV brakes, veered onto a small road, stopped, grabbed some blankets and our first aid kit, and ran toward the dusty, demolished Cadillac SUV. I hung back to see if I was needed, since I wasn't keen on being up close to the crash.

The contents of the car were strewn all over the field, including papers, coffee cups, clothing, and fast-food bags, not to mention the two occupants.

"You wrecked my fucking car! I am going to kill you!" yelled one guy, crawling toward the other.

"Shut up!" groaned the other guy, trying to push himself up with his elbow.

"You wrecked my car! Son of a bitch!"

Finally, the police, an ambulance, and a helicopter arrived. We left the scene, thinking that those two idiots ought to have been happy they were alive. Apparently, after a big night of partying at the beach, the SUV's owner had been sleeping in the passenger seat. His companion at the wheel had not been able to stay awake, either. Bruce recalled having noticed the truck as it sped by us a few minutes earlier and admiring how black and shiny that new Cadillac SRX was.

He admitted to me that as he witnessed the accident, he counted the flips with no concern for whoever was bouncing around inside, just like the example that I was now presenting. The cold details were what registered; empathy was absent. As I pondered this new discovery, I asked Bruce if he thought he was different from other people.

He responded, "I always knew I was different, but I didn't think it would affect anyone else."

Aaargh! Thirty-eight years of heartbreak for me as an intimate partner; the effect is immeasurable. "Anyone else" is me!

Thus began our journey into the world of Asperger's.

The first stop was to discontinue sessions with the current therapist on duty—Therapist Number Seven BD—a life coach. He had been recommended to me as a qualified hypnotherapist by another life coach, Therapist Number Six BD. Maybe hypnotism could "get the bad out of Bruce," like getting Mr. Hyde out of Dr. Jekyll. After several months, the life coach abandoned the individual sessions with Bruce and decided my input would be helpful. I was a reluctant participant, not only because of the expense but because I dreaded a repeat of the other failed counseling sessions. Bruce sat next to me like a lump on the couch as I fell into despair yet again, trying to get the guy to understand our elusive problems.

All ended abruptly with the life coach when we discovered Bruce had Asperger's syndrome. We were eager to share our discovery with him. Sitting together on the edge of the couch in his office, we both talked at once, recounting what we had learned. I am not sure if this fellow knew what Asperger's was. He said he did, but I was not convinced. This session happened to be our last in a series, and it was time to re-up for another $1,300, our third time doling out this kind of money. It was easy to see that this upbeat, enthusiastic, I-can-change-your-life life coach was not thrilled with our revelation. It was easy to pick up on his disappointment in losing the gravy train that these two older people provided. This meeting was not going as planned. Giving it his best shot, he tried to convince us to stay with him. All puppy-eyed, he insisted that he could help, but once we persuaded him that we had made a decision, he almost spat out, "Just go to an expert if you have to!"

We practically glided out of the office, happy and high, confident the nightmare would soon be over. How hard is it to fix this little Asperger's problem? Lunching on the deck of a riverfront restaurant, we felt our spirits soar like the marsh birds that darted in and out of the cattails and seagrasses.

For me, learning that Bruce had Asperger's was like being given a successful eye transplant after having been blind my entire life. I had fumbled in the dark for so long, trying to feel my way around, grasping at clues and questions and snippets of information, trying to paint a picture of what the hell was going on around me. Suddenly, there was light. There were forms and shapes. I could see what was going on. It was beginning to make sense.

We found a therapist who was Asperger-literate, Therapist Number One AD (After Diagnosis), Dr. Sunby. After she met with both of us, she said she wanted to talk to me solo. She informed me that she was not yet convinced that Bruce had Asperger's syndrome.

Damn! I had thought Asperger's was the key to our marital mystery.

I had finally been validated after trying to prove something was wrong for so many years; now I was getting pushback from the expert. She conceded, however, when I said, "He doesn't know when I stop talking and he is supposed to talk."

"Yes," she said, "people with Asperger's cannot have a reciprocal conversation."

Thank you very much, I thought.

Despite Dr. Sunby's doubts, Bruce scored high on the Baron-Cohen Autism Spectrum Quotient test, and the Asperger's designation was confirmed by a member of Asperger Alliance in our local community who knew Bruce.

Bruce saw Dr. Sunby for about a year. Every so often, I made a guest appearance in her office. The forty-five-minute time allotment was never enough time for me to explain the latest frustrations, fights, and miscommunications. Although Bruce was becoming less reactive and defensive, we were still dealing with the same issues. It felt good to know she understood Asperger's, even though she could not apprehend what I was experiencing. The few times we met with Dr. Sunby together, Bruce seemed to change into someone else for that hour, demonstrating the same chameleon personality he uses with everybody but me. Bruce was doing his same old snow job.

As evidenced before, ordinary problems become big issues in an Asperger's relationship. During the time Bruce was seeing Dr. Sunby, I was complaining to Bruce that he was leaving the toilet seat up. I asked him time and time again to put it back down. What woman wants to touch something soiled with butt sweat and little hairs? He would do it at our kids' houses and probably when we were visiting friends but not at home. I tried to explain that it was unsanitary and not good etiquette. It might be a guy thing, but what other guy insists that "it wasn't me" when he is the only guy living in the house?

One time, Bruce tried to blame our son, who had stopped by the house earlier, so I called him and asked, "Did you use the powder room toilet when you were here, Reid?"

"Nope."

"Well, Bruce, I guess it was the invisible man again."

I used the bathroom after Bruce in a doctor's office in New York City one time, and the seat was up when I got there.

"Bruce, you left the seat up," I said.

"It wasn't me," he answered. "Someone must have gone in after me."

"I am the only one who went in after you!" We were the only two people in the small office.

"Why are you mad about a toilet seat, for crying out loud? It is no big thing."

At this point, I was not mad about the toilet seat. I was driven mad by his gaslighting.

In a world where one person tries to cooperate with another person, this would be resolved easily. I would point out to Bruce that he was leaving the seat up and that it was unsightly and unsanitary, and he would respond rationally, "Oh, I didn't realize I was doing it."

"Okay, try to remember."

Then when he did not remember, I would say, "Bruce, you are still leaving the seat up everywhere you go, not just at home."

"I'm sorry, I just can't seem to remember."

"Maybe you should put a sticky note on the toilet."

Bruce will never admit that he is wrong and cannot internalize my injunction for him not to leave the seat up.

Now I know to say, "If you keep leaving the toilet seat up after you urinate, I am going to slam your penis in it!"

Bruce offhandedly told me, "Dr. Sunby laughed when she saw the note I left in the bathroom at her office. It said, 'If this seat is up, I didn't do it.' Hahaha."

My blood pressure soared, and stress hormones shot through my veins upon hearing him dismiss my pleading with such disdain. I cried, "You are making jokes when I am totally upset."

That was the end of his little chats and giggles with Dr. Sunby. *More worthless sessions with a therapist!* I had been counting on her help, but she was dismissing my feelings, too.

Bruce briefly attended a support group for aspies. I count this group as Therapist Number Two AD. Most in the group were very low functioning and had to live with their parents as adults. Bruce wound up being the mentor. He did give it a go, but it was the wrong approach. So long, Therapist Number Two AD.

I dove headfirst into the sea of knowledge that was Asperger literature, books by experts as well as wives married to men with Asperger's syndrome. Maxine Aston and Louise Weston were accessible and readily useful. Tony Atwood's *Complete Guide to Asperger's Syndrome* and Peter Vermeulen's *Autism as Context Blindness* (2012) provided a deep dive into the psychological complexities of the condition.

Bruce and I tried an exercise out of Maxine Aston's *Asperger Couples Workbook*. With color-coded strips of construction paper, we could indicate emotions that the other might not be picking up. We kept a stack on the mantel in our bedroom. Black was anger.

I thought of gluing yellow to my forehead to show how I was perpetually stressed.

In her book *Connecting with Your Asperger Partner*, Louise Weston says that if we have no expectations, we will have no disappointments. This advice is hard to swallow. Walk away when a fight escalates, she advises. Just walk away (Weston 2010). I am not good at this. I have gotten better at it, but when a meltdown is brewing, I still try to prove my point, as if I were talking to a neurotypical person. Maybe I should hold up a fiery red strip meaning *I'm losing it!*

Let's try working on Bruce's brain. We consulted with Dr. Daniel Kalish, a functional medicine practitioner in California who had treated me for my mold exposure. After using Bruce as a guinea pig in an experiment where he swallowed various neuro-transmitting amino acid supplements and no beer—bummer for Bruce—a urine test showed my hubby was dopamine deficient. This meant that he was not eligible for the amino protocols that might have regulated his brain processing and wiped out some of the Asperger symptoms. We had struck out with Therapist Number Three AD. Damn. I had hoped that Bruce could just take some pills and then we could have normal conversations.

Therapist Number Four AD treated clients with Asperger's, ADHD, insomnia, PTSD, and depression with neurofeedback, something suggested by the online aspie wives. Neurofeedback, also called EEG biofeedback, is a state-of-the-art, noninvasive, drugless method for teaching the brain to function in a more balanced and healthful way. To reach Therapist Number Four AD, we had to truck some distance through Pennsylvania hills and dales.

I was frustrated and crazed, as usual, when we arrived. While Bruce was plugged into the wires of the feedback machine, I spoke to

Therapist Number Four AD about Asperger's, and she made a lot of sense. When I told her that Bruce cannot say he is sorry, she replied, "Aspies feel shame, not remorse." Still, she felt we had a lot of positives going for us. "Don't throw the baby out with the bathwater," she advised. *Okay, I will hang in a little longer.*

Since I had issues of my own, I got plugged in several times to the feedback machine myself. "Let's try and get you sleeping better," she said. I thought of this treatment as a calming meditation. Neurofeedback also enhances peak performance at work or in sports. *Maybe I can make more of my putts if I do this.*

The long drive and cost became untenable, so we purchased our own feedback machine from a company called NeurOptimal. Four thousand dollars was a hefty price, but I figured out that we would actually *save* money if we both used it twice a week instead of trekking to the therapist's faraway office.

The machine displayed beautiful graphics on the laptop, but barely audible clicks would be heard when the user's concentration on the music lapsed. Even with graphic instructions, Bruce could not figure out how to hook himself up and never took the time anyway. It took me about forty-five minutes to hook it up, play the program, and clean up the electrodes, so now it sits in the closet. Goodbye, Therapist Number Four AD.

Meanwhile, Bruce and I were having more fights, so I decided to go back to Patricia Evans again. Fifteen years before, she had been Therapist Number One BD, and now she was Number Five AD. She is no-nonsense and told us in no uncertain terms what we had to do to save our marriage. Most importantly, the spouse must be willing to change. Bruce and I had to draw up contracts regarding both of our behaviors. Evans went so far as to say that we should record all our conversations, audio or video. This protocol proved to be too difficult for us.

While researching solutions, I encountered *Getting Past Your Past* by Francine Shapiro, who originated and developed EMDR therapy. So I sought out someone trained in EMDR.

Therapist Number Six AD lived nearby. After I tried to pour out all of our problems in forty-five minutes, he must have thought I was insane. Then he informed us that while he did have a certification in EMDR he no longer practiced it. Adios, Number Six!

Turns out there was another EMDR therapist living nearby. Soon after a nervous call to her office, I got a response from her husband, who was very nice, and now I had an appointment with Therapist Number Seven AD.

She was an attractive, stylish older woman, originally from South Africa, and an expert and international instructor in EMDR. Her office was located in a beautiful home. When we arrived for the first session, I drifted into a nervous collapse by this effort to make my marriage right, with the added duress of four months of illness. I had a lot to unload, but she was more interested in what Bruce had to say. He droned on and on about how he had earned money for college by freighting boxcars and any number of things while I was almost having a stroke right then and there. *Let's get to the point! WE need your help! What is this blathering all about?*

She asked if I was on meds and had a therapist. I answered affirmatively, though I was not on meds. That seemed to appease her. *Well, this isn't going well. Just lock me up in the asylum and wrap me in a straitjacket.*

Bruce never filled me in about his solo sessions with her, and I don't know whether he processed any of his childhood trauma, but for a while EMDR seemed to alleviate some of our misery. Hope was dashed again, however, as the year progressed and Bruce regressed. The latest small glimmer of light went out. I was the same broken record again, with Bruce being Mr. Innocent Nice Guy and me a woman who just imagines her problems. CADD is not giving me a break. Therapist Number Seven AD signed off on Bruce while I was in the throes of ongoing traumatic relationship syndrome.

We started with EMDR, we ended with EMDR, and in the end we succeeded only in spending half a fortune and going around in circles.

There was a foray with a Last Therapist AD (After Diagnosis), which ended as fast as it began. My daughter-in-law, who is a teacher, suggested a fellow in Milton, Delaware, who was often recommended by her school, and he worked with couples. I arrived armed with books about Asperger's, narcissism, EMDR, and other trauma therapies, which he refused to look at because, he said, "That's not the science I use."

We stared at each other from across the room in a long impasse, until I gathered up my collection and left.

That was not the most distressing thing about that day: June 4, 2015. It was the sad day that Beau Biden was to lie in state at the Delaware State Capitol. Since we were already halfway to Dover, we met up with Reid and our grandson Ethan to watch the mile-long motorcade and pay our respects. I saw then-Vice President Biden's solemn face in the window of a limousine as we stood with other bystanders on the highway, offering a salute with tears in my eyes.

We watched the casket being carried to the statehouse but did not stand in the receiving line, open to the public, because Ethan was too young. Beau was a great attorney general and would have elevated to high levels of government service. His early demise is a terrible tragedy.

Chapter 33

WASP STINGS

By June of 2009, I knew not only how my home had made me sick but why Bruce drove me crazy: mold and Asperger's. In our "for better or worse" marriage, the worsts were getting the better of our betters.

A couple of wedding invitations and a chance to visit Bruce's friend in Washington gave us a reason to escape these miseries. We fired up the RV for a Montana wedding and a gander at the Canadian Rockies. I was hale and happy at the first wedding, but I began to flag when we visited with Bruce's buddy in Spokane. By the time we reached Lake Louise in Banff, I was anxious, nauseated, and growing a rash on my torso. *Maybe the water in the RV is bad,* I thought. *Maybe I'm just tired; maybe the mold sickness is flaring.* After taking a shower and laying out my evening outfit on the bed, I did not have the strength to dress for dinner. While I crashed in bed, Bruce made one of his forays into town and bought me jewelry made by a local craftsman. Something was wrong. I was in the RV bed when I should have been dining at a cute upscale restaurant. By the time we finished with Canada and made it to my nephew's wedding in Minnesota, I was fatigued, inflamed, and buzzing with toxic reactions.

Back in Delaware three weeks later, the doctor said it was an allergic reaction. It was still a mystery, but I got a little better. In September, the same ailments reappeared, so I headed back to the doctor: same diagnosis without an answer. Then one night my eyes sprang open when I remembered how I had been stung by a wasp while picking flowers in my garden before the trip and, two months later, I had sat on a yellow jacket riding with me in my golf cart. I had been stung in the thigh, but I had finished the round and forgotten about it. I read up on wasp stings and found that they can cause serum sickness, a flu-like illness due to an overreaction in the immune system.

In November, while chatting on the phone with Reid, I slid open the door to our back deck and got stung again, right under my wedding ring. This time it was by a paper wasp. I could feel the venom burning in my veins as it traveled up my arm like an injection of Tabasco sauce. *Uh-oh, this can't be good.* It wasn't good for the wasp, either, crunched and dead at my feet. I took some Benadryl, but it was like pouring a bucket of water on a forest fire.

A week later, I had so many things wrong with my brain and body that I made a list to take to Dr. Ali in New York City. Without hesitation, he told me my immune system had gone overboard, but I left his office without any real idea of what to do to end this reaction.

With so much wrong with my brain and body, I got out of bed only to visit a parade of "ologists" of one sort or another. I saw a rheumatologist who sent me to a hematologist. He sent me for an onerous extended phlebotomy, during which they drew blood every few minutes for an hour. At least they had a video of a waterfall for me to watch to calm my nerves. They ruled out a severe blood disease. *Right, but what* is *wrong, for Chrissake?*

I am still shocked that a dermatologist I consulted did not pick up that my skin eruptions might be due to detox system overload and venom trying to escape through my skin as a last resort, creating sores, redness, itching, and burning so intense I could hardly sleep. I looked like I had hiked naked through brambles, poison ivy, and poison oak. Even after two years of tests by a functional doctor in California, who explained that my liver was not converting water-soluble toxins to fat-soluble toxins capable of washing out of my body, the dermatologist denied my experience. "That's a good story," he said.

Utterly fatigued and in a brain fog, I knitted, but I had to rest after each row of slips and purls. I could not even decipher the needle sizes spelled out in the pattern. I enlisted Bruce as my guide dog for excursions to the craft store. Bruce moved to an upstairs bedroom since I was too ill to have him in bed with me. Sometimes I did not think I would make it through the night. My mother-in-law gave us a brass bell as a souvenir from her cruise, and I propped it up next to the bed to alert Bruce if I felt I was going into a crisis. I never called him, but I wonder if he might have slept through my clanging anyway.

I had little appetite, so I ate a lot of soup. Bruce would carry soup to my bedside on a tray, but after repeatedly scalding my tongue, I learned to sit there stirring it until it cooled. I asked Bruce not to make it so damn hot, but it never sunk in. When talking to an aspie, I understood later, you have to be very specific: *precisely seventy degrees, please.*

One afternoon, he carried the bowl of soup on a blue translucent tray. He was naked, his genitals swinging under the tray and tinged with its blue color. He set the steaming soup down and walked off, bare butt bidding me toodle-loo. Sometimes things are so crazy that they are not crazy. *Please get me out of this place,* I thought, shaking my head and shutting my eyes. *I am trapped with an aspie and too weak to find professional help. How long will I have to endure this unreal reality?*

People thought I was lucky to have an advocate in Bruce, but Bruce was anything but, as I had to plead my own case. When a friend gave me the names of mold-literate doctors in Arizona and California, Bruce dillydallied before finally calling them. I learned that my immune system was stuck in permanent overdrive after having tried to fend off mold for seventeen years. My liver, gallbladder, and lymph nodes were congested, and I could not detoxify normally.

Then I discovered a scummy white growth on my tongue. Thrush, said my regular doctor, who prescribed a sublingual tablet. As I was trying to explain my symptoms, he suddenly slapped his laptop shut and told me I needed a brain doctor. I looked at him quizzically. He said, "You know, a psychiatrist."

I found something better for me than a shrink: Robert S. Ivker's *Sinus Survival: The Holistic Medical Treatment for Allergies, Colds, and Sinusitis* (2000). From this resource, I discovered I had candida albicans, a severe yeast infection that disrupts the healthy gut flora and creates general misery and a miscellany of symptoms. An allergy test later confirmed it, and my years of antibiotics created it.

To kill yeast and balance my gut, I had to avoid all sweets and any food such as bread, pasta, white rice, and potatoes that turn into sugar in the body. Worst of all, any fermented food, including wine, was entirely verboten. If I cheated on this diet, I got sicker. People thought I was on a weight-loss diet.

All through the winter of 2010, I walked in darkness. I would trudge out to our state park in the gray winter light and slog through snowy paths by the river, deep snow seeping into my old black winter boots. My weathered tan coat and corduroy pants blended like deer hide into the leafless woods. The thermometer seemed to always read twenty-eight degrees. I did not worry about rapists, deer hunters, or the cougars occasionally seen stalking the deep woods in the park. When a ray of sun appeared through the trees, I looked upward and repeated, "Healing light in, all that does not serve me out."

By this point, friends and family had decided I was merely depressed. They pleaded with me to take an antidepressant. They offered up gifts of lavender, stress-relieving items, and potions. They believed that it must be in my mind, just as the mold and Bruce's being off-kilter had to have been in my mind. Here I was again, alone in another situation where I was not being believed.

I just wanted to make it to New York City in April for the birth of my grandson. The day was creeping up too fast, and I was recovering too slowly.

Luckily, I had enough strength for the drive to the New York City hospital for my daughter's C-section. One of the most wonderful moments of my life was when my son-in-law burst through the double doors, his PPE all askew, with the moments-old baby boy in his cart. "Look at our son!" Poor Sally was getting stitched up while we were celebrating.

Every day was such a challenge that I had been thinking of ending my miserable existence. Toxins zooming around my brain did not help with rational thought. I planned to hide in a specific spot in the woods, drink a bottle of white wine, and eat apple pie à la mode, carrot cake, and a box of chocolates before checking out. The only problem was, I couldn't figure out how to check out. *Maybe I should just take a Caribbean cruise.*

While trapped in my bedroom during this illness, I listened to radio shows on my iPod and became acquainted with their hosts. In February of 2011, several of these radio personalities, activists, and politicians, including Mike Farrell, known as BJ in *Mash*, and his wife, Shelley Fabrares, plus Robert F. Kennedy Jr., were to be guests on a Progressive Voices cruise. I wanted to meet these people and hear them speak. When the cruise was scheduled to launch, however, Bruce would be away at Lake Placid, New York, skating with his synchronized skating team. But I would not give up on this cruise just because Bruce's calendar was perpetually jammed.

We went to a local travel agent, and she said it would be impossible for Bruce to join the cruise somewhere mid-cruise after his skating event had concluded. Instead of trying to find a solution, Bruce grinned and squirmed with his hands between his knees: aw, shucks. *What is this new weirdness?* I brought it up later. "She always flirts," he claimed, shifting the blame. Bruce does tend to mirror others' behavior, but if he thought she had been flirting, he had missed the mark this time. I had to pull him out of there by his ear—figuratively speaking—although we still had not figured out how to get him on this cruise.

Fortunately, I found a puddle jumper that could fly Bruce out of San Juan to the Turks and Caicos Islands, where the ship would be docked. He could not make reservations to catch the flight; he just had to show up.

Things were looking up. I managed to pack my summer clothes between rests in bed, but then I took a downturn. *I can't do this. I'm too weak.* I unpacked my clothes, hauled them back up to the attic, and collapsed in my sickbed. A few days later, I heard actor, musician, and radio host Hal Sparks with David Bender, the activist and radio host of *Politically Correct*, talking about flying down together for the cruise. I knew I just had to go, come hell or high water. Back up the stairs I lumbered, dragged my clothes back down, tossed them in a suitcase, and had Reid drive me to the airport to catch the plane for Fort Lauderdale. The only glitch after I got to Fort Lauderdale was the long wait for a hotel shuttle while the last drop of energy drained from my tank. I was afraid I would end up flat on the sidewalk.

When I checked in at the port the next morning, I felt like Wolf Girl coming out of the woods, not having seen any friends or socialized for a year. Tears streamed down my face as I walked up the gangplank, hoping my sunglasses hid my emotional display, and I kept my head low. Rooms were not yet available, so I found a pool, sat on a long cement bench, and proceeded to glance around. *Is that radio host Mike Malloy and activist David Bender at the bar?* They wandered over to where I was seated, and I overheard a political comment. It's them!

I inched over and said, "I am with the Progressive Voices Seminar. Are you Mike Malloy and David Bender?"

"Yes," they chimed in, "welcome to the cruise."

A server brought them complimentary champagne, and Mike offered his flute to me, which I accepted. *Game on! I am here, but will Bruce make it to the ship?*

At the meet and greet night, I met most of the speakers and, best of all, a woman who popped out of the opposite elevator simultaneously with me. We compared name tags and saw we were both in the Progressive Voices function. Her name was Gerry Bichovsky, from Chelsea in New York City, a beautiful, smart, world-traveled, and artsy woman who has become a dear friend to Bruce and me. When I told her my husband was coming, she thought that Bruce must be a delusion. Can you imagine I had a husband who would actually show up on the cruise ship in the middle of the ocean?

Bobby Kennedy's speech on climate change was the highlight of the trip. He had the most beautiful blue eyes. After the cruise, I heard a favorite host on the radio say the same thing about his eyes, and I thought to myself, *I know. I saw them, up close from the front row.* After Bobby spoke, I practically attacked him to get him to autograph his book *Crimes Against Nature*. In my down times, I open the book and am brightened by his autograph: "To April, Love Bobby." *LOVE Bobby!*

I had been cruising solo with this crowd when Bruce texted a picture of himself in a barbershop in Lake Placid, getting his beard shaved off. He had worn it to skate in character for a performance of *Fiddler on the Roof*. Then, the day before his arrival date, he texted, "Driving from Lake Placid to Newark Airport in a blizzard. Hope I make it." And now I wondered, *Has Bruce made it to Newark Airport in time for his flight to San Juan? Has he managed to catch the puddle jumper to Turks and Caicos where we will dock?*

As people were leaving the ship for some beach time, I looked down four floors from my veranda, which by some chance overlooked the loading area. Lo and behold, there was Bruce in his green-and-white flower print Tommy Bahama shirt, dragging his suitcase down the long dock and weaving through the passengers. *He's here! He's here!* I leaned over the veranda and yelled, "Bruce! BRUCE! Bruce!" as loud as I could, and finally he looked up. We both waved and took pictures of each other.

It was a long wait by the elevator, but when the doors opened, he rushed over to me, gave me a hug and kiss, and we laughed as he twirled me around in his arms—

No, that scene did not happen, not in my aspie world. When Bruce exited the elevator, he dropped his suitcase and said, "I told you I would make it." No hug.

I muttered, "Let me show you around the ship."

Still, he made it. Together Bruce and I engaged in the seminars, were credited as top conversationalists at the dinner tables, and had a ball hobnobbing with celebrity speakers. Onboard, we celebrated Bruce's sixty-fifth birthday, but the festivities were marred with news that on that very day, his favorite cousin, Judy from the Ohio crowd, had passed away.

Chapter 34

FIGHTS

While Bruce and I had our ups and downs, when we were down, the highs seemed like brief vacations from unrelenting brawls that drained me of energy, sanity, and hope. I never imagined I would have such horrible fights with a spouse, or with any person, for that matter. I know that spats and disputes are bound to happen in any marriage. But other couples fight about something tangible: an affair, physical abuse, too much time drinking at bars. Or, as my mom always told me, marital fights generally center around sex, money, and kids. In my case, something intangible would suck me into our arguments like quicksand, until I couldn't pull myself out. It was so foreign to anything that I had experienced as a child.

Deliberately or not, Bruce would goad or needle me until I took the bait. I would then try to reason with him—explain, explain, and explain whatever situation we were in using reason, examples, and analogies—but nothing ever worked. It seemed that he instinctively knew how to drive me nuts. Once the row was on, the most hurtful bile would spew from his lips. When I would try to imitate his words, I couldn't do it; it was so unnatural for me. Weirdly, he would sit in his chair, his body immobile and expression blank, while his lips moved autonomously like pieholes in a *South Park* character. Is this the way a movie director would play a fight scene? Who sits like a manikin to argue? Not me; I stomped and strutted around like a raging bull.

Once reason failed, I started hurling objects at Bruce, grabbing the closest things I could get my hands on. I slung framed pictures, couch pillows, and thick magazines. When I saw him unfazed by my attacks, I slammed and kicked doors and smashed kitchen utensils on the countertop until there were so many holes, it looked like the craters on the moon. By now, I was shouting obscenities and limping because of a foot I'd injured kicking a kitchen cabinet. Such fits wrecked a lot of things, especially my own health and well-being.

The mayhem usually erupted around dinner time because that was when the man was actually home. The simple act of cooking broccoli could be contentious, a real hurdle in marital relationships, as I have heard from *actually nobody*. Bruce liked to help prepare vegetables for dinner, which was fine with me, as I could be in another room on the computer or reading or out on the patio listening to the radio. But he could never figure out that some vegetables, like green beans or beets, need a lot of boiling or steaming, while frozen and cruciferous vegetables require only a very short time in the pot. No matter how many times I explained to Bruce what cruciferous vegetables are, he did not get it. You would think he was trying to learn the secrets of the universe. And often he would want to boil more than one at once. *Bruce, too much cabbage, cauliflower, and brussels sprouts in one meal will give you gas!*

The following incident illustrates our marital difficulties over vegetables. It seemed that we were having a normal evening. If I had known whatever I said or did would set him off, I would not have said it. This freakish folderol would have made a good scene in a telenovela on Univision.

I was listening to my radio show on my iPhone when Bruce asked, "Do you want me to prepare the vegetable for dinner?"

"Okay," I replied and went back to my show. I heard the sounds of Bruce opening and closing the refrigerator, running the tap, and clinking the saucepan on the stove. Then he went back to his TV.

After a few minutes, I heard the water at a full, bubbling boil and inquired, "Did you check the temperature? I hear it boiling."

"I'll turn it down."

After he settled back in front of the boob tube, the water was still at a broccoli-mushing boil. "Bruce, I can hear it still boiling."

"I turned it down."

"It's boiling too hard. You have to turn it down to low and see if it is still boiling hard. We have a new stove, and it is hotter than the other one. If it is boiling, it is on too high. You know, bubbles in the water."

"You cook it, then."

At this point, I should have realized that this conversation had veered off the rails, but I forged ahead: "All you have to do is look at the water and see if it is still boiling."

"I don't care how it is cooked."

"I've said this a hundred times. All the enzymes and vitamins will be boiled out." I felt that more than the broccoli was about to boil over and tried to cool things a bit. "It's okay, just check to see if it is boiling."

"Just because you like it another way doesn't mean it is right. Don't worry about it!"

"You are not supposed to boil the heck out of vegetables."

"I am not going to eat it anyway, and besides, you always criticize me," he snapped. Then he added, "We don't have a real marriage, anyway."

Let the games begin! Time for Bruce to employ his word salad and gaslighting skills. There is no logic, no reasoning, no explaining, and no resolution involved in these little family chats, which only succeed in making me act like a raving maniac. Or I could suck it up and eat broccoli mush.

We had a lot of fights in the basement or garage, because that's where Bruce would try to escape from me. Sometimes he went into a dark bedroom and lay down, staring at the ceiling, as unresponsive as a corpse. Mostly, he disappeared by roaring out of the driveway, only to creep back silently late at night. I would chase after him, yelling, "Fuck you, fuck you!" over and over, using a word that I had formerly found offensive and avoided, before all the stress disordered my sense of propriety. If only I had known a more terrible expletive, I would have used it. "Stop, you rude bastard!" I would yell. "If you walk out on me, DO NOT COME BACK!"

We must have been prime-time entertainment for the neighbors. Why watch a movie when the Hubbards' reality TV show was playing in their driveway? What did they think the time that Bruce bolted from the house after another of his provocations right before dinner, with me in hot pursuit? As he gained some distance from me—although we both could really run—I suddenly realized that I was armed with a box of frozen black bean and rice veggie burgers. I pulled the first frosted grenade from the box and fired away, thumping Bruce on the back of his head with the first try, but he turned around to deflect the second with his forearm just before it bopped him on the noggin. *Damn!* I grabbed another veggie burger from the box and wound up for a great Roger Clemens pitch, but I stopped myself mid-throw as the thought flashed through my mind: *This is my dinner!* So I gave up the chase and went inside, leaving pieces of veggie burger for the squirrels and birds while Bruce disappeared into the night.

My energy wasted, my sleep patterns disrupted, my adrenals overtaxed, and my nerves frayed like worn-out broom straws, it is a wonder that I didn't have a heart attack or stroke. I've read studies that for five hours after enduring intense stress a person is at a higher risk of both. My blood pressure and heart rate were often in the stratosphere. It's a good thing I am a runner, or I would have keeled over. I could feel my arteries gumming up with cholesterol and my elevated blood sugar fueling my fungal yeast disease. I might as well have been chasing a robber while eating a Mars Bar. Stress from ongoing traumatic relationship syndrome was flooding my body with inflammatory cytokines and stress hormones.

After our big rows, I would haul my shaking body into the bedroom and look for tranquilizers or sleeping pills. *Must be something here*, I would think, rummaging through the medicine cabinet. Hoping to relax a little, I would gulp down chamomile tea and herbal supplements like passionflower, lemon balm, kava kava, and valerian root.

In bed, I would lie on my back and repeat affirmations: *I am a calm, relaxed, fulfilled, and healthy person! I AM A CALM, RELAXED, FULFILLED, AND HEALTHY PERSON!! I am a calm, relaxed, fulfilled, and healthy person. I am breathing in love and light and breathing out all that does not serve me. Peace and serenity surround me at all times. I am a PEACEFUL PERSON!!* I had to count breaths for a long time to get my heart rate down. Sleep would elude me for days after a fight, even with a sleeping pill.

Hopelessness, anger, frustration, and confusion kept swirling through my brain. Plans to get out of the marriage would occupy my thoughts deep into the night. To stop my whirling brain, I started buying meditation, healing, sleep, and hypnotic CDs: *Sleep Deep. Sleep Now. Get Better Sleep. End Insomnia and Sleep Deeply. I Sleep, Sleep, Sleep Soundly Now. A Time for Sleep. Sleep Easy. Seeking Sleep. Relax. Release and Dream On. Heal Your Body. Inner Peace and Healing.* I can't sleep today without listening to a CD drawn from the voluminous collection boxed up by my bed or viewing meditation and relaxation videos on my iPhone.

And Bruce? He slept like a baby and never missed one minute of shut-eye. The next morning he would not remember what the fight had been about, and he would be in a generally happy mood, except for the slight annoyance of repairing holes in the door and pasting together vases and picture frames. How dare he be cheerful and upbeat? *Cheerful? How about a dozen red roses or divorce court?*

Instead of blood, Bruce sucked out my energy, like an energy vampire. He was full, and I was depleted. He had succeeded in releasing his built-up tension and restoring his sense of well-being. He had cemented the barrier that he had felt cracking, and he was in control. He denies his intent, and perhaps it was subconscious, but we played the same scene over and over. He would be nice as pie after a fight, though the niceties never lasted. I was duped until the next time Bruce needed an energy transfusion. *Walk away* is the advice. *Walk away when your aspie gets antagonistic.* It took me years to understand that I could not win under any circumstance. I was a fool to ride this merry-go-round and couldn't seem to jump off.

I did not understand at the time that immediately after Bruce would melt down, his brain would shut off, like the time he argued doggedly that we had not had quinoa for dinner the night before. He had been confusing quinoa with amaranth, which he never eats. When he would continue arguing (after his brain had shut off), he would have no idea what the topic was, like a person going blank during an exam. I could have been speaking Chinese; he was unable to process my words. What would start with his defensiveness would end with a huge fight, and then be forgotten by Bruce. He could go on with his day full of energy and calm while I felt exhausted and lost.

Now, I will not fight, at least not like that, because I don't want to die. I just want to heal my adrenals. Chronic emotional stress is one of the main causes of serious illnesses. I imposed a rule that if Bruce gets me upset, he has to pack his bag and leave for at least three days. Maybe I should kick him out for good. Who knows if that will be the final solution?

So far it has not been. Bruce always comes back, and I'm always too weak and worn out to resist. One time I swore to him that I was leaving. He must have believed it, because he appeared at my car window just when I was about to go into my therapist's office and stuck a letter in my face. He convinced me to give him another chance. As much as the words seemed loving, I realize now that it was only love bombing; he did not ever say he was sorry. And he couldn't change. Everything would be the same, and I was sucked back in. Psychologists who study narcissism call it *hoovering*, named for the Hoover vacuum cleaner brand.

I tried several times to end the marriage. When divorce would begin to feel possible, I would feel a huge weight lifted from my being. I did not know how I would do it, but I remember walking in our beautiful state park after a snowfall, grabbing a big stick, and writing "I AM FREE" over and over again in the newly fallen snow. Another time, I ran along the river in the same park, thinking, *This is really it; I will not have to endure this marriage anymore*. I ran and ran like Forrest Gump. I ran with my arms in the air. I twirled and ran, inhaling the light from the sun into my being and exhaling misery and suffering.

Chapter 35

FORTIETH ANNIVERSARY

By our fortieth wedding anniversary, Bruce and I had lived for two years with Bruce's diagnosis of high-functioning autism, which gave me some hope for our marriage. It is staggering how much things fell apart between anniversaries forty and fifty.

Although I was still recovering from my 2010 reaction to the wasp venom—which overloaded my (already imbalanced) gut, immune system, and detoxification pathways—I planned a golf trip to Copake Country Club in Hudson, New York. I was soldiering on the best I could. Besides, it would have been a shame to spend our fortieth anniversary lying around the house.

The golf course overlooking Copake Lake was scenic and in excellent condition. We were paired with a grandfather and grandson from New York City, which added levity, competition, and companionship to the round. That evening, a couple from Ireland wanted the usual tour of our RV and suggested that we join them for more golf, but I had to fabricate some excuse because of exhaustion. The on-site restaurant was upscale. As usual, we chose outside seating with a view of the course and were entertained by the golfers teeing off from the first hole. Bruce gave me a lovely ring, one with flowing ribs of gold cradling a ruby.

The next day, the town of Hudson was holding its annual gay pride parade, so after our anniversary lunch at an eclectic café, we joined the spectators. It was a lot of fun, especially watching the drag queens dancing at the park at the end of the parade route. It seemed like the whole town joined in the movin' and groovin'.

As we strolled back down the picturesque main street, we encountered two men in gowns sitting outside a restaurant and sipping beers. Even in my weakest moments I was able to move my mouth, so I said, "You guys look lovely!"

"Why, thank you," one replied, grinning ear-to-ear.

"Guess what?" I added. "It's our fortieth anniversary!"

"Fantastic! Come sit down!"

We made our way around the metal barriers, grabbed a couple of metal chairs, and ordered drinks, which they insisted on paying for in honor of the occasion.

One fellow was dressed in a hot-pink strapless gown with a beaded necklace hanging over his hairy upper chest. He sported gold sparkly sunglasses with wings spreading from the sides. The other fellow wore an off-the-shoulder, three-quarter-sleeved white satin wedding gown, with sunglasses and a pith helmet. They were straight but had decided to join in the festivities. They explained that one of their daughters had advised them where to purchase used gowns and they had hit pay dirt at the local thrift shop. While we were chatting, we were joined by the aforementioned fashion-savvy daughter and her boyfriend. It was a unique and memorable fortieth anniversary.

I did not anticipate the emotional deprivation that would weigh on me like a sack of nails over the next ten years. It should have been wonderful with both of us retired, but my adrenals slumped periodically. I'd rally, but by then our marriage had begun limping and then stayed lame. Bruce did not feel like the companion of our golden years that I longed for. He would be gone all day and almost every night. If he happened to be home and not jogging, golfing, working out at the track, or attending Delaware football games, he would be sitting in front of the TV glued to the news or sports. When I'd jog, I'd run the course and come home. When he would jog, he'd be gone all morning. When I'd go to the track, I'd do the workout and come right back. When he finished a workout, he would stay for a few beers and finally drag himself home at 8 p.m. If he had golf league at 5 p.m., he'd leave the house at 1:30 to get an extra nine holes in. A Delaware football game could start at 1 p.m., but he'd arrive at 10:30 a.m. to mingle beforehand and then would socialize after the game till the sun went down. I do not think he was trying to escape me but, rather, felt compelled to scrounge for supply. He could be married to Miss Universe or Nicole Kidman, and he would still be venturing out like Harrison Ford in *Raiders of the Lost Ark*.

I always ate dinner on the porch or poolside alone while listening to my favorite radio host, Norman Goldman, broadcasting out of California every night at six. Bruce had never been truly present, but now, with absolutely no distractions to direct my attention elsewhere, it was obvious to me that I was being ignored. He was self-absorbed in his own routine and had no ability or desire to change. This was for sure not the retirement I had pictured. *Let's go back to work so we can at least pretend we have a relationship.*

Thanks to my planning, we still went to road races, took RV trips, and dined with friends. Grandkids' birthdays, holidays, and the condo we owned in historic Brooklyn Heights offered some relief. We enjoyed some great days in that decade, but it wasn't enough. We tried to persevere, but the disappointments, frustrations, and heartbreaks added up faster than a Chinese abacus could flip beads. Asperger's syndrome can eat you up and spit you out. *How did I lose another decade?*

Chapter 36

NAME CHANGE

Our wedding and the women's movement arrived at the same time in 1970. When Bruce was in law school and I was involved in the Ohio NOW organization, I realized that I had made a mistake when I had changed my name to Bruce's when we married. I had never even liked the sound of April Hubbard, to boot.

My daughter says, "Flip it to switch it," and if it sounds weird, then it is...like Bruce Anderson. Why on Earth do we women give up our identity, as in the old days, from the father to the husband? I met one woman who decided to change her name from her married name but didn't go back to her maiden name because it was her father's. She chose "Rose" instead because she liked roses. It was entirely her own identity, and I thought it was wonderful.

When Reid was two years old and we were living in Toledo, Bruce, having no ego problems with me being a Hubbard or not, inserted a stenciled paper that said ANDERSON in an anniversary card as my gift, with instructions on how to make the change.

My mother-in-law was quite upset at the thought that I might change my name, and I wasn't too keen at that point not to have the same name as my children, although I witnessed name differences between mother and child all the time in the childcare business. So the idea settled somewhere in my memory bank to be withdrawn at a later date.

That date arrived when I sold my Mother Hubbard Child Care business. Yes, I sold out my beliefs for profit. People liked it that I was Mother Hubbard, *how clever*, and it sure was easier cashing checks at the bank when my name matched the name of my business. But, finally, in 2011, I was ready to make the change—mostly because the only time I cried at my daughter's wedding was when the newlywed couple was introduced as Sally and Bob!! Yay!! I always cover my ears when I hear "Mr. and Mrs. Joe Blow" or whatever. Did the woman get sucked into another identity universe? And to make it worse, she often has a career of her own.

Bruce helped me with the paperwork, but changing one's name is not an easy process. Not only is it costly, but notification of the name change must be placed in local papers to ensure that a person is not absconding with someone's money or a debtor trying to hide from authorities. I had no objection to my name change appearing in the paper, except for the gossip it might engender that I was getting divorced.

On the appointed day, Bruce and I went to the courthouse and sat down with a few souls sprinkled around in chairs. It looked like one couple was adopting a child, one woman was getting divorced, and the rest had their own reasons. I was called up first and opened the gate to the barrier that divided Your Honor from the rest of us lowly souls. He glared down at me and asked why I wanted to do this. I gave him a spiel about women keeping their own name and, with no response from him, added, "My daughter just got married, and she did not change her name." I was close to pleading at this point.

Finally, he said, "I can't see any reason to do this, but I can't see any reason not to." I wanted to smack him, but I didn't want to go to the hoosegow. He banged his gavel and pronounced, "Granted!"

As soon as I was on the other side of the gate, I pumped my fist in a YES! A woman came out later and told me how happy she was with my performance.

I had to go to the Social Security office to get a new card. The woman at the office kept repeating, "You are divorced." "No, I am not." "You are divorced." "No, I am not." Repeat ten times. She could not process this information. People still can't; I get all sorts of responses. A lot of women tell me their husbands would be too upset if they were to follow my example, and some hate their maiden names, but my Manhattan friend Gerry, who is in her eighties, just can't get it straight. Even though she is quite progressive in other areas, this is off her radar. All of her mail to me is addressed to April Anderson and Husband!

Chapter 37

MAJOR ASPERGATES

Major aspergates differ from mini and minor aspergates as much as train wrecks differ from fender benders.

I go temporarily insane over what Bruce does to my pretty roses. In the summer of 2019, Bruce was helping me cut back the deadheads on some drift roses we had planted at the front of our house so new blooms could grow, while pruning would have to wait until fall.

Bordering our driveway were taller pink knockout roses. I returned from errands the next day and found that Bruce had gotten it into his head to lop the tops off, as he had confused cutting deadheads with pruning, and there, scattered all over the driveway like tossed tissues, were my precious pink knockouts!

I freaked out, shaking and screaming. "Why did you do this?" I cried.

"I thought you wanted me to," he mewed meekly.

That's when I went totally, desperately, irrationally insane. I scraped up my poor decapitated roses from the asphalt and tried to mash them back onto the bushes. I ranted, I raved, I kicked, and I threw trowels, pots, and branches in frustration.

Another major aspergate involved our cats. When summer rolled around, we typically hired a lawn company to spray a "natural" concoction based on garlic to rid us of mosquitoes and ticks, and they didn't always warn us before I could hustle the cats inside and garlic fumes came up the side of the house. One golf league morning when I wouldn't be home, I reminded Bruce that the lawn company was coming and the cats must be inside when workers arrived. Unfortunately, he misunderstood my instruction, believing the cats could fend for themselves and escape when they heard the noise. Before long, he texted me that he was heading out, but nothing in his text told me the cats had not been brought inside. Meanwhile, the lawn guy came when our tiger cat Voter was asleep under the flowers, and she got soaked in spray.

I learned this only when a thunderstorm blew through and Voter, usually terrified of lightning, did not come inside for safety. I found her near dead, feverish, and unable to eat or drink for ten days. The vet thought she was a goner. I took her to his clinic every other day for fluids. Finally, she took a sip of water from the pool tarp and began to slowly recover. Only later did we learn that the incident had caused her to become nearly deaf. I had trusted Bruce to show some patience and watch over this production, and it almost cost us our pet's life, not to mention the thousand-dollar fee from the vet.

Sally was still a child when she won the school spelling bee and then the district bee. She went on to the state competition in Dover, the state capital. I reviewed the long list of words with her; once she spells a word, she never forgets it. We took a trip in the RV, and it was my turn to drive, so Bruce took a turn practicing the next words on the alphabetical list with Sally. Unfortunately, he neglected to go over the "s" words, one of which was "sauerkraut." Of course Sally got that word in an early round in Dover. She knew all the words other kids were given, but by the time her teacher had arrived to watch, Sally was out of the competition. I often ask people if they know how to spell "sauerkraut."

Bruce is inattentive when we are at the beach, shaking sand out of blankets and towels into the eyes of beachgoers downwind. I must always double-check that the beach umbrellas he puts up are secure and can't blow away. Bruce seems unaware when a breeze has kicked up and the canvas is flapping, snapping, and about to go airborne.

One day we met Sally and three-week-old baby Deven in Spring Lake, New Jersey, and were thrilled to be with her and the baby at the beach. We settled in with our blanket and chairs, and Bruce jabbed the umbrella into the sand. Then he and Sally walked down the beach to buy some food, leaving me with my sweet baby grandson, happily reclined in his carrier. For some unknown reason, I reached over to pick him up, and a split second later, a gust of wind whipped the umbrella out of the sand, bashing the carrier. I am certain Deven would have been severely injured if not killed had I not just taken him out. I was now frantic, holding the baby and screaming for Bruce and Sally, now out of earshot, while the umbrella tumbled down the beach. Some beachgoers grabbed it and brought it back. Bruce showed no emotion when I told him what had happened, even though I was shaking and ill from shock and embarrassment.

In 1999, I was excited to receive the Most Improved Runner Award from Pike Creek Valley Running Club, completing my first ten-miler a few weeks before. Usually a friend or spouse of the person receiving an award would write a piece for the dinner program about the recipient's accomplishments. Unbeknownst to me, Bruce was given this task, which was a recipe for disaster.

On the ride home from the banquet, I was happily balancing the beautiful green and gold wooden plaque on my lap when I read the bio he had written. I said tentatively, "Bruce, I don't see the 10K's from the Newark Turkey Trot and Wilmington Thanksgiving races—the ones you have done for ten years and that I finally ran instead of the 5Ks." Sensing impending doom, he did not utter a word. I began to get anxious. "The Turkey Trot is hard and hilly, but my personal record? Why would you list the Turtle Strut in Myrtle Beach as a credit? That was my first 10K and practice to see if I could do the distance. I was reading historical markers in front of the old beach cottages, for crying out loud! You listed my worst time, not my best!" He had to pick TURTLE strut. Doing the races meant a lot to me but apparently not to Bruce. *How can he be so self-involved that he cannot remember races that we did together?* Before the banquet, he did ask me some random race questions, but he obviously didn't process the answers. Since the Turkey Trot course is a block from my street, I have run it often in races and training, forever reminded of this slight, which Bruce has never been able to explain.

Another time we skied at Mount Ascutney, where we parked in a lot beside one of the ski runs. Bruce went to the RV for his peanut butter and baloney sandwich and left the door open. He never likes to close car or RV doors, preferring to let the cold air and gas fumes inside. Bebo, our part-German shepherd who loves the snow, took off, gallivanting near the run as I watched helplessly from the lift. He could have been killed or injured, as the bottom is not visible to a skier flying down the hill, who could have been hurt as well. I yelled hysterically to Bruce in a futile attempt for him to hear me. Life seemed to move in slow motion as I watched the impending doom. Finally, I was freed by the lift and skied down to the parking lot just as Bruce finally noticed the dog was missing and got him back inside. My nerves had taken a big hit, while Bruce calmly sipped his beer.

Bruce erected a wire fence around our vegetable garden, but he neglected to remove or cover the sharp prongs buried where he had cut the gate, and I got a nasty puncture wound through my sandals. I was prescribed strong antibiotics that gave me stomach aches, damaged my gut flora, and escalated my yeast problems. For a week, I sat in bed with my foot elevated to avoid a blood infection, and for several more weeks, I limped around. On the brighter side, on the golf course

I got to ride in a golf cart with a red flag, indicating that I was handicapped and therefore allowed to park near the green.

My dad's eightieth birthday was July 4, 1999. I was ill from the mold, yet I did not know then why I was sick, so I was anxious and in a bad state of mind. We invited a lot of people to the bash, and I was worried that I wouldn't have the energy to go through with the party. Bruce said he would help and not to worry, as I could just "whistle" when I needed him. It seemed a goofy thing to say, but it gave me the courage that I could host this celebration, which would be particularly difficult since we were setting up outdoors by the pool and I would need to make repeated trips to the kitchen up the long flight of stairs.

Dad bought a top-line steak filet for $200 and gave us explicit instructions on how to cook it, emphasizing that it had to be taken out of the freezer and warmed up for an hour before putting it on the grill. While Dad was opening gifts, I asked Bruce to start on the meat. He kept ignoring me as he drank beer and socialized.

I said, "What about whistling if I needed you?"

He made fun of me in front of a couple of guy friends. He insinuated that I was nagging and said he would do it when he wanted, that he knew what he was doing. I remember it was a nasty comment, and I felt the same fear as I had years prior at the Rathbun Ruckus in Toledo. All the women climbed up to the kitchen and helped me put out the buffet food, which was a feast, but when Bruce brought up the meat, it was too rare because he had not started it on time. He put it back on the grill, and we had to clear the table, cover food, and either put perishables in the refrigerator or keep them warm in the oven.

Again we organized the buffet and Bruce brought up the meat, which was still too rare, so we had to repeat the whole production. I was upset with the party getting screwed up and ready to collapse from stress and exhaustion. We finally ate, much later than planned, and set off the fireworks.

The next day, I found the baked bean casserole that Dad had prepared still in the microwave; it was one of his specialties. I was heartbroken that it had not been served and had gone bad to boot, but I had been too tired to remember it. Bruce had completely let me down with no empathy regarding my health or diligence as a good host. I went to bed feeling alone and discouraged at his rude behavior.

We entertained a lot, but there were other times when things went south. At one backyard cookout, Bruce stayed at the horseshoe pit or otherwise occupied, so our neighbor Harmon stepped in and cooked the sausages on the grill. He seemed to know I needed help, and he was probably eager to eat!

The last dinner party we had at Amaranth, I wanted it to be special. I worked hard on the menu, table settings, and floral centerpiece. I reminded Bruce that I needed him to help in the kitchen since it is not the most organized place in the world. At the end of the main course, Bruce refused to get up off his butt at the end of the table, so one of the husbands, realizing that I needed help, pitched in to clear the dishes and serve coffee and dessert, exactly the scenario I had been trying to avoid. Bruce's excuse later was that he had been in a conversation, but again he had ignored my wishes when I had trusted him not to aspergate me. I have no idea why I persist in entertaining, but I guess most of the time it worked out.

Once when we were visiting Bruce's good friend in Washington State, I warned him not to mention politics since we were not on the same page as his friend's wife. We spent a pleasant couple of days golfing, dining, shopping, and touring their lovely home and neighborhood before Bruce casually blurted out a political remark. I could've strangled him as he sat in front of me in the car. His comment had undone my careful tiptoeing around politics and ended my enjoyment of the things our friend's wife and I have in common. *What was he thinking?* The dam burst, and the gal and I got into a heated discussion, disrupting our nice visit. The two guys jumped out of the car to hide in the underbrush.

We loosely adhere to the common idea that a man's work is the tool shop, garage, and basement while a woman's work is in the finer rooms in the house. But this plan often gets muddled, especially when the tool shop, garage, and basement are neglected and become woman's work.

Our garage was under the house. The steps to the landing for the back entrance were stained and dirty, with cobwebs peeking out beneath the risers. I thought a quick wash was in order, so I asked Bruce if he would do it. While I prepared dinner, Bruce busily worked in the garage. No arguments or hassles. Smooth sailing for once.

After dinner, I got changed for bed when I heard a loud yell and terrible crash coming from the direction of the garage. I raced to the stairway landing, and there was Bruce lying face down on the cement floor, one arm bent to his forehead, broken glasses in hand, the other arm by his side. One leg was bent, too, with the other straight. I pictured a yellow chalk line drawn around his body, as in a crime scene. Blood was seeping out of his head, but he had moaned, so I knew he wasn't dead. Next to him was the large brown plastic trash can that usually sat at the top of the landing, with recycled magazines and newspapers strewn all over him and the garage floor. The strange, colorful scene looked like a Jackson Pollock painting.

"Oh my God! Are you okay? I am going to call an ambula—aaah! Help!" I bumped and slid on my butt down the stairs and crashed to the floor next to him, my pink-and-yellow nightgown covered in something gray and sticky. *Now who is going to call the damn ambulance?*

Still lying on the floor, Bruce mumbled, "I forgot I painted the stairs."

Oh, that little Asperger's and memory thing. "You PAINTED the stairs!" I yelled. "Why couldn't you just clean them like I asked?"

"I grabbed the trash can to try and break my fall," he muttered.

"Is it that hard to just clean the stairs? They didn't even need painting!" I said as I picked up copies of *Newsweek, Ms.* magazine, *Golf Digest,* and our daily newspaper from his body.

The blood was coming from a cut caused by Bruce's glasses, but he never got any medical attention. My nightgown was ruined. The stairs had to be repainted, and our kids said it was hilarious, "after we knew you guys were okay."

Bruce's Maintenancemobile had survived many a repair by duct-taping random parts that barely held together. It served its purpose: carrying tools and supplies out to rental properties and the Mother Hubbard Daycare centers. Most Sundays Bruce took off alone, blaring his polka music on a radio show (which reminded him that he had once danced the polka). Sometimes I could not avoid joining him in the car, so I suffocated on musty dust and got bruised by shot shocks.

We looked like Ma and Pa Kettle in that thing. I thought of plastering the back window with a sticker: "My other car is a Cadillac," which was true. One morning we bounced over a rutted shoulder to buy a watermelon from a farmer selling produce. Apparently we looked so poverty-stricken that the guy felt sorry for us and insisted we take one at no charge.

Often the rusty seatbelts wouldn't hook. One time Bruce took a hard left, and I slid across the cracked fake leather seat and toward the door, which popped open. I was nearly dumped out onto the highway. My fingers clawed at a piece of torn fabric, holding it like a rock climber grabbing a crevice, and thus I was saved from a dire aspergate.

When the old Chevy was hauled off for parts, our neighbors mourned with us.

The new deck of our renovated home on Amaranth needed cleaning—a simple wipe down. I heard water blasting and splashing and looked out the back door to find Bruce power washing it. Quickly, I read the manufacturer's online instructions for deck care, which clearly stated there was to be absolutely NO power washing on composite material such as what our deck was made of. Too late: the $30,000 deck had lost its rich brown tone, it was now flecked everywhere with tiny white splotches, and I was disconsolate.

Pool care—to introduce another aspergate—is not Bruce's forte. At Amaranth, our pool had been turbid for two years. Bugs floated on the surface, and it took me a half hour to scoop them off. Since we had had the pool for many years without having previously experienced this problem, I suspected something was wrong. Bruce thinks problems will disappear by themselves, and he did not want to have the deck dug up. When we spent time at a friend's pool, I saw that their water was crystal clear, and I asked Bruce why our pool did not look like theirs. Finally, he hired a pool company that discovered a pipe from the filter to the pool had been broken at a ninety-degree angle, so all the bugs and muck had been accumulating without filtration for two years. Yuck! I felt terrible about how many kids or other swimmers like me could have gotten sick because of this.

Our eighty-five-year-old friend, Gerry, who lived in Manhattan, came to Delaware for the first time. I planned a perfect weekend: appetizing dinners, sightseeing, and enjoyment by our pool and yard. Bruce prepared his pancake specialty, something he had done perfectly for forty-seven years. As we dug into each pancake, we found a reservoir of raw batter. How had this happened? Was this just a glitch that had popped up with his pancake-making skills? We didn't get our hearty breakfast.

That afternoon, after more sightseeing, Gerry and I had time to relax, so I convinced her to don her bathing suit and sun hat and come to the pool. I had been preoccupied with other arrangements and did not notice that the water was not clear. Gerry decided to try the water, so she walked down the steps and into the pool, swirling the water with her arms. At that moment, the pool filter went off, and the skimmers opened up, jettisoning the day's debris. Three dead frogs floated by with their gross, white bellies turned up to the sky. I usually catch frogs, snakes, and bugs without issue, but I was horrified that this city woman had been exposed to these amphibian cadavers. Bruce was on the golf course, so I scooped them out, but the swim had been ruined.

A few days passed, and the pool guy informed us that the cleaning unit—coincidentally called a "frog"—had not been changed as needed and was covered with sediment. Bruce had assumed that it lasted all summer. Reid was astounded at the condition of the filter. The pool guy advised that we not let our grandson in the pool, or he might get an ear infection. Too late again: he already had one.

Without any forethought, we picked bike week in Daytona to take a travel trailer trip to Florida. The plan was to go to the Arnold Palmer golf tournament in Orlando and then visit my cousin Lynda, our friends Carole and Ted, and other friends scattered around the state during the winter. Bruce had booked the lodgings for the RV. Exhausted by the drive, we arrived at a campground packed with a beer-drinking, leather-wearing, boisterous, tattooed, and *frightening* crowd of bikers. I couldn't believe the campground owner had even taken our reservation. I convinced Bruce not to stop and talk to the owners but to get away fast, which wasn't easy, as the road was blocked by Harleys and their drunken riders.

Some miles away, we parked in a church parking lot. I took a phone call from Reid, so I was distracted while Bruce called other campgrounds. I told him, "Ask them if they have bikers!" We drove another forty-five minutes to a fairground with some campsites. After the long process of registering, we were finally being escorted to our site when a company of woolly bikers roared in.

"What did you say to the people in the office?" I asked Bruce.

"I asked if it was quiet."

"Why didn't you ask if there were bikers?"

The guy escorting us got angry and grumbled, "These are good people."

"I smoke marijuana," I inform the guy, "and I have a tattoo, too. I need to sleep, and they are partying and noisy."

Bruce never said anything, so I was the bad guy again. Why can't Bruce have my back and say, "This is not what we were looking for. Thank you very much"?

Unbelievably, things got worse. We had almost zero gas in our car that had pulled the long trailer. Stressed and drained, I wondered, *Now what?* We were told the whereabouts of a gas station, but we could hardly find it, could hardly fit in it, and found it crammed with bikers. Bruce struggled to get us out of the place while bikers and curious spectators gawked. Meanwhile, I called for refuge. Campgrounds? All closed. Hotels? Booked with bikers. *Are we gonna drive around all night?*

Somehow, I reached a trailer park in Deland, where a woman named Cathy took pity on us and said we could hook up our electricity to her laundry room. She met us at the entrance to the dilapidated place, and after back-and-forth maneuvering, we got hooked up. Cathy was our angel. She cleaned the small bathroom and laundry for us and showed us how to reconnect the electrical plug when the electricity failed. We gave her money that she desperately needed to get to Tennessee, where her dad was dying. In the morning, we decided to stay another two nights and give Cathy another hundred bucks. We could've gone to a real campground, but she was so kind. It was a kind of miracle that we were able to help each other in a time of need. I will always remember Cathy, one of the forgotten souls in this country.

In the terrible winter of 2015, when I needed a boost recovering from two flu viruses, sinus infections, and bronchitis, Bruce had to administer injections of minerals and vitamins sent by Dr. Ali. I didn't want to have a reaction, so I started with low doses, which I wrote down on a sheet of paper: five millimeters of magnesium, two millimeters of selenium, so much of vitamin B-12, and so on. Dr. Ali's office neglected to send zinc, so we began without it. When we added the missing zinc, Bruce stopped magnesium. I have no idea why. When I realized the error, it was too late to go back and catch up because I had only so many needles. "For want of a nail, the kingdom is lost," they say.

It must be noted that the term "aspergates" in no way implies a lack of intelligence. Bruce can figure a sum in a split second. He won a math scholarship to college. He is a keen bridge player, and he has done well as a lawyer. But he forgets to predict consequences. Cause and effect and simple instructions pass over his head, or in one ear and out the other. To an aspie, storing general information is a waste of brain space. After hundreds and hundreds of these aspergates, it is not only the event but the anticipation that keeps me riled, anxious to stay one step ahead of my aspie. When I fail, I am as frustrated with myself as I am with him, and each occurrence is stamped on my brain. Bruce, too, is on alert and overly cautious about making a mistake, but good intentions tend to slide, and we are unable to evade these unpremeditated, though unforgettable, accidents.

So now you know why I tried to mash those severed knockout roses back on their stems and how much I crave a re-do on every blessed aspergate. If only I could have stayed ahead of my aspie's messes 20,000 times, how much misery I could have forestalled and been healthier, stronger, and saner.

No roses for the rest of the summer. By the end of September, amazingly, some did rebloom, but Bruce replaced those old bushes with new ones, which are very small but should be fine in a couple of years.

Chapter 38

MOVING BUT NOT GROOVING

Even though Bruce would hightail it to his cheapo motel for a few days after a fight, each respite was short-lived. By winter of 2012, after forty-two years of escalating clashes, our relationship had become toxic, and my nerves were screaming for a break before they finally broke. One of our apartment units was vacant, so Bruce had a place to live longer-term, though it was sparsely furnished, with no cable TV, as any motel would have had, and no box spring for his bed.

I almost lost my resolve, as I had done so many times before, watching him pack his things and load his car, especially when he carried the box containing his collection of watches, the bands peeking out like little serpents writhing in all directions.

A few days later, I caught his image in the glare of my headlights in a parking lot. I leaned on my horn: BEEP! Startled, he jumped, but when he saw it was me, we both laughed, something we had not done together in a long time.

Before long, there he was, following my car as I found a parking space at the restaurant where we would have our first date since he had moved into his apartment. Dressed in tan slacks and a teal sport coat with gold buttons, he escorted me inside, where we met good friends who knew nothing of our situation. Despite horrible fights and unbearable pain, we could transform into our social "fun couple" role as easily as sliding into a pair of old slippers. We could do this in our business roles, parent and grandparent roles, sport and activity roles, and any other role required for this transformation. It was natural for us, and it did not feel like "faking it" because we had done it for so many years.

After a pleasant dinner, Bruce drove us a short way to a University of Delaware theater to see a show where we would rejoin our friends. I put my right hand on his left hand and said, "Hello, husband." He looked at me warily, and I could hardly blame him, considering the screaming and yelling I'd done when I had kicked him out of the house. I just felt like touching his hand because I have always liked the shape of his hands. On his right hand was his college ring. It was his habit to always wear that ring, so he has had the stone replaced many times over the years. On his left was his large gold wedding band, the one he had saved by nixing the anesthetic when his finger had been stitched up after he had slashed it while climbing off the RV.

The play was a comedy, which lifted our spirits as we laughed with our friends at the onstage antics. Bruce drove me back to my car, and I headed home alone to my big house, empty but for my cats, while he returned to his spartan flat.

Meanwhile, my health was in the tank, and I was so sick of being sick. Dr. Shrader felt that I must've still been too sensitive to our house despite the renovation, so he urged us to move out. His staff told me they had never heard him give that advice before, and we took it to heart. In fact, the mold no longer resided in the house, but it had settled in my cells and organs. This we would not learn for seven more years, long after we had sold our beautiful "House of Sunshine." We said goodbye to my vast flower gardens, our pool and jacuzzi with the peach-colored deck, and our lovely property sloping gracefully down to the woods and river. This was during the housing crisis, to boot, and we sold at a humongous loss.

I did need to stay free of mold, though, so we hired Frank, the owner of the mold remediation company, as an advisor to the builder of our new house. *No more damp walls, please!*

Trying to assuage our sadness about moving, we picked a unique house design with pods or wings that surrounded a courtyard protected by pretty wrought iron gates and graced with lots of stone and pavers. We planted flowering trees and worked up a vegetable garden. We had solar panels installed and added geothermal heat. Our small pool was called a "spool," a combination of spa and pool, which spewed out tons of bubbles. Peace symbols in every form were a major theme, including our specially made wrought iron peace door knocker.

One of the pods comprises Bruce's bedroom and bathroom. My large, yellow bedroom, decorated with butterflies, flowers, and birds, makes up the pod on the other side of the house. I wonder what people thought when we gave them a tour, since they had no idea that Bruce has had his own bedroom since 2010 at Amaranth, and it was obvious we didn't share one now.

Our living apart magnified befuddlements caused by Asperger miscommunications.

Working with the builder while Bruce lived elsewhere reminded me of a situational comedy in which the characters caused chaos by covering up a secret.

Thinking we'd settled on a time to meet the contractor at the construction site, we often arrived in different cars at different times. The builder asked us which floor molding we had picked out; we each pointed to a different one on the sample board. And when the bewildered fellow questioned us as to which color floor tile we had selected?

"Green," I said. "Blue," Bruce said.

Now everyone was discombobulated.

I read in *AARP The Magazine* that older people who build houses are setting themselves up for a heart attack. With chronic stress, marital stress, and organizing the move, housebuilding was an excruciating challenge for us. I look back on the winter and spring of 2011–2012 through a brain fog that's perforated with memory lapses. I am sure I was suffering some sort of nervous collapse.

Once construction was nearly completed, we were overwhelmed with packing and preparing Amaranth for sale. One day, while Bruce was still living in his apartment, I was about to head out the door but decided to check our phone messages: "This is Dr. Bi#z#*wski's office." I almost deleted the garbled voice, but I understood enough to know it was meant for Mr. Hubbard. Bruce took the time to listen and respond to the message, which was from the office of a new gastroenterologist. The regular doctor had died, and this office had taken over his practice. They said it was time for Bruce's colonoscopy. Much to my surprise, Bruce made an appointment in March of 2012.

I was his driver that early morning and waited and waited for word about his progress. I worried as patient after patient who had gone in before Bruce tipsily emerged from the building with escorts to meet their drivers. Where was Bruce? Had an assigned escort forgotten about him?

Finally, I was directed to the recovery area, only to find the poor doctor professing exhaustion while propping himself up on the door frame. He had removed a couple of polyps, but one was flat and kept slipping around the colon, he told me. Flat polyps are more difficult to see and easily missed. More than likely, by finding that polyp, Dr. Bi#z#*wski saved Bruce's life. The doctor said that Bruce could not exercise for two weeks, and biopsy results would be forthcoming.

We simultaneously exclaimed (with appropriate pronouns), "But he has a Caesar Rodney Half Marathon in two days, and he has a twenty-seven-year streak!"

A streak means the person has run the same race every year. Bruce had two other Delaware race streaks going as well. We argued and fussed, but the doctor, who thought we had lost our marbles, convinced us that Bruce would hemorrhage and be carted off in an ambulance if he tried to run.

A few days later, I ran into Betty, a runner friend, at our natural foods store where she was collecting gift certificates for the Lung Association of Delaware, who happened to sponsor the Caesar Rodney Half Marathon. I told Betty about Bruce's plight of missing the race and thus ending his streak. She suggested he contact the race director, who was also a friend, and arrange to run the course as soon as he was allowed. A well-known runner had kept his streak alive by doing that very thing, completing the course with a witness, but there would be no statistics since the run could not be officially timed. It took some convincing by me to get Bruce to agree.

"What do you have to lose?" I argued. "Go for it!"

Bruce contacted the race director and told him his intentions. Bruce got permission, but he was told that he needed to run the course as soon as possible after his two-week rest period was over.

On the day of this big event, Reid rode his bike the 13.2 miles alongside his dad, and Bruce's friend Ray joined him for the last seven miles. I parked in downtown Wilmington to wait at the finish line. Bruce had only had time to run five miles twice for training, first having to recover from his colonoscopy. On top of that, he'd had one of his rare colds. He was not in good shape for a hilly half-marathon, so I was worried and paced in the middle of the street by the town square, peering down the big hill that was the torturous last quarter mile to the finish. It was Sunday and with little traffic, so I stood there feeling like I was experiencing a dramatic movie scene.

I texted Reid: "How is dad doing?"

He texted back: "At mile 9. He is getting tired."

I texted Sally: "I think I just killed your father."

Come on, Bruce! Come on, show yourself! I glimpsed some movement way down the hill, and up he came, step by step, so I joined the crew and ran alongside him. When he reached the finish line, Bruce hugged Ray, turned to me, and said in a flat tone, "I told you I could do it." No hug again. We all went to a local pub for a celebratory lunch. Bruce kept his streak going for thirty years.

Soon after that success, Bruce came into our bedroom at Amaranth where I was packing, looked at me, and gave me a thumbs-down sign. That was always my sign for the results of several breast biopsies, and, luckily, I could always give him a thumbs-up when I went to the waiting room after talking to the doctor. I immediately knew what he meant: cancer! We hugged and cried.

We worked tirelessly getting Amaranth ready for sale before Bruce went under the knife. With a heavy heart, I walked through every room several times—remembering how our party guests could admire themselves in mirrors or view our lovely woods through fabulous windows—before walking out the door for the last time.

The weekend of Mother's Day 2012, we hired a truck and recruited friends, my brother, and our wonderful Amaranth next-door neighbors, and somehow we got all the belongings to our new house. I had no idea how hard the move would be. I was overwhelmed and, as usual, didn't feel all that strong, so I could not keep one step ahead of my aspie. When I wasn't looking, Bruce had our crew put all the outdoor furniture—seventeen chairs, four tables, and accompanying umbrellas—in the basement. *Holy crap! Now we have to haul all this stuff back out. And there's our china, crystal, and silver under the chairs down there. They go in the dining room, Bruce, with the dinner table!* Also, the tools ended up in the kitchen.

Everything was now out of the truck, but with Bruce's surgery looming, I would be the only one who could unpack, move boxes, and try to sort out the whole mess. I convinced Bruce to leave his apartment before the surgery and take up residence in the new house.

Let's give it a go. Maybe the setup with the pods and separate wings will provide relief from Asperger troubles.

Part of Bruce's colon was removed on May 18, 2012. Sally and the grandchildren came down from Brooklyn. Bruce endured a lot of pain, but as he is known to do, he recovered quickly, although he was forbidden to lift anything heavy for three months. I know he didn't plan cancer and surgery, but there I was again, dealing with the worst timing ever.

Our volunteers were terrific, but eventually we were left on our own with piles of boxes that I had to push and drag around the house, not to mention all the patio furniture that I had to carry back outside.

Before we knew Bruce had cancer, we had ordered fencing to go around the swimming pool. We were to install it ourselves, which seemed like an economical option at the time, but now Bruce was out of commission. Then one fellow we hired to install it bonked himself in the head with the post-hole digger and contemplated suing us because he said he'd suffered a severe brain injury. We paid his medical bills, but the required-by-law fence was still not installed. Two little boys lived next door, and it was dangerous for the pool to be accessible to them, so we warned the parents and hoped we didn't find any bodies floating around. Eventually, we got the fence up.

We needed a lot of help while Bruce was recovering, and we just couldn't find it, even though I made a dozen calls trying to hire any able body. I was literally begging for help. Reid had injured his back, so even my own kid wasn't available. There'd been many bad breaks setting up at our new address, and stress was taking an unknown toll on me, a toll that I would pay and pay.

Chapter 39

BURNOUT

With the new house built, I thought I was through with chasing cures for serial health crises, but I was wrong. Still, I was to find unexpected relief in an off-beat pastime, one that provided me new lessons in compassion and in life.

I had no idea why I could barely get one foot in front of the other or why I felt so weird. I had dodged the bullets of mold in our Amaranth home, mold in our RV, the rounds of rows with Bruce, the dread of losing my aspie to cancer, and the stress of building a mold-free home. My strength almost restored, I ran a 5K road race along the beautiful Brandywine River in Wilmington, Delaware, although the ride home upset my progress. My running friend had come to the race from out of town, and I was anxious to show her our new house. She offered to drive me there, a forty-five-minute trip. To my terror, however, she careened her little vintage Honda down the interstate at a high speed, windows open because she had no AC, and there was a high outdoor mold count to add to the mix. She veered off the exit ramp, ignoring my warnings of vigilant Newark cops, and sped through the town limits—dodging the vans parked on the road as parents unloaded their college kids and belongings—and zoomed out like some urban rally racer. I was sure that we were going to crash and that I was breathing my last breaths.

We didn't crash, but as I found out a year later, my adrenals were down for the count after all my heaped-up stresses. That ride might have been the last, triggering dose of cortisol, the fight-or-flight stress hormone pumped out by our adrenal glands. We inherited this response from our less cerebral progenitors, who needed a chemical signal to tell them to get the hell out or fight for their lives. A sustained fight-or-flight mode has ramifications. The ability to generate cortisol will flag, and I was particularly susceptible to the effects of depleted cortisol. The functional medicine doctor I was working with in California claimed I did not have adrenal fatigue, at least not at the level my tests had registered. All the same, I had many of the clinical symptoms: unrelenting fatigue, body aches, anxiety, insomnia, and hypoglycemia (low blood sugar), to name a few. In sum, I was both wired and tired.

I read vociferously about adrenal exhaustion, especially in the articles by Dr. Lam, an expert in the field. For decades, I had endured all four categories of stress: toxic exposure, relationship problems, ongoing gut infection, and overexercise. People continue to function for years in the early stages, crashing and recovering, flirting with adrenal insufficiency. That had been me. Unfortunately, medical doctors were knowledgeable only about Addison's disease, which John F. Kennedy acquired due to the stress of the PT boat battle in the Pacific. "America Runs on Dunkin" is an apt slogan for a nation now fighting burnout with sugary overstimulation.

By then, my body was breaking down by being in a near-catabolic state. No matter how much food I ate, I kept losing weight. I dreaded the scale and kicked it when it showed another pound gone. I became self-conscious about my looks and had to pin or sew my waistbands so that I would not trip on my pantlegs as the waistbands slipped off my waist. I was skinny as a skeleton. The only good thing about being that skinny was the great deals I got on clothes sized two and four, but I wanted to be chubby, or at least a little round around the edges. Adrenal supplements such as licorice and adaptogens are usually helpful, but I did not improve after taking them. Informed by research and shaken by my deterioration, I was convinced I needed replacement hydrocortisone.

I contacted a naturopath online who specialized in adrenal problems. I was instructed to again obtain a saliva test and send in my samples. This time, the results were definitive: I had adrenal fatigue.

On June 12, 2014, Bruce and I drove to Brooklyn to visit our daughter, who lives a very busy life, but I managed to get her to lunch as well as get her attention. "Sally," I said, looking at her from across the little table, "I am very ill and think I am dying, and if I don't die, I am going to kill myself."

She was dumbstruck and horrified, quickly making an appointment for me with a doctor in New York City who seemed promising. I remember struggling to negotiate my way across the Broadway traffic to her building and thinking that I was not going to make it. In her office, I leaned back in the chair with my head resting against the wall. As I had feared, the two visits I had with her turned out to be unproductive.

"Why don't you go back to that integrative doctor you saw before you found the mold?" Reid said. So we went back to Dr. Majid Ali.

We were a motley crew heading up the West Side Highway that August. Sally was physically sick to her stomach about my condition, Bruce was lugging around a scarecrow wife, and I was again battling for my life. Even though many of Dr. Ali's videos and articles suggested hydrocortisone for adrenal exhaustion, he did not say anything about such a treatment to us. I had to ask him for the prescription.

"Oh, do you want some?" he asked.

Darn tootin'!

My seventieth birthday was coming up in October, but although I was now taking the hydrocortisone regularly, I was still too exhausted to plan a party. Coincidentally, Sally told me she would be passing through Wilmington on the way from Washington, D.C. and could stop by to say happy birthday. I pulled myself together and rented a private room at a restaurant near the train station and invited close friends to join Sally and Reid's family. Everyone was wonderful to answer the call on short notice, to bring lovely cards and gifts, and to provide excellent company.

While cutting my cake, I unwittingly licked the frosting on my big number seven candle, which elicited ribald laughs and off-color jokes from the crowd. One of the typically risqué fellows missed the scene, so I called him over and camped it up, licking off more frosting, which tickled his fancy. For three hours, I was the real April, not the feeble wreck I'd become. Following the party, I resumed my low-key regimen, and, by the middle of December, I was getting stronger and adding needed pounds to my spindly frame.

This past year of misery, I thought, was finally over, but I was wrong. I managed to contract the swine flu at my eye doctor's office the first week of January in 2015. I had never had it before, and I hope I never get it again. It was terrible, but luckily I made it through without complications, even though at seventy-plus I was considered an "at-risk" patient.

I had been out of bed and out in the world less than a week after my swine flu episode when Bruce thought he might be coming down with something himself. That morning, as I stood beside him in the kitchen while he was making coffee, he suddenly turned and coughed directly into my face just as I was taking a deep breath. If a person wanted to transfer germs, they could not have planned this interaction better. Bruce spewed 3,000 droplets of flu-laden saliva at fifty miles per hour right into my lungs. *Oh crap!*

"Bruce," I cried, helplessly trying to wave the spray away, "why didn't you cover your mouth or turn away?"

"I can't control my coughing," he stated.

Three days later, I was back in bed with the seasonal flu while Bruce was hardly ill. During the next few months, I contracted a sinus infection, a severe case of bronchial pneumonia, and another sinus infection.

Barely making it to the doctor's office with bronchitis, I was seen by an intern. It was around St. Patrick's Day, and he was a short, red-haired man dressed in Kelly green pants and a checkered green tie. He looked to be all of twelve years old, and, in my delirium, I wondered how a leprechaun had gotten into this office. Still, he knew enough to send me for an X-ray. An hour later, I got a call back from a non-leprechaun doctor who told me I was very ill. It was frightening how frightened she was.

I had never coughed so much in my life or had such severe mucus from a sinus infection. In the middle of this mess, I called Dr. Ali, who was appalled at all my illnesses and suggested that I come to terms with my own death. That is a scary remark from a doctor! He recommended that I read books about Buddhism. I not only read books but listened to a Great Courses class on the topic and placed statues of the Buddha around my house and yard.

Dr. Ali sent me a bag of needles and vials of vitamins and minerals for Bruce to inject into me in hopes of giving my immune system a boost. In May, we went to our co-op apartment in Brooklyn, which I had not visited in over a year. I remember walking four blocks to The Loft, a clothing store, but I was so weak I could hardly nudge myself forward. I looked at my legs to see if they were moving. My body had deconditioned from the once-great shape I had been in.

I had tried everything, and I was ripe for experimentation and maybe a little criminal activity. What I got was a little more compassion for myself and for others, too.

During those awful months in 2015, Delaware's first medical marijuana dispensary was due to open. More out of curiosity than commitment, I read the qualifications for a card: terminal illness, cancer, HIV, pediatric epilepsy. I initially dismissed the idea, as it did not seem to fit me. However, I was in a bad way, so Bruce checked out Canna Care Docs, a screening service for people who needed a card, even though their physician would not fill out the application form. At that early date, many physicians were afraid of getting involved with cannabis.

Even though Bruce and I had never been into the pot scene, I was convinced that cannabis offered many health benefits. And I clearly needed help, especially with sleep, as I was taking only catnaps at night and functioning in a zombie-like state all day. We decided to apply. However, contacting all the health practitioners that I had seen in the last twenty-five years was like pulling teeth, as was convincing them that they would not be directly involved in my scoring medical marijuana. It was challenging and stressful for me to gather all the proper documents and make copies. Eager to get my new card and irate with the absurdity of the process, I became especially frustrated with our new fax/printer/scanner, which decides not to fax/print/scan at the most inopportune times. I cursed and banged on the thing, a similar reaction to when I flung my health records around my car before we discovered the sickening mold in our house.

I finally got all my diagnoses and paperwork together, and soon I found myself nervously watching the Canna Care Docs intake employee thumb through my records. She set some aside and marked others for my interview with the medical doctor, who said *YES*. I qualified! My prescriptions for Lyrica for fibromyalgia pain, doctors' notations of constant body aches and pains, and cachexia disorder, the wasting disease explicitly listed in state code qualifying conditions (I had consistently low BMI weight), met the requirements. I am indebted to those health practitioners who wrote letters and cooperated with my requests for digging up my health records.

Despite my successfully obtaining a card, we were outraged by the injustice of anti-marijuana laws and went all-in with the effort to legalize cannabis. We joined Delaware National Organization for the

Reform of Marijuana Laws (NORML) and lobbied with the cannabis advocacy group to legalize all marijuana and end its prohibition. I discovered that anti-weed hysteria had been a political tool in the 1930s to scare people with tales of degenerate Mexicans bringing it into the United States and spreading it among good Americans to undermine their moral fiber.

Bruce and I participated in marches for legalizing cannabis and wore weed-leaf green. Ever the law-abider, I did all this before I had had my first puff. Ironically, before I got my card, I slipped slightly south of the law. During these demonstrations, I encountered a woman who stuck a small bag of a cannabis variety called Trainwreck in my hand. I stashed it in the glove compartment of our car, and then Bruce and I ended up following a state trooper, which was disconcerting, especially given Bruce's propensity to nearly rear-end the car in front.

At this stage, I was still wary of the stuff but managed to pass my stash of Trainwreck to a waiter I'd struck up an acquaintance with. He knew a lot about foot reflexology and alternative health protocols. When I told my daughter, she texted me, "You gave pot to your server?"

The dispensary opening was behind schedule. I had the card but not the cannabis, which I desperately needed. I met another fellow who stuffed a tiny piece of crumpled paper with his phone number into my hand. Not knowing what exactly was up, I talked Bruce into giving him a call. It turned out that we could get cannabis from him. Bruce and I knew nothing about this underworld. The man was quite nice, and he told us that he had gone through a terrible time with addiction to hard drugs and that cannabis had saved his life.

I bought a PAX 3 vaporizer and learned how to grind the cannabis buds, pack them in, and clean the machine. Pens with cannabis oil cartridges are the easiest for me. I began sleeping better, got stronger, and slowly reentered the race scene, even though I was plodding at the beginning. When I earned a medal in my age group, I visited my dealer, gave him a big hug, and showed him my medal. We both teared up.

He helped me so much. Everyone I met connected to cannabis, from the underworld to the activists, to the employees and patients at the dispensaries, had been kind, smart, and caring.

Delaware's First State Compassion medical cannabis dispensary centers opened in June 2015. They are all bright and attractively decorated, contrary to what one might imagine. They have expanded greatly since the beginning, although we had to fight for supplies back then. I met all sorts of people who were helped by cannabis, especially with pain, anxiety, appetite, and getting off heavy prescription drugs. I always gave everyone respect. Many of the customers had endured rough lives, illnesses, and injuries.

When I arrived at the dispensary one day, an unshaven middle-aged man was lying in a wheelchair inside the front entrance, waiting for a ride.

"Do they have any Pineapple Fields today?" I asked him. Pineapple Fields was a popular strain at that time.

"They had it when I bought some, ma'am."

"Thanks."

By the time I got to the counter, it was all gone.

I teased the fellow as I left: "Hey, you bought my Pineapple Fields. Now they are out."

He took me seriously. "Sorry," he said, offering me his bag. "I'll trade you my Pineapple Fields for what you got."

We would have to do the exchange in the parking lot to comply with the rules. I watched him prop himself up and wheel out to the late December cold. That simple act of kindness was the best Christmas gift I received that year.

Another time, a poor young guy also in a wheelchair helped me figure out some new strains from Israel. He was only twenty-seven and in pain from sitting in the chair on disintegrating bones. He winced each time he had to readjust his weight. He told me that when he was seventeen and racing a Motocross bike, he had been the leader in the last lap when he crashed and crushed his spine. And he had been about to sign with Honda. I empathized with him for his terrible turn of events. I doubt whether he is alive as I write this.

Happily, a dispensary opened closer to me in Newark. One day I was going in to get my medicine when a shaggy-haired fellow stopped me. He was heavily tattooed and wore a sleeveless muscle shirt, long mismatched shorts, and a dirty baseball hat. He asked if he knew me. He thought maybe it was from his job when he could still work. I could tell that he was proud of the work he had once done and hoped to talk about it. Before, I would have run from a character like this, but now we talked, and we figured out that he had seen me at the other dispensary. *These are my people, people who have fallen on challenging health problems.* I learned a lot about courage, suffering, survival, and compassion at the dispensaries while enjoying the alleviation of my own misery.

Bruce had the idea that I should make my medical marijuana card the wallpaper of my phone. *Maybe not!* My goal in life was not to be so ill that I needed the state of Delaware to reissue me a card every year. But it has been an enlightening, albeit unwanted, journey, and I have tried to educate people about cannabis. It was not to be the end of all our problems, but it was good for Bruce and me to collaborate on getting other citizens and me our cannabis, and my grandkids think it is a hoot that Grandma buys pot.

Chapter 40

TRAVEL TROUBLES

My spine is frozen, my fingers are numb, and where the hell is Bruce? He's never around!

The darn snow was so wet that my granddaughter's boots wouldn't clamp into her skis. I didn't think my seventy-one-year-old body could bend over one more time or board the kiddie's magic carpet ride just in time for the yellow spot. The little ones didn't know how to ski but gave it their best shot. My son-in-law and daughter-in-law did not ski well enough to teach them, so Grandma and Reid were giving it their all.

Grandpa, on the other hand, was wandering around recovering from retina surgery. He had been skating in a Richmond, Virginia, competition when he went blind in one eye. He managed to finish the performance and drive back with me monitoring his condition and arranging for an emergency appointment with an ophthalmologist. This blindness was due to complications from cataract surgery, which had required a series of injections in his eyeball and resulted in his retina going south. I suspected heavy drinking had eroded his eye health, but who was I to know? His doctor had barred him from getting on skis, but couldn't Bruce at least acknowledge we were having a bad time instead of just standing there acting as though he hadn't a care in the world?

I had done the yeoman's work of calling, coordinating, and making reservations to get both families at this ski lodge to celebrate Bruce's upcoming seventieth birthday, February 10, 2016. Now I could have used the man's help picking up the grandkids scattered around the bunny slope and giving me a break to do a few runs with my kids for old times' sake. I thought, *I know it's not really his fault, but the man's afflictions hang on him like dust on that kid in the Charlie Brown comics—Pig Pen.*

To me, it was a pattern. *Didn't Bruce pass a kidney stone the morning of Dad's Fourth of July birthday party?* For that event, I had been expecting a crowd of thirty at the house, so I had had to sprint home from the hospital and tear around like a maniac to prepare for our guests. Just in time for the party, Reid picked up his dad, who was happy-clappy on pain pills and beer at that point. Not to mention, he had had colon cancer surgery right before we moved to the new house, forbidding him to do any heavy work. His cloud of dust billowed around me.

Somewhat recovered from the birthday ski weekend, Bruce and I headed out in our RV for the Hilton Head Island Running Festival—for many years a winter ritual, this time it would be the warm-weather leg of Bruce's birthday celebration. The eye doctor had nixed the half-marathon for Bruce but said he was A-OK to join me in the short race. *Woohoo!*

I always set a goal to rest and sleep well the first night in a campground to save my low energy reserves for vacation activities. Invariably, however, something would go wrong, such as traffic jams from car crashes, overturned trucks, car fires, and ten-mile backups from construction, which made me wonder how people with children and dogs on board who didn't have a traveling bathroom like we did coped in such situations.

In addition to the normal travel stresses, we generated our own vexations.

For example, on one trip, while planning for us to stop in Atlanta on the way to Pensacola, somehow Bruce missed the fact that the campground he had chosen was members-only, gated, and primarily residential. After discovering this inconvenient fact, we circumvented Atlanta city limits for hours, searching for someplace to park. We finally found a dilapidated, run-down place with muddy, rutted roads and no amenities, nothing like a normal campground. I don't remember how we checked in and never saw an employee.

Unable to find a working electrical outlet, we pulled in and out of spots with Bruce dragging out the cord and me praying for a light to go on inside. Watching our every move were scary characters sitting in small groups by fire pits scattered around like volcanic ash or forest fires. I was sure that they were using drugs and drinking moonshine and just hoped they kept their distance and did not venture from their tents and rusted-out trailers. Their poor skinny dogs roamed about aimlessly. We locked up and escaped at first light the next morning.

When we acquired the trailer, somehow neither of us knew to buy a cover for the slide-outs where rainwater accumulated. We discovered this necessity for a cover during our first night on the birthday trip to Hilton Head when we activated the slide-outs upon reaching the campground and water began dripping in. Although we immediately began mopping it up, we soon realized that the bed linens had been soaked down to the mattress. Luckily the campground had a nice laundry room, so we spent the evening running the dryers, but it was not what I would call a relaxing evening. When I finally got to bed, I had to crunch over on the part of the mattress that was not wet. I could have cried at the mess.

The last thing I needed now was another crisis, *especially this first night on the road, please!* I would sleep in the double bed, and

I suggested that Bruce take the couch, but he chose the overhead bunk instead. I curled up in the darkness for a restorative rest.

KA-BOOM!!!!! A deafening crash woke me from a dead sleep. *We are being bombed by a terrorist!* That was the crazy thought that first registered in my brain. I jumped from the bed and slid the dividing door aside, calling, "Bruce! Bruce!" I hit the light and was stunned by the sight before my eyes. Bruce was lying on the floor, his butt in the air, underwear stained with urine, blood oozing through fingers that cradled his head like a leaky basket, and wounded animal moans issuing from his mouth. I was horrified! He wasn't dead, not yet anyway. My hands were shaking so badly, my fingers could hardly punch out 911, but I got through to a dispatcher who told me to put a compress on Bruce's bloody head and stay on the line.

Bruce did not form any coherent words, moaning and groaning like the grinding of some broken motor: "Oo-ooong-ng-ng-ng!" I have never forgotten those torturous sounds. The EMTs found us in fifteen minutes. Good damn thing we were parked at the campground entrance instead of at one of the sites on the winding dark roads in the back. Bruce was not responsive to the EMTs or to me.

He had fallen off the six-foot-high bunk onto a wooden dining table and then bounced to the floor like a big exercise ball: *THUMP! THUMP!* The EMTs were relieved to find out that he had not fallen all the way from the RV rooftop outside. I might not have made much sense talking to the dispatcher, but what the hell would a seventy-year-old man have been doing on top of an RV at midnight?

Bruce screamed as they lifted him into a sitting position on the couch. Bulging from his head was an enormous goose egg—yet another blow to his head that he has survived. Bruce must have the hardest noggin on Earth! His hair was sticking straight up, he was trembling, and his unlucky front tooth was broken yet again. "Put a blanket around him. He is freezing!" I implored the EMTs, but they were preoccupied with Bruce's ability to communicate.

Bruce had no idea where he was and kept slurring, "Wha-where am I?"

"You're in a campground," I explained.

"A c-campground? Wha-why am I in a c-campground?"

The EMT asked, "How old are you?"

No answer.

I pointed to the big Happy Birthday sign stuck on the window and cried, "This is his seventieth birthday!"

Off went Bruce in the ambulance. There was no way I could drive the RV in the dark of night somewhere near Rocky Mount, North Carolina, and anyway, I was quivering like a leaf and close to vomiting. The EMTs called on the way to the hospital to tell me that Bruce was coming around. He had his cell phone with him and called me over and over from the hospital to ask me what had happened, unable to understand his circumstances.

"You fell! You fell! Turn off your darn cell phone. Just rest and don't run down your battery."

This was one time I truly experienced the benefit of my medical marijuana, which I use as a sleep aid. I lay down under the covers, took some puffs off my vaporizer, and instantly quit shaking and stopped feeling nauseous. I still could not sleep, but I rested all through the long night hours. The hospital sent Bruce back in a cab at around 5 a.m., having informed him that he had bruised a rib or two. We both slept for an hour.

When we woke, I said, "Bruce, I am calling Reid. He can rent a car and drive down and then drive us back to Delaware tomorrow."

Bruce would have none of it. He declared that he was heading to warm weather, even though he was in pain. Well, he seemed okay, and after all, it was his birthday. However, I should have known from experience that he has little self-awareness. He certainly wasn't wallowing in self-recriminations. *And it isn't MY freaking fault*, I had to remind myself. *I told him to sleep on the couch. Huh! Since when does he listen to me?*

So I gave in and drove most of the way to Hilton Head. *Goodbye, good rest on the first night of a trip; hello, crashed adrenals.*

Back on the road again, we pieced together the probable cause of this calamity. Before his eye surgery, Bruce had been instructed to turn on his side to protect his detached retina. Now that it was reattached, sleeping on his side was no longer necessary. However, his turning habit had been well-imprinted, and he had turned over again, not considering that he was lying at the edge of a bunk six feet above the floor when he rolled. We argue to this day that his four beers and no dinner had a lot to do with this disaster. He had intended to have popcorn with his beer, his favorite meal, but he had forgotten to bring the oil to cook the popcorn, so he had gone without the food part of his repast.

I applied tons of Bengay to Bruce's back and chest and wrapped him in Ace bandages like a mummy, but he was still in terrible pain. Then, despite his prescription pain patches and pills, Bruce managed to drive the RV. We finally arrived at our favorite Hilton Head campground and marina and dined early at the Sunset Grill overlooking the inland waterway. Or, rather, I dined while Bruce just sat there, nauseous due to having consumed pain pills like candy. The horrible ordeal kept rerunning through my mind like a bad movie, and right there at the table, I began sobbing spontaneously. I had the mental pain; Bruce had the physical pain. He has no memory of his fall; I have PTSD from it.

The next day, Bruce thought he might be able to putt with his new putter, a birthday gift from Reid, so we headed out to a golf course. But he could not even handle a putting movement without wincing in pain, so he just rode around with me on the golf cart for nine holes. After golf, we picked up more pain remedies from the pharmacy since things were not improving. I learned that I'm a crappy caregiver, too. I have no aptitude for dressing a grown man, especially stuffing his big wide feet into socks and shoes.

Bruce looked nasty with his missing front tooth and huge discolored goose egg. We were compelled to repeat our story whenever we interacted with strangers, such as the two women in my age group I met at the Hilton Head 5K race. They were very sympathetic to Bruce's plight. As stressed and tired as I was, I managed to win a nice medal, but the drive home was an arduous feat.

X-rays later revealed that Bruce had slammed into the floor so hard that his rib cage was caved in on one side, with five ribs cracked and two bruised. Remind me never to use that North Carolina hospital—where they had proclaimed that he had simply bruised a rib or two—again for an emergency. Bruce felt like crap and could hardly move from his chair.

While his pain slowly receded, his breathing became more and more labored, prompting Reid and me to insist that Bruce go see his doctor. The doctor discovered that Bruce's resting heart rate was pounding away at 160 bpm, so Bruce was hustled into an ambulance lickety-split and raced to the hospital. His chest cavity was engorged with fluid, causing a strain on his heart. They drained a coke bottle's worth of goo from his chest. Before we could say "pulmonologist," however, another bottle of brown stuff refilled his lungs. To stop the coke factory running in his chest cavity, Bruce underwent another procedure. In this one, a pulmonologist lined his lungs with talcum powder. Good news: it worked!

Bad news: his heart's upper chambers began beating too fast, causing an atrial flutter. Even with the brown fluid gone, there was no respite. Bruce required two heart cauterizations to slow and regularize his heartbeat. Since then, a few more episodes have popped up from time to time, like unwelcome guests, so back to the hospital we go with Bruce.

Bruce is now under the care of both a cardiologist and a pulmonologist and takes medication for his heart. He suffers from shortness of breath, a constant cough, and a loss of stamina. I know it could have been worse, like brain damage, a spinal injury, or death, but this terrible accident was a turning point in Bruce's life. I could never get back in that RV again because of the memory, so we sold it. In our new Sunseeker RV, Bruce sleeps two feet from the floor.

It felt like déjà vu all over again when we took a trip recently to Hilton Head, South Carolina, Bruce's front tooth broken like a cracked iceberg. He had chipped it while chomping on an ear of corn, having gotten his mouth too close to the metal prongs on the handy little corn-on-the-cob holders. At least he didn't have a big goose egg on his head or broken ribs this time, so we enjoyed golfing, the beach, and running the Run Forrest Run 5K at the Shrimp Festival in Beaufort. I have no idea if the people we encountered wondered why he hadn't gone to the dentist, but he got the tooth bonded a few weeks after our return.

As for Bruce's terrible bunk fall, ironically it finally unkinked Bruce's neck, which had been subluxated ever since he slammed helmet-first into a tree years ago while riding downhill on his dirt bike. The universe works in strange ways.

Chapter 41

THINGS FALL APART

The bright colors of Bruce's life were dimming like a fading rainbow after a summer rain. His topple off the RV bunk accelerated a slow decline that started when he retired from his law practice and progressed with a cascade of health issues. Drinking beer and golfing most days, combined with his less-than-stellar eating habits and reckless behavior, was finally catching up with Superman. His general approach to life was deserting him, and he was forced to admit that he had to join the rest of us feeble mortals. It didn't sit well with him.

Bruce was making a lot of mistakes, which made him both frustrated and volatile. He was losing muscle and had developed a beer belly, not to mention that he was getting older. The easy magic was gone. He seemed to be folding into himself, and possibly into a state of narcissistic collapse. Meanwhile, I was hanging onto a marriage that felt like a branch pulling loose from a collapsing cliff side.

During this decline, we decided to go to the Run from the Sun 5K in Avalon, New Jersey, to support our friends who owned Races2Run, the sponsor. Initially Bruce had no plans to participate, but he got caught up in the excitement and registered despite his condition. The night before the race, we headed out to dinner but first wanted to stop by a liquor store because most of the area restaurants had BYOB policies.

Our friends had given us explicit directions to the best liquor store with enough parking for an RV, telling us to park at the end as we entered, but Bruce just cruised by the spot as I shouted, "Stop!" *How can he not see this space?* So we got ourselves stuck in the small crowded part of the lot, irritating the throng of booze buyers entering and exiting the store and parking lot. I finally jumped out and took off on foot to get to the restaurant on time because they had told us they would not hold our table, but I got lost and walked a half mile out of my way. Oh well, I got to tour downtown Avalon. I felt like I was trying to make my way through a corn maze of confusion and negativity by the time I finally huffed and puffed through the restaurant door.

When the host was about to seat us at a communal table outside, I said, "Bruce, there are going to be other people sitting here, and I am too tired to make polite conversation."

"Nobody else will sit here," insisted Bruce, which was obviously not going to be the case on a crowded summer weekend, but we sat down anyway. *What is it with these weird pronouncements that come out of nowhere, based on nothing rational and with no acceptance of responsibility on his part?* Immediately, the host seated a young couple at our table. They got to hear our interactions when Bruce dumped an entire cup of gin into his tonic. I said, "No wonder you used to be drunk in five minutes sitting in front of the fireplace at Amaranth after work."

"I won't drink anything, then," he snapped. But he did drink it, and I had to calm him down as those poor kids were trying to enjoy their summer dinner.

He was slow to finish the race the next morning, and as I waited, I saw a police officer answer his phone at one point. I feared it might have been a "runner down" call. A call about Bruce. When Bruce finally did cross the finish line, he collapsed on the curb. When I managed to get him to the RV, he collapsed on the bed there. At the awards ceremony, Bruce could not even chew the pizza. I mean, he was totally tuckered out, no longer the competitive runner of yore who could conquer the mighty Survival of the Shawangunks triathlon and celebrate afterward like a hungry bear. Nonetheless, his later version of events was that I had made him lie down and the pizza had been leathery.

Our summer routine had always given us focus, but things were falling apart. In Rehoboth Beach, where I had first met Bruce so many years ago, we were to run a race on Saturday sponsored by the SPCA, and we planned on running another on Sunday when there would be a kiddie K for children eight and under. We were excited that Reid was meeting us there so our grandson could participate, but we woke up late.

"Bruce!" I yelled. "What happened to the alarm?"

"You always wake up!" he yelled back.

"You mean to tell me you NEVER set your watch for any of our races?"

OMG, I thought. *We better not miss the kiddie K after Reid drove all the way to the beach. Races start on time.*

We rushed frantically to get ready. Bruce opened the door and slammed it, swearing up a storm: "Damn! Shit! Fuck! It is too humid!"

Well, it's August and it's Delaware! Why is he so angry and agitated? We gotta cooperate, get coffee, and get going!

Suddenly it was just too much: this shower of crazed talk utterly shattered my world. I shielded my ears with my hands and cried, "You make me so unhappy!"

It was such a shock to finally hear those words that I think they stunned both of us. Such simple words I had never said before. For decades, I had discussed, explained, and persuaded, trying to reconcile our conflicts. Now this was my reality: "You make me unhappy!"

Our grandson ran the kiddie K and proudly wore his medal. We mingled with the runners, and I think I acted normal, but I did not feel normal. How I did not die out there running with my biotoxin illness, my stress overload, the eighty-four-degree heat, the high humidity, and my seventy-three-year-old body, I will never know. I was numb on the drive home. Obviously, I could not continue like this, but I knew that no one could help me. I had to help myself.

Bruce stayed quiet for a few days and then announced that he would go to our Brooklyn co-op. I supposed he expected me to calm down while he enjoyed life with our daughter and grandkids and then returned home in a few days to continue life as usual. *Not this time, buddy!* I was determined to put the brakes on this cyclical, depressing scenario, so I told Bruce that he had to move out for good. He didn't seem surprised or try to argue.

Coincidentally, our neighbors who lived in our co-op building in Brooklyn emailed that they would love to buy our place if and when we were ready to sell. It would be an easy sale because we would not need to make any of the required renovations and could just turn over the key. I wrote back, "Sold American!" as the tobacco auctioneers used to shout. Meanwhile, our close friends were selling a rental condo in Newark and were dumbfounded when we made an offer. Bruce was quite helpful as he applied his lawyering skills to set all the wheels in motion and reassured our friends that we still loved each other. *Does he really believe this or even understand what love means?*

It was August 2018, and we had two and a half months to live in this peculiar manner, waiting until the condo was ready. I had to stay resolute and not vacillate in my decision, but Bruce made it easier for me since he was still in a mental and physical downward spiral.

In September, we camped in the Outer Banks of North Carolina, hoping to reduce my outdoor mold exposure where there was only sand and sparse vegetation. It didn't work. I don't know whether it was stress with Bruce or that I was still carrying mold in my body, but I remained very tired. Coping with Bruce was putting me over the edge, beginning with when he left me in the RV for a half hour to check us in, "yabbering" with the staff and then returning to the

RV knowing the workers' life stories and first names. *Okay, talk to everyone but me.*

I needed to rest once we settled in, so off Bruce went to shop at a permanent GOING OUT OF BUSINESS store. He returned with his plunder of hats, souvenirs, and a new beach umbrella, but he pitched a fit when I told him that Reid had given us a new umbrella, which was in storage with the beach chairs. I guess he had failed to notice it or had not paid attention when Reid had told us about it, so now his big savings deal was not a deal at all. He slammed down the umbrella on the picnic table and became overly agitated because there were no refunds. I helped him exchange it for a beach chair. *It is only an umbrella! This is not normal behavior for a grown man.*

Golfing is usually fun for us, but when we hit the fairways, that didn't go well, either. Bruce insisted on getting the soup deal at the clubhouse instead of grabbing a sandwich in the RV. Trouble was, the sign said, "Soup and Sandwich Special." He missed the sandwich part clearly printed on the sign and became flustered to learn of his error.

"The sandwich will take a while to cook," warned the server. *Oh boy.*

We rolled up to the first tee just in time, but in a state too frenzied to meet new golf partners. "We shouldn't be paired up with anyone, as I am tired, I will need to go slow, and you have been spraying shots." I don't know why those words popped out of my mouth, but "mere anarchy" was "loosed upon the world"!

Bruce was angry the whole round. When he hit a good shot, he snarled, "Is this a spray? Is this a spray? I don't spray shots; Reid does!"

When I hit a ball into the rough, Bruce wheeled the golf cart around and around in circles trying to find my ball until I became dizzy and ill from the bouncing.

"Stop driving like this!" I implored.

"Do you want to drive?" he snapped. I've sure heard that before, but it wasn't while I was in a golf cart.

With my ball stuck somewhere in the weeds and people coming up behind us, I rushed to hit my pitch shot onto the green.

"I need another club," I mumbled. Bruce replied in a silly singsong falsetto, "Why don't you just say, 'Bruce, will you please get me my sand wedge?'" By then, I felt like I was dealing with a sociopath. I was shaking inside and pleaded with him to calm down as he wavered for the rest of the day between exasperation one moment and a peculiar composure the next.

We sat on the beach, ate out, and toured the area, but it continued to be a balancing act of grabbing bits of fun, me fighting the mold inflammation, and avoiding arguments and meltdowns. All in all, a pretty crapola vacation.

At home, my coping skills unraveled like a frayed dishtowel as Bruce continued to pick on me and spew antagonistic remarks from his living room chair while sitting as stone-faced as a ventriloquist talking through his dummy. I frequently found myself clapping my hands tightly over my ears and screaming at the top of my lungs so I would not hear the vile noises coming from his mouth. One night I went to the front door, threw it open, and screamed and screamed out into the night. *Good thing no one was out walking their dogs. They might have called the cops!*

It is hard to commit to separation or divorce with an aspie husband, but I knew that I would die if this continued. My kids would be planning my funeral if I kept trying to survive this onslaught of verbal abuse, word salads, and gaslighting. I had no choice but to stand firm as I had not done for the last forty-eight years. No more wishy-washy sitting on the fence. No more love bombs, hovering, or quiet mutterings of "I'm sorry."

Our co-op settlement in Brooklyn Heights was Tuesday, October 30, a sad day, as I loved our little place in that beautiful historic neighborhood. Nonetheless, we were pleased that the couple that bought it could now have the whole floor for their family, whom we had come to know during our six years as Brooklynites. Reid and a friend drove a rental truck to the co-op and returned to Delaware with our stuff.

In one day, we had completed moving all the contents into Bruce's new condo, and now a chapter in our lives was closed.

Bruce needed to find what could give him peace, better health, and less anxiety. The code he had lived by had been slowly eating away at his soul like termites on an old log. He was all moved in on Saturday, November 3, 2018. Surprisingly, on Sunday, Bruce called me to golf with him and a friend, and I did. The next week, we ventured out together for a chrysanthemum show at Longwood Gardens and then went out to lunch. Although so much had changed, the thread of familiarity still ran through our lives.

Chapter 42

TOXIC

"In my world, you are toxic."
How many people are told, "You are toxic"?
I guess I'm Typhoid Mary.
"You are toxic."

So answered the functional medicine doctor in California when I asked him what to tell friends who wondered why I was sick. It's true, though; my cells are full of mold toxins that still kindle inflammation thirteen years after remediation and moving into a newly built, mold-free house. Every six months, I took a complex and expensive organic acid urine test from Genova Diagnostics. The results were always the same: brain inflammation, inability to properly detox through my liver, and problems with stress and energy production. My immune system was hosting a mold exposure-induced three-ring circus called chronic immune response syndrome (CIRS). Under the CIRS big top are chaos and inefficiency in my immune system and chronic inflammation in multiple organs and body systems.

As with Asperger marriages, little was known until recently about sick building syndrome, the main source of my CIRS. Dr. Neil Nathan's book *Toxic: Heal Your Body from Mold Toxicity, Lyme Disease, Multiple Chemical Sensitivities, and Chronic Environmental Illness*, published in 2018, has been extremely helpful, and I wish I had been privy to this information in 2007 when we found the nasty black stuff. *Beginner's Guide to Mold Avoidance* by Lisa Petrison and Erik Johnson, published in 2015, has also been very helpful.

One-quarter of the population, including me, has the HLA (HS) gene, which means our bodies do not make antibodies to the mold toxins that render them harmless. I have a gene snip called MTHFR, which my mind reads as MoTHerFuckeR but actually stands for methylenetetrahydrofolate—whew! My detox pathways operate at a level about 50 percent below that of normal people, so efforts in eliminating toxins are compromised. This double genetic whammy makes me the last person who should have inhabited a moldy home!

With the critters in my circus running wild, I was initially treated with strong antifungal prescriptions such as Sporanox, Diflucan, Nizoral, and Nystatin. Disastrously, the die-off of microorganisms was too rapid, producing a strong Jarisch-Herxheimer reaction. Mold, yeast, and fungi (interchangeable terms) were being killed off faster than I could detox their by-products through my lymph nodes, liver, and gallbladder to rid them from my body. Toxins were swimming around in my blood and brain like leeches in a stream, and it was a horrible feeling.

The worst side effect was feeling woozy or drunk without having drunk alcohol. Alcohol is broken down into water and acetaldehyde. Yeast also produces acetaldehyde as one of the more potent toxins. One time I hallucinated after taking the smallest dose of Sporanox. Reid and I were looking at a house with a Realtor, and I lost consciousness while remaining upright. I could not see the living room, but through a yellow hue I saw my feet trying to move as if plodding through quicksand. I must have returned to some level of consciousness because we finished touring and Reid drove me home. Confused, I later called Reid and asked if we had ever gone to see the house. He informed me that we had indeed taken a tour, but he had noticed I had remained fixed in place and stopped talking, at which point he had waved his hand in front of my face.

Equally perplexing was an incident during a golf outing with a friend after I had taken half a tablet of Diflucan. My goal was to kill the mold with a tolerable level of the antifungal. During the round, however, I had the oddest impression that my body was present but my brain was not. (I know, I could say that about my normal golf game, but usually I am at least on the planet.) After our round, when I tried to order a sandwich at the deli, the glass shelves and counter began drifting and spinning before my eyes. *Just order a sandwich, say anything,* I urged myself, struggling not to look as weird as I felt. I have no idea if my golf friend noticed that her partner was off-kilter.

With my liver congested, my lymph nodes had to pull too much weight, and eventually they broke down. Instead of a mammogram, I always get a thermogram, which avoids radiation. A technician takes a picture of my breast tissue using an instrument like the one my mold remediation team used to detect heat. Heat means inflammation. My breasts have been fine, but the surrounding lymph nodes were congested for five years, though they are now cleared. In addition, two lymph nodes in my right armpit became enlarged, with the result that one of them was removed—unnecessarily, it turns out. I was awake through the whole horrible procedure but relieved to find the node was noncancerous. Now I have edema in my hip, and I miss that darn node.

In June of 2019, a doctor in Manhattan pulled up my recent mold test on his computer. He leaned back in his chair, put his hands in his lap, and told me, "You have severe biotoxin illness. All categories of mold or mycotoxins in the urine test are present." Today, mold is often treated with herbal supplements such as oregano oil, garlic, and caprylic acid and binders such as activated charcoal and bentonite clay.

Prescription drugs, health practitioners believe, provoke die-off reactions that set back healing efforts because of the stress on the body. For me, even herbal protocols can provoke a reaction. It's like taking an upper, combined with an anxiety attack, fatigue, heart palpitations, blurring eyes, itching skin, and achy muscles. The umbrella diagnosis is CFS/fibromyalgia, which often makes me feel like I have an endless flu.

I worry that I will not survive golf outings, visits by guests, lunch dates, road races, or vacations. My energy is so depleted by early evening that I am usually in bed by 7:30 p.m., so I can forget about nighttime activities. I joined the gray-haired crowd at theatrical matinees long before I had gray hair. On the plus side, I don't have to worry about getting a restaurant table at 5 p.m.

Hiding my unusual sickness is laborious and stressful, but it is too complicated for people to understand. Even that doctor in Manhattan told me I was "catastrophizing," making me feel not believed even by the person who should have most understood my illness. People mistake my immune reaction to mold for seasonal allergies, which are called Type IIgE reactions, but my reaction is Type II IgG. I would not have spent hundreds of thousands of dollars on the sneezing, stuffy noses, and itchy eyes of hay fever, even though I know how uncomfortable that can be because I experienced it myself when I was younger. As with Cassandra syndrome, I am understood only by those on the toxic mold CIRS Facebook forums who suffer the same fate.

Sometimes I overcommit, and then I panic when I feel my lifeblood running out of me. On one such day, as I teed up to drive a golf ball, a wave of exhaustion passed through me. I muttered the f-bomb as I stared at the ball, willing myself to hit it. My conscientious golf partner had come up behind me to watch the ball. I don't know if she heard me, but if she did, she probably thought, "Boy, she is really freaking out over this little par three!"

My cabinets are filled with more supplements than a health store. I choke down fistfuls daily. I keep our local compounding pharmacy in business by ordering hormone replacements for estrogen, testosterone, progesterone, DHEA, pregnenolone, and hydrocortisone. My holistic doctor in Brooklyn says they keep me going. I call myself the "bionic woman."

The COVID-19 protection equipment has been standard with me for years. Fall mold is high in humid Delaware, and I wear an N95 mask, baseball hat, nose filters, nostril gel, and wraparound sunglasses. Dry, windy days cause the mold to fly, often hitching a ride on pollen. When anyone remarks, "Isn't this a nice breeze today?" I tense up and think, *I will be sick tomorrow!* To find a dry climate, I would have to move two thousand miles away to Colorado, Arizona, or Idaho—or maybe a tent in Death Valley? I do not want to relocate in my mid-seventies. That would be exile with a capital E!

If I could be free of the mold, I could be free of my reliance on Bruce. Without CIRS, I could also cope better with his Asperger's syndrome. I would not become so angry and resentful that my self-absorbed Asperger husband could not feel empathy for his sick wife. I feel that half of my adult life is forever lost, having evaporated hour by hour, day by day, like the morning dew.

I still brood on what might have been had Bruce put two and two together when he was told about that lawyer's illness from mold. *Bruce got a bang out of chatting with him about my illness,* runs the tape. *Got narcissistic supply putting in his two cents, but no supply from connecting that lawyer's mold disease to MINE, a connection that dissipated somewhere in Bruce's Asperger fog.*

An interesting protocol called low dose allergen therapy was developed by Dr. Butch Shrader and recently modified by Dr. Ty Vincent as low dose immunotherapy. It treats illnesses that are not infections but, rather, immune reactions, such as those that occur with Lyme disease, rheumatoid arthritis, hay fever, other inhalant allergies, Crohn's disease, irritable bowel syndrome and other gut problems, skin problems like psoriasis, rosacea, and acne, and the list goes on. A very diluted dose of the offending pathogen is given, as in homeopathy, and you develop a tolerance for whatever ails you.

Even autism has been successfully treated. *Hey, Bruce, want to give it a go?*

In 2011, I contacted a holistic doctor in Brooklyn about low dose allergen therapy, and she asked that I first consult with Dr. Shrader. Unfortunately, his office was in Santa Fe, New Mexico, and we made the four-thousand-mile trek––the trip during which the front of our RV blew off. I wish Bruce had stepped up and thought about our situation and the fact that a simple phone consultation might have done the trick instead of driving thousands of miles, but taking the initiative is often absent in aspies. When we arrived at Dr. Shrader's clinic, he was in his office playing solitaire, thinking we were going to be a phone consult. Who would be so dumb they would drive across almost the entire country for nothing?

I am still working on this protocol with the holistic doctor. Well-intentioned friends say, "I hope you feel better," but in thirty years I have not "felt better." I have been admonished for "looking good," as if I were faking. I just don't look like someone in a TV ad for Nyquil. Those who suffer as I do say, "We don't fake being sick; we fake being well."

No one understands how this illness breaks you, not just physically but financially, emotionally, and mentally. I find comfort in this poem by Kathi Lubin Orendain (n.d.):

TOXIC BLACK MOLD

It will take your life
And turn it upside down,
The ringing in your ears.
Will be a constant sound,
I shall steal your happiness,

And replace it with enormous pain.
Life as you know it,
Will never be the same.
I will take your mind.
Lock away your reasoning,
Leave you without mobility
I'll take away all agility
You will know my wrath,
With every step you make.
Everything that's yours
Is now mine to take.
I will steal your vision
Your laughter and your sanity.
When I am done with you,
They'll be nothing left of vanity.
No longer will you care,
If your house is a mess.
A day where you shower and cook
Will be your new success.
I'll take your job,
Your money and your car
Look in the mirror…
Are you losing your hair?
Your quality of life,
Is mine to devour.
I hope you like the
Taste of lemon sour.
I'll take and I'll take
Till you've nothing more to give.
Then I'll dig down deeper
And steal your desire to live.
You'll trade your favorite foods,
For a hand full of pills.

Then suffer the consequences,
As you sweat in your bath
Through the chills.
Friends will think you're crazy.
Doctors will send you away,
Leaving you to fight alone,
Each and every day.
Oh yes, I'm deep inside you.
And I'll be here for all of time.
I am your worst nightmare.
I am Black Toxic Mold.

Chapter 43

FIFTIETH ANNIVERSARY

Hordes of happy revelers hugged, kissed, and cheered as the ball dropped in Times Square:2020! The lights in New York City sparkled like all the stars in the Milky Way. I watched the excitement while standing in front of the television in my bathrobe and slippers. But I was feeling a sense of dread for this new year because it was the year of our fiftieth wedding anniversary. I thought if I could stop time from passing and keep June 20, 2020, from showing up on the calendar, I would not have to face the fact that I had lost fifty years, that I had spent a half century in a marriage that could not be normal. The months passed, and I couldn't figure out if divorce before the date would free me of this anxiety. *I have fiftieth wedding anniversary anxiety*! I was stuck in quicksand, not being able to decide or move forward to solve this dilemma. I wanted it to go away.

Winter passed, and we had a great RV trip to Tampa, Florida, where we ran in the Gasparilla running festival. I was excited to place second out of thirty-two women in my new age group of 75–79. We had a lovely golf day at the Babe Zaharias historic golf course and visited old friends. We planned another fun trip to the Virginia Beach Sports Fest, held on St. Patrick's Day. Meanwhile, the calendar pages were flipping over like shuffling cards. I shoved the beginning of summer back into the recesses of my brain. If I kept busy and didn't think about those five decades of marriage, maybe the anniversary just wouldn't happen.

How about a world pandemic to distract me from the still-creeping date of our fiftieth? That would do it, especially when I became ill on April 1and remained sick all month. It was a scary time for me, and the whole country was freaking out. I think I got COVID-19 when I was treated by a doctor who did not wear a mask, just before we all received the proper warnings. Bruce brought me food and did errands. He wore an N95 mask and stayed clear of me. Everyone kept asking, "How did Bruce do?"

He doesn't live with me, so lucky for him.

When my strength returned, I had a month and a half to get divorced, run away, or hide in the closet. I checked the legal grounds and the time it would take for a Delaware divorce. If we had not lived together or shared a bed for so many months, we would've qualified for an uncontested divorce. *Well, we sure qualified!*

I sat Bruce down by the computer, and we looked up do-it-yourself divorces. Being an ex-lawyer and having handled a few divorces, Bruce called the court and found out they were slammed because ofCOVID-19 and had no idea when our divorce could be finalized. It could take months. *Oh shit, when June 20 arrives, I'll still be married to this man who is on the spectrum.* Bruce went along with all my frantic efforts to escape the marriage. Why didn't he just say, "I don't want a divorce," or "I care about you," or anything at all about it? He later explained that he would not *initiate* it, but if it's what I wanted, he would go along with it.

So we changed course and decided to go to Hilton Head for an anniversary week vacation. Maybe it wouldn't seem so real if we're away, I thought, but my daughter wanted to bring the grandkids to visit that weekend. Serendipitously, Newark Country Club—to which we belonged and the place where we had held our wedding reception—was holding an outdoor Beatles band concert. We took it as a sign to live and let live, and I could think of nothing better than being with my kids and grandkids for this celebration.

If we are going to do this, let's go in style and make it fun for everyone, I thought. We weren't going out to a lovely dinner or hosting a party, but it seemed fun and fitting to dress up, and Bruce was game. He had black shorts and a long-sleeved black dress shirt from one of his skating costumes, so all he needed was a tie. I suggested a white straight tie, which we nixed, thinking he would look like a mobster. He felt a bow tie would do the trick, so I bought one online. I wore a gauzy white flowing top with a soft pink skort and the pretty carved pearl birthstone pendant that Bruce had given me for the occasion. From our local florist, I ordered a boutonniere and wrist corsage of white and pink roses, which replicated my original bridal bouquet. Our entourage included Reid, Sally, and three grandkids, who were gussied up as well. We unintentionally made a grand entrance, because we were late and the concert guests were already seated in a semi-circle of camping chairs around the lawn.

I don't know how I thought we could sneak around the crowd unnoticed in our garb, so I began showing the folks the pictures of our wedding party and the reception fifty years ago. "Look how the old clubhouse is exactly the same," I exclaimed, "but we sure have changed."

The band leader announced our anniversary during a break in the performance, and the club manager presented us with a bottle of champagne and filled our glasses for a toast, with the whole crowd chiming in with a toast and applause. They have no idea how much that meant to me. The journey had been very hard, a fact that no one at the concert was privy to. I was stumped by the repeated question, "What's your secret to staying married for fifty years?" I joked that it was drinking wine, but the secret was dark: mold spores growing in walls made me so ill that I could not leave a difficult marriage.

The day passed, and I did not suffer a mental breakdown or fall into depression. Sunday was Father's Day, and our grandson Ethan had turned nine a few days before, so we had more gifts and balloons to add to our anniversary bunch. This jumble of festivities helped draw focus away from the half-century milepost and relieved my anxiety. I watched the balloons deflate with a deep sense of regret that I could not seem to get off this roller-coaster marriage.

Meanwhile, Bruce had his life back, ensconced in his condo, walking twice a day, working out at the track Tuesdays, and golfing with friends.

Chapter 44

SURRENDER

I try to imagine how our lives might have turned out if I had not gone to the beach that rainy day fifty-one years ago and that young sailor Bruce had not spied me near the waves. As with a near-miss head-on car collision, I would never have known the unimaginable grief that was in store for me. This thought has haunted me for years. Someone else would have wandered into my life, maybe not on a beach, but somewhere. My other-life marriage might have survived the high divorce rate, or perhaps not. "What about the kids?" friends ask when they hear my fantasy. "Surely they've been worth the hardship?" My heart grows heavy, and tears well up to think about it, but I answer, "I would have had other kids. I would never have known my sweeties in the first place."

Bruce would have gotten married and had children, but I bet he'd eventually have gotten divorced and possibly remarried. Only a woman with a personality disorder like his would have stayed with Bruce, both of them living their own self-centered lives.

And what about the successful career path I followed? Could I have done it without Bruce's assistance? My mother always said I was a "self-starter," so I think I would have been hustling somehow, but this time with a neurotypical mate.

As for Bruce, it has become apparent as I have written this memoir that I have "dragged him through life." My therapist suggested this expression after only our second meeting. While Bruce was on course for law school through his own initiative, it was my parents' contacts that got him the job clerking at a small office, which he ended up owning. Thus, it is at least initially through them that he acquired a range of connections and enjoyed a freedom he would have missed had he been swallowed up in the corporate world.

He told me once that he was content living in a house like the one Dickie, our Down syndrome charge, shared with us in Toledo. *Geez, how about a nice house with a lovely yard, a patio, a pool, and a view of the woods?*

I envision him happily consuming his daily popcorn and beer. A pan-fried steak meal suited him just fine when we met, and the highest-carbohydrate selection on the menu remains his first choice. *Make that a Reuben sandwich, please.* Would he have cared that he was overweight? Would he have been a diabetic when he was in his thirties?

I wonder if he would have finished multiple triathlons each year, run the Boston Marathon, skated in a synchronized team, hosted outlandish parties, become an RV traveler, been an activist, worked for a political candidate, or invested in real estate. Without me, he would have avoided all the hassles of developing and maintaining childcare centers. I think he would have been content with a simple, uneventful, and unhampered routine. I was eager to share kids, a house, and a marriage with someone, but Bruce would have drifted blissfully through life in Minnesota with a Stepford wife.

I enlisted him once to grab a shovel and get some Queen Anne's lace from the side of a two-lane road near our house. The white flowers were a pretty accent in my zinnia arrangements. While he was digging a batch out, a county cop stopped behind us and got out. "Are you digging up a dead body?" he inquired. I don't know what Bruce said to the officer, but when the officer got back into his car, Bruce asked me, "What fine mess have you gotten me into now?"

In the early years, Bruce was gone a lot with shift work in the navy, law school, and studying for the bar while law clerking. My mother made a prescient joke that we got along well because we were rarely together. Absence lets the heart avoid Asperger's.

Why didn't I leave after only two or three years, when Bruce was in the navy in Virginia? Why didn't I move out with toddler Reid the first time Bruce threw the playpen in the car and drove recklessly to the beach, snapping at me that I was out of line to even question his driving? Sadly, it never crossed my mind. Women's liberation was still around the corner, there was a terrible war raging, and autism awareness was in its infancy. Verbal abuse was an unexplored topic. And who did I know that had divorced when they had a toddler? I was busy teaching childbirth classes and taking care of the family. Besides, we had mutual friends, Bruce was nice to people, and he got along with my parents. I made up excuses, hid behind a curtain of denial, and hoped for change.

I need to believe that I would have had the courage to break away if I had not gotten sick later in our marriage; the mold illness had sealed my fate.

What is a genuine mutually caring relationship like? I wondered. Maybe I could try GrayhairSingles.com. Maybe not. Ever since Bruce moved out three years ago, I have been on my own, and now I am accustomed to not being accountable to any living soul except my cats and perhaps the black vulture family I feed on my patio. I question whether I could share my life with anyone after so much solitude. Years ago, I was struck by an article about released prisoners of war who return to their wives and families. The wives had been independent for so long they could not resurrect their marriages with the past dynamic, and they divorced. Still, I am more than curious about what a genuine, neurotypical relationship might be like.

At no time since we separated has Bruce proclaimed that he misses the house, let alone that he misses me. Despite the separation, we share holidays, birthdays, golfing, trips to Brooklyn to see our daughter and grandkids, playing in the pool with grandkids, and random events and activities. He stops by most days to get the newspaper, do errands, work on rental properties or banking affairs, help with projects big and small, and service the RV and cars. We chat about the goings-on with friends, townsfolk, and the nation.

As I see him, he is neither happy nor sad. Rather, he seems frozen, an emotionally flatlined person without passion, joy, or laughter. He is still serious, as if he were suppressing anger like that old Boy Scout robot: helpful, square, and rigid. He has never expressed regret such as, "Why didn't I marry someone who could deal with Asperger's syndrome? Or someone who didn't bug me to participate in family life, eat better, stop drinking, call my mother?"

Our close friends and family know we do not live together. It's easier to avoid explaining this whole Asperger's thing to the general population, but it spills out sometimes. For example, I was running in our state park when two male runners passed me. One said, "Hi, April. Say hi to Bruce," and added, "if you see him." *If you see him?* It was relatively early in our separation, and I thought I was hearing things. How could this guy, whoever he was, know that Bruce and I didn't see each other on a daily basis?

Turns out it was a longtime runner friend that Bruce sees at weekly track workouts. "Why the hell did you tell him?" I asked Bruce, thinking, *He was blabbing to runners at the track?* The problem is he tells people we "just don't get along." *Say what?*

I have had three of our mutual male friends look at me like I was a piranha, probably thinking I must be the meanest person in the world to have kicked Bruce out of the house. When we chatted, and my eyeballs didn't glow red or my head didn't spin on my neck, they seemed to relax and understand I was the same old April. I take this as a variety of that nagging Cassandra syndrome. Mild-mannered Bruce will always fool people. I witness his childlike, overly polite, and nonthreatening attitude. "That's his modus operandi," I say. Even he admits that he will put on a good face for people. I will criticize some kiss-ass thing he said to someone, and his response is, "It works for me," so I am forever fighting Cassandra syndrome. Me bad, Bruce nice.

I learned an interesting phenomenon throughout the years. People become invested in us as a couple, presumably because we add life to any race, golf game, or party. "What a fun couple!" they'll gush. Apparently it is not difficult to appear to be like a loving, married couple. Just show up together at some social affair and then leave together.

In December 2019, we took a seminar cruise, sponsored by *The Nation* magazine, to the Caribbean. Bruce and I are both Tiger Woods fanatics and attended his Hero Championship in the Bahamas just a few days before the ship left from Fort Lauderdale. We booked with a friend, who had to back out at the last minute, leaving Bruce and me to muddle through an unaccustomed week of total togetherness. We slept in separate staterooms, which we kept secret to avoid the hassle of explaining our weird situation, but it turned out interesting and fun.

When we were posing for formal-night photographs, the cheery female photographer kept trying to push us together for a shipboard romance portrait rather than a snapshot of two stiff stand-offish creatures out of Grant Wood's *American Gothic*. "Sir, hold her hand. Ma'am, lean closer, lean closer."

Finally, I said, "We don't like each other!" We didn't like the photos, either.

A similar thing happened at the hospital when Bruce underwent a lung procedure after being injured from the RV bunk fall. He was suited and hooked up, ready to be wheeled away, with me standing by his bedside. A "Nurse Ratched" breezed in and began giving me orders regarding how I was to sit in the waiting room and stare at the monitor to watch for updated texts. Feeling like I'd been arrested, I accommodated myself to her authoritarian manner. *Yes ma'am, yes ma'am, okay ma'am.* Then she said, "You can kiss him goodbye now." I stood still for a long awkward moment. *No ma'am.*

We have never been what people imagine, and many friends still cannot accept the reality that our marriage is not normal. "But you do love each other," people will say. "You have a history." "Things will be better."

It seems so odd that no one notices how those subtle gestures of intimacy are missing between Bruce and me. I am highly sensitive to other couples' interactions, their smiles, touches, fleeting glances, and inside jokes. *Honestly, did anyone EVER see Bruce give me a hug, put his arm around me, take my hand, look at me and smile, or—OH, NO—kiss me?*

I cannot seem to interact with anyone without their saying, "Say hi to Bruce."

I want to say, "*You* say hi to Bruce!"

I hate hearing it. I tense up. *We have a problem going on here, for God's sake, not to mention he doesn't give a fig who says hi to him.* Worse, he does not bother to bring me a *hi* from those he runs into, which puts me in some pretty awkward situations. "Did Bruce tell you I saw him the other day?" *No.* So I have to fudge it. And he recently told me that he himself does not like to hear someone bid, "Say hi to April."

I understand that resentment and anger serve only to hurt me. Accordingly, I strive to heal my mind and body by reading from spiritual coaches such as Eckhart Tolle. From Joe Dispenza (2012), I learn how one might rewire the brain and restore the immune system. I listen to Glenn Harrold's meditation CDs and Facebook programs and read the teachings of the Buddha and Deepak Chopra. I get great comfort and advice from other aspie wives online. Being able to communicate with other women in my situation has been a lifesaver. I try to think positive thoughts and give myself strengthening affirmations.

To reduce PTSD, I watch EMDR videos, which suggest that while we cannot change an event, we can change how we respond to and think about an event.

After all this instruction, viewing, and contemplation, sometimes after just five minutes with Bruce, my good intentions can vanish like a magician's trick, and I am pissed! Then off Bruce goes to golfing or some other activity, seemingly unfazed, while I am left struggling to patch up the shredded remnants of my life.

I am still in emotional limbo but hopeful that I will soon cease to be *spellbound*. I learned this term from Dr. Abdul Saad. He explains that "spellbound" is the mental state of an abused person who is overstressed and trapped within the abuser's orbit, not unlike those afflicted with Stockholm syndrome (Vital Mind Psychology 2016). Unfortunately, I did not know precisely how to cease being spellbound or trauma-bound.

How to negotiate conflicts with someone with a personality disorder was not part of my upbringing. Psychologist Les Carter describes it in his YouTube video as *trained incompetence*: "You didn't know what you didn't know" (Carter 2020).

In the end, there was no way to fix Asperger's syndrome or narcissistic traits embedded in childhood. It was a losing battle that practically killed me. The stress of the fights, the dashed hopes, and the thousand little heartbreaks and disappointments had no cure. No amount of therapy, counseling, amino acids tests, neurofeedback, life coaching, or hypnosis could change Bruce.

I am truly a candidate for Al-Anon, as Ray tried to tell me years ago. It is not just for people in a relationship with a chemically dependent person; it is also for those partnered with any difficult person who causes them physical and/or emotional illnesses. Spouses like me feel outraged, anxious, afraid, rejected, and perpetually sorry for themselves. I needed to accept that I cannot control Bruce's brain or behavior. I needed to accept the Al-Anon three C's: "I didn't cause it, I can't control it, and I can't cure it."

I should have heeded Earnie Larson, as reported in Melody Beattie's *Codependent No More: How to Stop Controlling Others and Start Caring for Yourself*: "If the relationship is dead, bury it!" Regarding people like me, Beattie writes, "We flew in the face of reality . . . shaking the dreams at the truth, refusing to believe or accept anything less. But one day the truth caught up to us and refused to be put off any longer. This isn't what we planned, asked for or hoped for. It never would be . . . The dream was dead, and it would never breathe again" (Beattie 1992, loc. 3459, Kindle).

I could have learned this lesson from Mother Goose: "For every ailment under the sun/There is a remedy, or there is none;/If there be one, try to find it;/If there be none, never mind it."

I gave too much and tried too hard and became codependent. I needed a comeuppance or a whack on the head. I have a quote from Winston Churchill on my refrigerator: "Never, never, never give up." I didn't give up when I knew I was sick. I didn't give up when the two banks rejected my application for a loan to build my first freestanding childcare center. I didn't give up competing in grueling races. I didn't give up writing this book. I didn't give up when I knew something was wrong with my husband. For almost fifty years, I didn't give up trying to fix our marriage. But now, I am waving the white flag of surrender.

Chapter 45

SORT OF

Something happened the fall after Bruce and I separated that perhaps captures the pathetic peculiarity of our relationship. We had driven in the same car to vote in a local school referendum and stood at the table to sign our voting cards.

The volunteer opened the registration book, pulled out two cards, and asked if we were together. She was flummoxed by our reply.

In unison, we answered, "Sort of."

Sort of.

Good grief! The answers to all our introspection, floating beyond our grasp like dandelion seeds blowing in the wind, had been condensed into these two words. We had a "sort of" marriage, a "sort of" separation, a divorce where we will be "sort of" friends or relatives. But "sort of" is not whole or complete; it is as pitiful as a deflated wedding balloon. It was certainly not what I aspired to at the dawn of my womanhood.

I grieve for my young self. I think that is the hardest part for me in the declining years of my Asperger marriage. I grieve for the heartbroken newlywed, the lonely, confused young wife and mother lost in a turbulent sea and trying to stay afloat. This person seems detached from who I have now become. I see her apart from me, standing at a distance, and I want to take her in my arms and console her, give her strength, have her voice that fell on deaf ears be heard. My young self wasn't equipped to handle meltdowns, verbal abuse, and rages. Her brain and emotions were scrambled on a daily basis. She was like David facing Goliath, but with no sling or sword against gaslighting, word twisting, narcissistic behavior, and autism. Now I am hardened, tough, cynical, and educated. It takes a lot to fool me these days, but years ago it was like taking candy from a baby.

It is particularly upsetting to me when I look at three photographs of Bruce and me from the summer of 1969, the summer at Whiskey Beach. The first is a picture of us in a huge hug, probably the one and only spontaneous embrace from Bruce I was ever to receive. In the second, Bruce is playfully splashing water on me while I am kicking up my heels in the shallow ocean surf. The third photo hurts me the most. We are walking in the sandy parking lot, and I am wearing my bright flower print baby doll beach cover and floppy pink hat. Bruce is holding my hand and leaning toward my face in order to hear what I am saying. He is smiling.

This is the person I thought I was marrying. But Bruce's playful attitude turned into a serious one overnight.

Joking, teasing, and kidding would occur too seldom for me to count on. Smiling, listening to my words, and holding my hand would be rare. Our Whiskey Beach courtship was an illusion. I want to go back in time and grab that happy girl by her other hand and pull her away to safety, to another life. My heart will always ache for that other, younger me.

For New Year's Eve 2014, Bruce and I made last-minute reservations at an upscale restaurant in a town nearby. He donned his best blue suit jacket and colorful runner's tie, and I wore a flowing black silk and velvet top, a gift from my fashion-conscious daughter. I loaded up on my diamonds, which are usually cached in a drawer. We were gussied up, as my mom would say. Our gourmet dinner was a subdued affair. Candlelight flickered across the faces of other diners, and I caught snippets of muted conversation. I pined for our old partying days at Amaranth or a dinner dance, but at least we were out, trying to celebrate.

After dinner, we headed home and hustled out of the cold into the new house. We stood in our small foyer by the front door, which divides my bedroom wing from his, and looked at each other. For us, there would be no sitting on the couch under a blanket, holding hands and watching the ball descend above Times Square. We gave each other a quick light kiss, and Bruce emotionally choked out the words, "Happy New Year." Close to tears, we withdrew to our own rooms.

END

EPILOGUE

By Deborah Lawrence

April 2020

I was happy and you came along
You joined in my dance and sang with my song.
You talked of together in your wedding vow,
But now it's so clear you never knew how.
Your world of overwhelm, fear and dread
And constant anxiety in your body and head.
I've striven and given, supported and tried
But day by day a piece of me died.
Repeatedly snapped at, and then just ignored
My interests and company showed you were bored.
Selfish and cruel our home became jail
I'd sob home returning, our marriage a fail.

You've peopled all day so return home a mute
Every day is the same timetable, always the same route.
I've cried and I've begged till I'm shamed on my knee
Locked in your world, my needs you don't see.
I'll do my duty and pour out my care
But you look right through me, don't acknowledge me there.
I've given and shriveled to the size of a seed
Craved for an ounce of you knowing my need.
Over dramatic!! I'd scream to be heard
But only one way, your final word.
No one would listen, no one understood
"He's a kind man, he's always so good"
So I was the problem, I was so wrong
Still I silenced my voice and bit hard on my tongue.
And smaller I shrank, so far from me
Not a bruise on my body or a cut did you see
Just the pain in my heart and a stamp on my soul
Trying to survive became my end goal.
Yesterdays promise turned to scorn the next day
Feeling so battered, I crawled slowly away.
I knew I was in danger, I didn't feel safe
But where to get rescued? Where is that place?
Away from you. The seed can now flourish
With air I can breathe, and myself I can nourish
I regained my voice, my laugh and my song
But to dance truly heartfelt? . . . that won't take long

OX

BIBLIOGRAPHY

Andrew. "You Are Not Alone." NARCDAILY. Accessed March 27, 2022. YouTube podcast. https://www.youtube.com/c/NARCDAILY YouAreNotAlone.

Aston, Maxine. 2008. *The Asperger Couple's Workbook: Practical Advice and Activities for Couples and Counsellors*. London and Philadelphia, PA: Jessica Kingsley Publishers.

Attwood, Tony. 2015. *The Complete Guide to Asperger's Syndrome*. London and Philadelphia, PA: Jessica Kingsley Publishers.

Baron-Cohen, Simon, Sally Wheelright, Richard Skinner, Joanne Martin, and Emma Clubley. 2001. "The Autism-Spectrum Quotient (AQ): Evidence from Asperger Syndrome/High-Functioning Autism, Males and Females, Scientists and Mathematicians." *Journal of Autism and Developmental Disorders* 31: 5–17. https://doi.org/10.1023/a:1005653411471.

Beattie, Melody. 1992. *Codependent No More: How to Stop Controlling Others and Start Caring for Yourself*. Center City, MN: Hazelden. Kindle.

Boroch, Ann. 2009. *The Candida Cure: Yeast Fungus and Your Health*. Los Angeles, CA: Quintessential Healing, Inc.

Carter, Les. 2020. "The #1 Reason A Narcissist Has Power Over You." YouTube video, 14:25. July 2nd, 2020. https://www.youtube.com/watch?v=5bY9wS5G3ww.

Dispenza, Joe. 2012. *Breaking the Habit of Being Yourself: How to Lose Your Mind and Create a New One*. Carlsbad, CA: Hay House.

Dyer, Wayne W. 2001. *Your Erroneous Zones: Step-by-Step Advice for Escaping the Trap of Negative Thinking and Taking Control of Your Life*. New York: Harper Collins.

Evans, Patricia. 1992. *The Verbally Abusive Relationship: How to Recognize It and How to Respond*. Holbrook, MA: Adams Media Corporation.

Hubbard, April, and Clementine Hayburn. 1988. *Daycare Parenting*. NY: Bart Books.

Ivker, Robert S. 2000. *Sinus Survival: The Holistic Medical Treatment for Allergies, Colds, and Sinusitis*, 4th ed. New York: Tarcher/Putnam.

Jong, Erica. 1973. *Fear of Flying*. New York: Holt, Rinehart and Winston.

Lowen, Alexander. 1985. *Narcissism: Denial of the True Self*. NY: Touchstone.

Marshack, Kathy. 2009. *Life with a Partner or Spouse with Asperger Syndrome: Going over the Edge? Practical Steps to Savings You and Your Relationship*. Shawnee Mission, KS: Autism Asperger Publishing Co.

Mendes, E. [Eva Mendes]. (2015). *Marriage and Lasting Relationships*. London and Philadelphia, PA: Jessica Kingsley Publishers.

Nathan, Neil. 2018. *Toxic: Heal Your Body from Mold Toxicity, Lyme Disease, Multiple Chemical Sensitivities, and Chronic Environmental Illness*. Las Vegas: Victory Belt Publishing.

Orendain, Kathi Lubin. No Date. "Toxic Black Mold." Personal communication.

Petrison, Lisa, and Erik Johnson. 2015. *A Beginner's Guide to Mold Avoidance*. Paradigm Change. https://moldavoiders.com/books/.

Shapiro, Francine. 2013. *Getting Past Your Past: Take Control of Your Life with Self-Help Techniques from EMDR Therapy*. Emmaus, PA: Rodale Books.

Tolle, Eckert. 2005. *A New Earth: Awakening to Your Life's Purpose*. New York: Penguin Books.

Vaknin, Sam. 2015. *Malignant Self Love: Narcissism Revisited*. Czech Republic: Narcissus Publications.

Vermeulen, Peter. 2012. *Autism as Context Blindness*. Shawnee, KS: AAPC Publishing.

Vital Mind Psychology. 2016. "The Childhood Origins of Narcissism." YouTube video, 16:56. December 6, 2016. https://www.youtube.com/watch?v=SeVj_0r0swg.

Weston, Louise. 2010. *Connecting with Your Asperger Partner: Negotiating the Maze of Intimacy*. London: Jessica Kingsley Publishers.

RESOURCES FOR READERS

Atkinson, Angie. YouTube videos on toxic relationship rehab. https://www.youtube.com/c/AngieAtkinson/videos.
Crook, William G. 1987. *The Yeast Connection: A Medical Breakthrough*. New Orleans: Pelican Pub Co Inc.
Crook, William G, Carolyn Dean, and Elizabeth B. Crook. 2007. *The Yeast Connection and Women's Health*. New York: Square One Publishers.
Durvasula, Ramani. YouTube videos on narcissism. https://www.youtube.com/c/DoctorRamani/videos.
Evans, Patricia. 1993. *Verbal Abuse: Survivors Speak Out on Relationship and Recovery*. Holbrook, MA: Adams Media Corporation.
_____. 2003. *Controlling People: How to Recognize, Understand, and Deal with People Who Try to Control You*. Holbrook, MA: Adams Media Corporation.

———. 2006. *The Verbally Abusive Man, Can He Change?: A Woman's Guide to Deciding Whether to Stay or Go*. Holbrook, MA: Adams Media Corporation.

Grannon, Richard. 2020. "Covert Narcissists SECRET CrazyMaking Communication Weapon They Use to ABUSE." YouTube video, 12:37. April 24, 2020. https://www.youtube.com/watch?v=q6vlnfdo5jI.

———. 2019. "How Covert Narcissists Use Word 'Salad' as a Tactic." YouTube video, 8:37. October 6, 2019. https://www.youtube.com/watch?v=P5x4A_-MaIU.

Hagland, Carol. 2010. *Getting to Grips with Asperger Syndrome: Understanding Adults on the Asperger Spectrum*. London and Philadelphia, PA: Jessica Kingsley Publishers.

Kalish, Daniel. 2012. *The Kalish Method: Healing the Body, Mapping the Mind*. CreateSpace Independent Publishing Platform.

Lam, Michael. Dr. Lam Coaching (website about adrenal fatigue). http://www.drlamcoaching.com.

National Institute of Mental Health. 2018. "Autism Spectrum Disorder." https://www.nimh.nih.gov/health/publications/autism-spectrum-disorder/index.shtml.

Partner Support. 2014. "The Burden on NT Spouses and Children, OTRS." Asperger Partner. http://www.aspergerpartner.com/the-burden-on-nt-spouses-and-children-otrs.html.

QueenBeeing. Website about narcissism and toxic relationships. http://www.QueenBeeing.com.

Saperstein, Jesse. 2010. *Atypical: Life with Asperger's in 20 1/3 Chapters*. New York: Penguin Group.

Simone, Rudy. 2009. *22 Things a Woman Must Know if She Loves a Man with Asperger's Syndrome*. London and Philadelphia, PA: Jessica Kingsley Publishing.

Talbot, Shawn. 2007. *The Cortisol Connection: Why Stress Makes You Fat and Ruins Your Health and What You Can Do About It*. Alameda, CA: Hunter House Inc Publishers.

Teitelbaum, Jacob. 2007. *From Fatigued to Fantastic*. New York: Avery Publishing.

Vital Mind Psychology. 2017. "How the Narcissist Destroys Your Physical Health." YouTube video, 10:39. July 13, 2017. https://www.youtube.com/watch?v=mrDnVIkzOz0

Vital Mind Psychology. https://vitalmind.com.au.

———. YouTube videos on narcissism. https://www.youtube.com/channel/UC_P8aFACl-VqJl0flQPGMQQ/videos.

Willey, Liane Holliday. 1999. *Pretending to be Normal*. London: Jessica Kingsley Publishers.

Wilson, James. 2002. *Adrenal Fatigue: The 21st-Century Stress Syndrome*. Petaluma, CA: Smart Publications.

ACKNOWLEDGMENTS

Starting from a few scribbles in a notebook ten years ago as a novice in this memoir-writing business, I am thankful for the early help I received when I began taking baby steps forward. I owe a debt of gratitude to freelance writer Marjorie Dorfman, who answered an obscure email from me and generously gave her time to review several rough draft chapters. Her frank and sound critique pointed me in the right direction.

JoAnn Balingit, a neighbor and ex-poet laureate of Delaware, encouraged me to push ahead when I told her my rough draft was terrible. "Rough drafts are supposed to be terrible!" she said.

Amy Lynn Durham was my first writer helper when I had not yet found my voice or narrative arc. Amy is the real deal; a kind, caring, and talented writer; the foundation of the finished product; and the creator of the font design for the book cover. We worked together for almost three years, which was a long time for her to deal with my tears, angst, ramblings, and indecision about how best to frame the memoir. She lives in Canada, so we spent hours (before Zoom) holding the phone to our sore ears. Amy, thanks so much!

While I was still fumbling for direction, Laurel Marshfield, owner of Blue Horizons Communications, Rehoboth Beach, Delaware, jumped into the fray and offered new perspective and encouragement, which I sincerely appreciated.

My intuition brought me Phillip Bannowsky, writer, poet, professor, actor/director, and retired autoworker. The manuscript had been sitting in hiatus for over a year in a cardboard box when I got a sign from the universe advising me to call an old friend. The friend knew Phillip, who, after some convincing, took on my project. Phillip and I met for two years. We laughed, cried, fussed, and wore our brains out. When I was past the crying stage and into the anger stage, he put on a therapist hat and calmed me down whenever I was triggered by a memory. Love and gratitude to Phillip for his creativity, coaching, collaboration, and computer knowledge with formatting a manuscript.

Thank you to Paula Perselo, who had the difficult task of being the first editor. She did a spectacularly thorough job.

Thank you to early readers Sherry Hanlin, Mary Grace Kayatta, and a few anonymous souls who gave me great feedback.

Much appreciation to Jenn T. Grace and Bailly Morse at Publish Your Purpose (PYP), along with Cornelia (Nelly) Murariu for her stellar cover design and Nancy Graham-Tillman for her expert and patient proofreading. PYP, a woman-owned company, is knowledgeable, supportive, and accessible to new authors with a dream.

Luck from the universe guided me again when I chose an editor who freelanced for PYP. Noël King and I bonded in mind and spirit as we proceeded to finalize the memoir. I was tired and losing motivation, but her wonderful editing skills and encouragement that the book was a good read and well worthwhile gave me the boost I needed to get to the finish line. I couldn't have done it without you, Noël, and that is not a cliché.

Thank you to all the wonderful women on the Yahoo and Facebook Asperger's forums who gave me strength every day to complete the project. Their heartfelt posts, strength of will, determination, and fight for themselves and their families are an inspiration to anyone who has an autistic relationship challenge.

The deepest love to my kids, Reid and Sally, for warming the cockles of my heart during my coldest moments. Thank you for giving me Amelia, Deven, and Ethan, grandkids extraordinaire. Their dad stands fast in his declaration that we sure had a lot of fun.

ABOUT THE AUTHOR

April Anderson lives in Newark, Delaware, home of the Fightin' Blue Hens, with her rescued cats. Her favorite pastimes are golfing, snow skiing, road racing, and growing lots of pretty flowers. Her website is www.aprilanderson.net.

CPSIA information can be obtained
at www.ICGtesting.com
Printed in the USA
BVHW071515200522
637649BV00011B/69/J